THE MAKING OF EASTERN EUROPE: From Earliest Times to 1815

This volume, together with its companion, *EASTERN EUROPE: AN HISTORICAL GEOGRAPHY, 1815–1945*, traces the historical geography of Eastern Europe from earliest times to the present day. It draws on indigenous sources which have not been widely studied in the West to provide a wealth of detail about the development of landscape, settlement patterns, towns, political units and economic behaviour and about their interrelationship. The frequency with which political boundaries and other patterns have changed in this area makes the picture that emerges very complex. The region has never achieved political unity and the author accounts for this in terms of internal political, geographical and cultural division and of the importance of external influences and forces at key historical moments.

David Turnock is Reader in Geography at the University of Leicester.

THE MAKING OF EASTERN EUROPE: From the Earliest Times to 1815

DAVID TURNOCK

ROUTLEDGE
London and New York

First published in 1988 by
Routledge
11 New Fetter Lane, London EC4P 4EE
29 West 35th Street, New York NY 10001

Printed and bound in Great Britain by Mackays of Chatham PLC, Kent

British Library Cataloguing in Publication Data

Turnock, David
The making of Eastern Europe : from the earliest times to 1815.
1. Eastern Europe. Geographical features, to 1815
I. Title
911′.4

ISBN 0-415-01267-8

Library of Congress Cataloging-in-Publication Data

Turnock, David.
The making of Eastern Europe.

Bibliography: p.
Includes index.
1. Europe, Eastern — History. I. Title.
DJK38.T87 947 88-15842
ISBN 0-415-01267-8

Contents

To Serban,
for his friendship and encouragement

Figures

Acknowledgements

My thanks for assistance in writing this book go in the first place to numerous fellow academics without whose contributions this work of synthesis would be quite impossible. Although it has not been feasible to extend the referencing beyond English language publications I am very much aware of the formidable amount of literature available in East European and other continental languages. It is also a pleasurable duty to record my gratitude to Mr A.A.L. Caesar and Mrs H.G. Steers at Cambridge University and Professor R.E.H. Mellor at Aberdeen University for stimulating and encouraging my interest in Eastern Europe to the point where such a work as this could be contemplated. But I am also grateful to a number of my contemporaries, in Eastern Europe and elsewhere, who share my interests: for example my colleague here in Leicester, Professor Derek Aldcroft, has helped me a great deal through his fund of bibliographical material. The maps have been prepared most expertly by Mrs Kate Moore, Mr David Orme and Mrs Ruth Pollington while the typing has been efficiently completed by Mrs Carol Deacon, Miss Susan Haywood and Mrs Pat Jinks. My wife has loyally supported me in my endeavours and made many valuable comments for the improvement of the typescript.

David Turnock
Leicester

Introduction

This book is concerned with the historical geography of a part of Europe which had very limited coherence as a distinct region before 1945 when, as a consequence of the Second World War, Germany and her sphere of influence in Central Europe was split by rival socio-economic and military alignments. A new political barrier appeared which seemed 'from both sides of the fence rather like a frontier in the old Roman sense, separating civilisations that consider each other as barbarian'.[1] Historically however it is convenient to follow the thinking of W.J. Cahnman in recognising two great socio-political fields of east and west, the former defined by the Soviet boundary of 1939 and the latter in terms of the ninth century Carolingian Empire.[2] Between the two fields lies a 'marchland' territory extending from Scandinavia through the North European Plain and south to Pannonia and the Balkans, a belt in which various independent and mutually antagonistic powers have emerged.[3] The term 'shatterbelt' might also be applied, to indicate an area with conflicting state or great power interests.[4] Despite (or perhaps because of) strong external cultural stimuli: Frankish and Byzantine (Catholic or Orthodox) or Western and Ottoman, it has never been possible for this region to be unified either within itself or through annexation by powers in the east or west. As E. Fischer points out, there were forces striving for unity but they never accomplished their goal.[5] A.P. Vlasto thus refers to the 'soft centre' of Europe inhabited predominantly by Slavs through which a frontier between east and west would have to be drawn, a frontier which 'would reflect in its oscillations the relative vitality ... of east and west expressed in their bids for the spiritual allegiance of the Slav people.'[6] In the late ninth century a strong impulse from

Figure 0.1: Countries of Eastern Europe today

Source: Modern atlases

the east penetrated as far as Moravia but a political frontier could not be drawn so far to the northwest and by early eleventh century the tide had turned. A crown for St. Stephen in 1000 marked Hungary's establishment as a Catholic bastion, subsequently reinforced by the economic importance of Venice and the expansion of German settlement. And after the havoc wrought in Constantinople by the crusading movement in 1204 Latin unity in the Balkans was further frustrated by the rise of the Ottoman Empire under whose wing the Orthodox Church was able to find sanctuary.

Cultural and ethnic anomalies, thrown up by a complex historical evolution, have consistently impeded unification during the Medieval and modern periods. Since Medieval times the greatest potential for unity has arisen through German leadership, which became most assertive during the nineteenth century with the emergence of an economically powerful German Empire acting in concert with the Habsburg and Ottoman empires.[7] Yet the simultaneous rise of nationalism in the Balkans, drawing strength from both Russia and the west, posed an overwhelming constraint so dramatically projected by the tragic waste of two world wars. It is interesting to recall that for the German geographer, J. Partsch, 'the threefold belt of the Alps, Middle Mountains and Northern Lowlands dominate the landscape and scenery of Central Europe: wherever one of these elements dies out Central Europe comes to an end'.[8] But the topographical idea, with its transitional landforms and intersecting trade routes, was then lined up with the area of German civilisation and economic penetration. G.G. Chisholm reinforced this view in a thoughtful review of Partsch's book. He saw clearly that unity came not from landscape but rather from German and Austro-Hungarian economic and political interests.[9] It says much for the arrogance of nineteenth century imperialism that F. Naumann could write at the height of the First World War to advocate a massive power bloc embracing over thirteen million square kilometers and extending as far as the Asian frontiers of the Ottoman Empire and the overseas territories of the Netherlands.[10] He rejected any notion of ethnic superiority for Germans or Magyars and emphasised common interests. Although the desired treatment of non-Germans might differ from that actually meted out by the advancing war machine there was no understanding that the force of nationalism would never allow the German

Kernland to integrate with such a vast alien periphery. Chisholm clearly saw the vulnerability of such an edifice to Russian attack.[11] And his words were certainly prophetic, for the Russian advance has duly taken place and apparently destroyed any validity that the notion of Central Europe may have possessed.[12] For the foreseeable future the problem of Central Europe has been resolved and one consequence has been the creation of a tier of eight communist states which on the whole (recognising here the ambivalence of Albania and Yugoslavia) have become associated with the eastern bloc (Figure 0.1). According to S.B. Cohen this area constitutes part of the domain of Eurasian continental power which stands in a state of dynamic equilibrium with the trade dependent maritime world.[13]

The Russian advance has done more than merely undermine the regional coherence of Central Europe. It has brought a sharp change in foreign policy by the powers of Western Europe. There can be few reappraisals quite as decisive as the one which replaced British and French collaboration with Russia in two world wars with the present ideological and military confrontation. Such a change was clearly anticipated by H.J. Mackinder in the development of the 'Heartland' theory to warn of the danger for the west that would emerge from the union of the Heartland and 'Eastern Europe'.[14] Of course the controlling power is the USSR, rather than Germany as Mackinder supposed, and the prediction that such a union would ultimately lead to the assumption of world power by the Heartland power has not been vindicated. The vulnerability of the Heartland to nuclear attack inhibits any dramatic advance for the time being and provides a technological basis for an effective containment strategy, provided there is the political will in the 'Rimland' to exploit it as a basis for effective negotiation.[15] Nevertheless Mackinder was surely right to point out that a solution to the problems posed by the central powers would bring more challenging questions to the fore. Unfortunately any conscious effort to act on this advice immediately ran into a great dilemma, for while an alliance with Russia against Germany ran the risk of Russian expansion into the centre of Europe and the takeover of the whole of Eastern Europe as Mackinder defined it (that is the area from the Urals approximately to the Lübeck-Trieste line) there was always a chance that a rupture in relations between Russia and the western powers would precipitate a German attack on Russia or else bring out a closer union between them on the lines of the nineteenth century Holy Alliance.

Out of the dilemma has come an Eastern Europe with unprecedented ideological unity. The union may not be entirely harmonious, for nationalism has not been suppressed and serious divisions have occurred in both political and economic matters.[16] Yet the current view of Eastern Europe has become sufficiently conventional to warrant a historical geography text complementing material already available for both Russia and Western Europe.[17] Such a work is necessary to examine the region's marchland or shatterbelt status, both as an exercise in its own right and as a context for studies of the post-1945 period, concerning problems and strategies which often arise directly out of past experiences. However in view of the large scale of the project it has been found desirable to divide the work into two volumes. This volume deals with the making of Eastern Europe up to 1815, while the subsequent modernisation of the region is dealt with in a companion work: Eastern Europe: an historical geography 1815-1945.

PHYSICAL BASIS FOR MIGRATION AND SETTLEMENT

The settlement history of Eastern Europe cannot of course be divorced from the complex physical geography although the significance of the regional environment is not to be measured in simple terms.[18] Table 0.1 reveals that there are substantial areas of high ground: 23.2 percent of the land lies above 500m. with the proportion much higher in the southern part (37.1 percent) than in the north (11.6) However, given the lower latitudes and higher sunshine levels in the south much of the mountain zone has a significant agricultural potential and there are valuable mineral deposits too. The four Balkan countries and the southern half of Hungary have mean July temperatures in excess of 20 degrees centigrade; and with the exception of Baragan, Dobrogea and Moldavia rainfall exceeds 50cm./20 inches. Certainly in prehistoric times there do not appear to have been any major constraints on settlement. While the Mediterranean with its tideless seas and extensive coastlands, conducive to stock-rearing and arable farming, was of the utmost importance in early cultural, economic and political developments it is equally evident that 'the variety

Figure 0.2: Aspects of settlement and physical geography

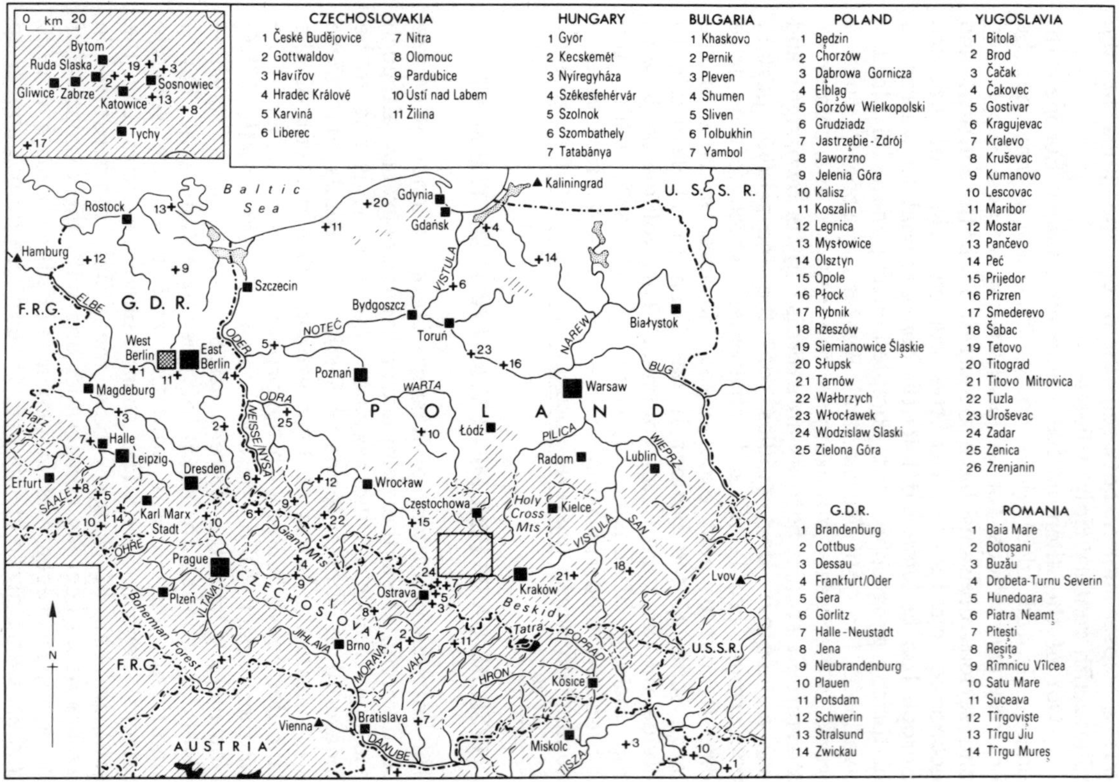

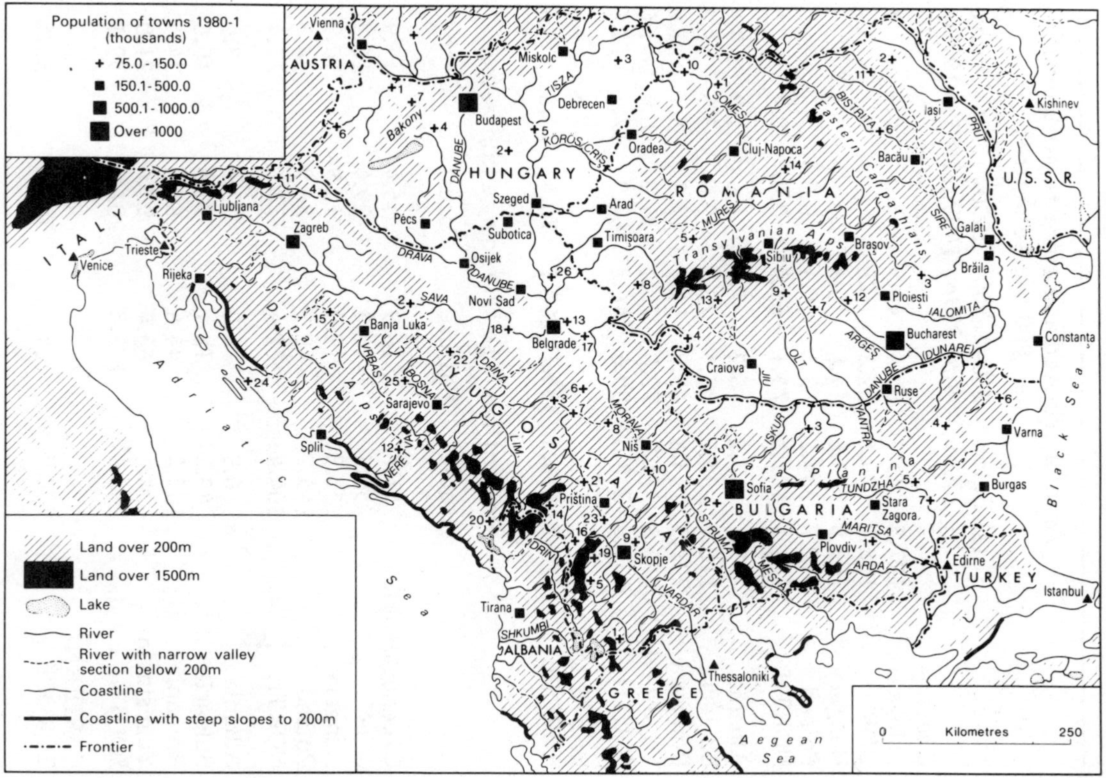

Source: Modern atlases and statistical yearbooks

Table 0.1: Relief and land use

	Area distributed according to altitudinal zones '000 square metres						
	Total	Below 200m	200-499m	500-999m	1000-1499m	1500-1999m	Above 1999m
Czecho-slovakia	127.9	15.1	68.4	40.9	3.0	0.4	*
GDR	108.2	74.6	22.8	10.8			
Hungary	93.0	77.6	14.8	0.6			
Poland	312.7	234.2	69.1	9.1	0.3		
NORTH	641.8	401.5	175.1	61.4	3.4	0.4	*
Albania	28.7	7.2	6.2	7.5	5.6	1.9	0.4
Bulgaria	110.9	35.2	38.5	23.2	9.6	3.5	1.2
Romania	237.5	103.8	63.9	45.9	17.8	5.1	1.0
Yugoslavia	255.8	71.8	72.0	70.1	34.0	6.9	1.0
SOUTH	632.9	218.0	180.6	146.7	67.0	17.4	3.6
EASTERN EUROPE	1274.7	619.5	355.7	208.1	70.4	17.8	3.6

	Present land use '000 square kilometres			
	Arable	Pasture	Forest	Other
Czechoslovakia	51.7	16.9	45.4	13.9
GDR	50.2	12.3	29.4	16.3
Hungary	53.3	12.9	15.9	10.9
Poland	149.2	40.3	86.9	36.3
NORTH	304.4	82.4	177.6	77.4
Albania	6.0	6.2	13.5	3.0
Bulgaria	43.8	18.1	38.4	10.6
Romania	105.0	44.6	63.4	24.5
Yugoslavia	78.8	63.4	92.6	21.0
SOUTH	233.6	132.3	207.9	59.1
EASTERN EUROPE	538.0	214.7	385.5	136.5

* less than 0.1

Source: J. Breu 1970, Atlas der Donauländer (Vienna: Osterreichisches Ost- und Sudosteuropa Institut) and statistical yearbooks.

of relief, the availability of navigable rivers (particularly the Danube) and above all the frequency of either grassland or easily cleared open woodland on loess soils made much of central Europe and the Balkans a corridor for early movement', clearly separated from the Mediterranean by the Dinaric Alps and associated structures.[19] Migrants found their way into Eastern Europe from the Aegean via the Morava Vardar corridor or from the Black Sea, with westward movement possible either along the Danube or across the steppe-lands which gave ready access through Silesia towards the Elbe and via the Carpathian passes to Pannonia. Perhaps the amber routes best exemplify the role of Eastern Europe in transmitting new cultural elements across the steppes and North European Plain, thereby nourishing such remarkable responses on the continental periphery as the Scandinavian Early Bronze Age. But with regard to political development it is evident that there have been several distinct natural regions with resources capable of inducing a powerful sense of unity which has complicated the emergence of stable larger units.

However any review of early settlement must acknowledge that the Middle East was the important diffusion centre so that the southern parts of Eastern Europe were the first to be affected by prehistoric migrations. The northern zone of coniferous and deciduous woodlands must have appeared relatively unattractive on account of its peripheral position in relation to many of the early cultural developments. However the Germans and Slavs were eventually able to colonise the whole of Eastern Europe's largest lowland zone and initiate economic developments which emphatically eclipsed the south in late Medieval and modern times. This relative revaluation of the resources of the northern and southern parts of Eastern Europe could be seen simply as an accommodation to the emergence of Western Europe as the centre for innovation and the market that could draw surplus primary production most easily from areas immediately adjacent. But it also is evident that the fuel and mineral endowment in the north was particularly suitable for diffusion of the Western European industrial revolution with the hard coal of Moravia and Silesia, the soft coal of Bohemia and Saxony, an abundance of salt and a useful endowment of iron ore and other minerals. In the south light industries were more backward technologically and therefore less competitive, while the relatively high transport costs to West European markets reduced the profitability of international trade and encouraged the persistence of traditional social structures. It is therefore the access between Eastern and Western Europe that is crucial in conditioning development options rather than the resource endowment of Eastern Europe per se.[20] Although power was concentrated at the Baltic approaches, the northern areas were much more closely in touch by virtue of the navigable rivers draining to the Baltic and North Sea whereas in the south the Dinaric barrier complicates access to the Adriatic and the Danube, with its many navigational problems, drains southeastwards to the Black Sea which is then some 6000km. from the great ports of Western Europe. Thus the plight of the Balkans in modern times, as the periphery of an inevitably backward empire, is underlined. The Ottomans, like the Byzantines before, tried to interrupt the trade flows between Western Europe and the Orient but they were unable to capitalise on their successes and the Ottoman economy drew relatively little benefit from the interaction.

So it is established that while Eastern Europe has always been eminently congenial for settlement and economic development it is handicapped by remoteness from the major shipping lanes of the Baltic and Mediterranean (and even greater inaccessibility in relation to the Atlantic theatre in modern times). Highly favoured districts capable of functioning as ecumene for state development have been compromised by the potentials for continental and global power which usually place Eastern Europe in a marchland position, either between the gates leading the Baltic and Black seas or else between the sea power of the west and the land power of the east. But within Eastern Europe it is clearly relevant to discriminate between north and south, separating the territory of Czechoslovakia, the GDR, Hungary and Poland from the rest.

It is also worth pointing out that for the south (Albania, Bulgaria, Romania and Yugoslavia) the popular term 'Balkan' may be used as an alternative label. This is a rather enigmatic regional name, basically derived from a Turkish word indicating a heavily wooded mountain ridge. It seems to have been first used by A. Zeune in 1789 wishing to avoid both the political label 'European Turkey' and the obvious clinical alternative 'Southeast Europe'. However there has always been a certain imprecision as to the true limits of the Balkans.[21] The mountain core of Bulgaria and Macedonia is rather too restrictive: at least it may be supposed that fairly civilised hill country (with forest and meadow) is included because the word dagh would be more appropriate for wild and rocky terrain.[22] However despite Zeune's sense of political detachment there is little doubt that the label has been appropriated for the European possessions of the Ottoman Empire. Connotations of disunity (as well as backwardness) have arisen and may be attributed to incomplete conquest by both the Byzantine and Ottoman empires and the considerable amount of decentralisation tolerated by the latter, to the point where attempts to overhaul the administration after the Young Turk revolution merely provoked further resistance and the outbreak of the Balkan Wars which reduced the Turkish stake in Europe to the Istanbul-Adrianople bridgehead. Well might M.I. Newbigin ask in 1919 'where racial purity does not exist (and) where stable nationality has not developed what form of human group is possible?'.[23] Since the First World War the link with politics has continued and the famous Yugoslav geographer J. Cvijic (1868-1927) had no scruples about advocating the Danube-Sava-Isonzo line as the northern limit to accommodate the new political realities.[24] Most recent usage has included the Danube plains of Romania and finally, to harmonise with state boundaries, the whole of the latter country. However the progressive enlargement of 'The Balkans' serves to magnify the disunity of the area (even without considering Greece and Turkey). Despite its geographical centrality there is little prospect of Belgrade playing the same role in future as Sirmium did in the Roman period.

METHODOLOGY

The chapters in the two volumes cover quite long periods of time so that broad themes can be developed without excessive repetition. In the companion volume Eastern Europe: an historical geography 1815-1945 the present geography is seen as the outcome of a desperate effort by the new nations in the marchlands of Europe to organise their defences and accelerate the process of modernisation. And in turn the belated manoeuvrings of the inter-war years are rationalised through the tight grip maintained through the nineteenth century and into the eighteenth century by Habsburg, Ottoman and Russian imperialism. But the later chapters of this present volume demonstrate that failure to modernise is not only the consequence of core-periphery antagonisms within the empires but more fundamentally the result of inability to match the progress of Western Europe enjoying the benefit of unhindered access to the oceans. The study of Eastern Europe in the Middle Ages is therefore able to demonstrate the change in relations with the west as the overland trade routes were eclipsed by the seaways. And finally the Medieval states must be seen as the outcome of Dark Age migrations and the prior transfer of technology from the Middle East. In view of this stripping off of overlays there might be some justification for the organisation of chapters in a regressive sequence, working back from the present deeper and deeper into the past. Some work of this kind has been done in France but in Britain there is a strong consensus against such practice.[25] J.L.M. Gulley found it appropriate to take his readers backwards through time to trace the origins of the various elements making up the Wealden landscape of southeast England.[26] But given the long timespan of most of the periods adopted in this book it seems that the mental leaps required by the reader to connect the end of one period with the beginning of the previous period would be too daunting to countenance. And the function of the book as a historical study of Europe's shatterbelt also justifies a conventional sequence of chapters.

Such is the philosophical ferment over 'explanation' in geography today that any writer needs to clarify his position. The view taken here is that established facts must claim priority and to that extent the case for positivism seems fundamentally unanswerable. However human behaviour should be understood as well as explained and to that extent the idealist stance, seeking to relate actions to ideas, is adopted.[27] But it is deployed very much as a critique of positivism and not as an alternative.[28] Arguably it is desirable to go further and recognise the importance of individual initiative in a wider structural context introducing collective values or ideology. Particularly controversial in this context is the Marxist view of socio-economic development related to the three stages of feudalism, capitalism and socialism. Marxism is superficially attractive in the sense that a progressive method is necessary to trace the modernisation of societies in a specific territorial framework evolving through Medieval and Modern times.[29] And it is not unreasonable to deduce through historical materialism a progression from local subsistence to regional and national specialisation on the basis of comparative advantages and to combine with this a pattern of social evolution from feudal interdependence to a more sophisticated relationship between free peoples and welfare states. But the obsession with class conflict as a prelude to revolutionary upheaval not only devalues cultural and political forces of change but burdens the study of past periods with such an emphasis of evil and injustice as to inhibit objective appraisal. Furthermore it is quite unacceptable academically to equate Marx's socialism narrowly with the theory and practice of those regimes which claim to act in his name. Hence the perspectives of many East European scholars based on the assumption that the socialism imposed by their ruling communist parties was bound to emerge and that the capitalism sustained under former East European governments was a transient aberration cannot be appreciated.

Finally it is always a problem for the geographer to decide on the optimum level of spatial referencing. For this work the prominence of research on broad themes by historians and the lack of familiarity with topographical detail on the part of many readers effectively forces a somewhat generalised approach, compromised only by a judicious sprinkling of case studies. Major topographical features are usually assigned their English labels and this conveniently avoids the need to mention the range of titles used by the various peoples of East Europe through centuries of fluctuating political organisation. For settlement names the problem cannot be so easily overcome. English names are used for capital cities throughout the book but all other settlements are given the proper name appropriate to the period. However to make for easy linkage with the present nomenclature the present name is also supplied on the first occasion in the chapter that each place is mentioned. Problems of course still arise, as with the multinational empires of the eighteenth and nineteenth centuries where the language of the imperial power is usually recognised rather than those of subject peoples.

NOTES

1. J. Gottman 1973, 'The significance of territory' (Charlottesville: University Press of Wisconsin) 143.
2. W.J. Cahnman 1949.
3. A.E. Moodie 1956, 'Eastern Marchlands of Europe': W.G. East and A.E. Moodie eds. 'The changing world:

studies in political geography' (London: Harrap) 60-79. The term 'marchland' was previously used by H.G. Wanklyn 1941.

4. W.G. East 1961, 'The concept and political status of the shatter zone': N.J.G. Pounds ed. 'Geographical essays on Eastern Europe' (Bloomington: Indiana University) 1-27.

5. E. Fischer 1956, 'The passing of Mitteleuropa': W.G. East and A.E. Moodie eds. op. cit. (note 3) 67.

6. A.P. Vlasto 1970, 308-9.

7. E. Lewin 1916, 'The German road to the east: an account of the 'Drang nach Osten' and of Teutonic aims in the Near and Middle East' (London: Heinemann).

8. J. Partsch 1905, 'Central Europe' (London: Frowde) 2.

9. G.G. Chisholm 1904, 'Review of J. Partsch's Central Europe' Geographical Journal 23, 242-4.

10. F. Naumann 1916, 'Central Europe' (London: P.S. King). See also H.C. Meyer 1946, 'Mitteleuropa in German political geography' Annals Association of American Geographers 36 178-94; H.C. Meyer 1955; H. Ormsby 1935, 'The definition of Mitteleuropa and its relation to the conception of Deutschland in the writings of modern German geographers' Scottish Geographical Magazine 51, 337-47; K.A. Sinnhuber 1954, 'Central Europe-Mitteleuropa-Europe Centrale: an analysis of a geographical term' Transactions Institute of British Geographers 20, 15-39. For other ideas on federation see M. Hodza 1942, 'Federalism in Central Europe: reflections and recollections' (London: Jarrolds); R. Schlesinger 1945, 'Federalism in Central and Eastern Europe' (London: Kegan Paul Trench Trubner & Co.).

11. G.G. Chisholm 1904, op. cit. (note 9). See also W. Lacqeur 1965, 'Russia and Germany: a century of conflict' (London: Weidenfeld & Nicolson).

12. E. Fischer 1956, op. cit. (note 5).

13. S.B. Cohen 1968, 'The contemporary geopolitical setting: a proposal for global geopolitical equilibrium': C.A. Fisher ed. 'Essays in political geography' (London: Methuen) 61-72. Also S.B. Cohen 1973, 'Geography and politics in a world divided' (New York: Oxford University Press) 59-89.

14. H.J. Mackinder 1904, 'The geographical pivot of history' Geographical Journal 23, 421-37; H.J. Mackinder 1919, 'Democratic ideals and reality' (London: Constable). See also A. Hall 1955, 'Mackinder and the course of events' Annals Association of American Geographers 45, 109-26; J.R. Smith 1943, 'Grassland and farmland in the cyclical development of Eurasian history' Ibid 33, 135-61.

15. C. Gati 1974, 'East Central Europe: touchstone for detente' Journal of International Affairs 28, 158-74; C. Gati 1981, 'Worker assertiveness: western dilemmas'; J.F. Triska and C. Gati eds. 'Blue collar workers in Eastern Europe' (London: George Allen & Unwin) 283-94; R.B. King and R.W. Dean eds. 1974, 'East European perspectives on European security and cooperation' (New York: Praeger); R. Kintner and W. Klaiber 1971, 'Eastern Europe and European security' (New York: Dunellan); E.N. Luttwak 1983, 'The grand strategy of the Soviet Union' (London: Weidenfeld & Nicolson); J. Pinder and P. Pinder 1975, 'The European Community's policy towards Eastern Europe' (London: Chatham House). For consideration of emigre pressure groups see G. Ginsburgs 1959-60, 'Hungary and Hungarian exiles' Journal of Central European Affairs 19, 227-59; C.D. Harris and C. Wulker 1953, 'The refugee problem of Germany' Economic Geography 29, 10-25.

16. See for example R.R. King and J.F. Brown eds. 1977; J.M. Montias 1969, 'Obstacles to the economic integration of Eastern Europe' Studies in Comparative Communism 3-4, 38-60; L.P. Morris 1980, 'Dependent independence: Eastern Europe 1918-1956' History Today 30, 38-48; P. Summerscale 1981, 'The East European predicament' (Aldershot: Gower); P. Summerscale 1981, 'Is Eastern Europe a liability to the Soviet Union?' International Affairs 57, 585-98.

17. W.H. Parker 1968, 'Historical geography of Russia' (London: University of London Press); C.T. Smith 1967. The post-war restructuring of Eastern Europe has called for a new generation of text books. Geographers have been slow to respond to the challenge although the first major contribution (R.H. Osborne 1967) has since been followed by others offering treatment with either a regional bias (N.J.G. Pounds 1969) or a thematic orientation (R.E.H. Mellow 1975; D. Turnock 1978). Much the same situation arose after the First World War with textbooks on current affairs making an immediate appearance: like R. Butler 1919, 'The new Eastern Europe' (London: Longman); and geographical synthesis coming only later, most notably H.G. Wanklyn 1941.

18. C. Embleton ed. 1984, 'Geomorphology of Europe' (London: Macmillan) 152-9, 214-30, 355-86.

19. W.G. East 1966, 'An historical geography of Europe' (London: Methuen) 51.

20. S. Rokkan 1980, 'Territories centres and peripheries:

towards a geoethnic-geoeconomic-geopolitical model of differentiation within Western Europe', J. Gottman ed. 'Centre and periphery: spatial variation in politics' (London: Sage Publications) 163-204.

21. F.W. Carter ed. 1977, 7-14.

22. D.G. Hogarth 1913, 'The Balkan peninsula' Geographical Journal 41, 324-40; F.R. Maunsell 1906, 'The Rhodope Balkans' Ibid 28, 7-30.

23. M.I. Newbegin 1919, 'The human geography of the Balkans' Geographical Journal 53, 221-3 (quote p.113).

24. S. Culibrk 1971, 'Cvijic's sociological research into society in the Balkans' British Journal of Sociology 22, 423-40.

25. A.R.H. Baker 1968, 'A note on the retrospective and regressive approaches in historical geography' Erdkunde 22, 244-5.

26. J.L.M. Gulley 1960, 'The Wealden landscape in the early seventeenth century and its antecedents' (London University: Ph.D. thesis).

27. L. Guelke 1982, 'Historical understanding in geography: an idealist approach' (Cambridge: Cambridge University Press).

28. J.N. Entrikin 1976, 'Contemporary humanism in geography' Annals Association of American Geographers 66, 615-32.

29. M. Quaini 1982, 'Geography and Marxism' (Oxford: Blackwell) 171. See also R.J. Johnston 1983, 'Philosophy and human geography: an introduction to contemporary approaches' (London: Arnold) 87-121.

Pre-Medieval Eastern Europe

to c.1000

1

The Region in Prehistory

There is much that is speculative concerning the relations between the various cultures recognised in prehistory. It is only in the Iron Age that there are clear hints about the existence of sharp class differences in society and the importance of central places to coordinate administration and defence for incipient states made up of apparently loose groupings of tribes. But what is clearly distinct about this whole period is the relatively advanced state of the Balkans compared with the northern half of Eastern Europe, and indeed compared with Western Europe for much of prehistory.[1] The eclipse of the Balkans, culturally and technologically, over the last thousand years is part of a radical turnaround in relationships between the Middle East and Western Europe. The diffusion centre can be seen shifting from the Middle East to Greece and Rome in the course of prehistory and subsequently the shift has continued into northwestern Europe. Although inevitably tributary to Greece, with an excellent position for trade in the eastern Mediterranean reaching out to the Adriatic, Black Sea and Lower Danube, the Balkans enjoyed considerable opportunity. There was significant economic growth and a measure of political consolidation among the Thracian tribes which the Romans felt obliged to interrupt. At times the Balkans showed a capacity for innovation, providing the culture hearth for the Urnfield peoples and the base for their migrations to both the east and west, although the underlying theme of the chapter is the spread of advanced cultures from the Middle East, Europe's peninsula status and the role of the Balkans in the diffusion process.

NEOLITHIC SETTLEMENT

It is perhaps inappropriate to deal with the very earliest cultures, not least because the process of adaptation to a changing environment at the end of the Ice Age does not seem to generate significant themes relevant specifically to Eastern Europe. But it is likely that the area was already transmitting cultural impulses from the east since an Asian origin is proposed for the Aurignacian culture which once embraced the whole area from the Crimea through the Hercynian lands into southern France. However the amelioration in climate transformed an open countryside into a relatively well-wooded environment and cultures became more localised within groups of small and widely scattered communities: C.T. Smith suggests the possibility 'that the greater resources of the forest, the decline of long-distance seasonal migrations over open country and the isolation of groups within a forested environment combined to bring to an end the uniformity over wide areas which seems to characterise the Upper Palaeolithic world of open vegetation, wide-ranging game and communal hunting'.[2]

Various artifacts have been found in Pannonia on sandy 'islands' surrounded by waterlogged floodplains and at Backa Palanka and Peres in Vojvodina there is evidence of the population's dependence on deer, goats and pigs. Similar evidence comes from the Dinaric Alps and especially Crvena Stijena in Montenegro, while in the Iron Gates the emphasis on small game (in addition to pigs and red deer) and fishing seems to have allowed an unusual degree of sedentism. On the North European Plain the landscape of mixed oak forest, lakes and marshes created further scope for a combination of hunting, fowling and fishing, as indicated by evidence from Hohen Viecheln on Lake Schwerin for a large kill of auroch, elk, red deer, reindeer and wild boar along with water fowl and fish.[3] Cultivation and stockrearing, along with the manufacturing skills in ceramics and textiles which comprise the Neolithic revolution, may well have emerged out of problems over food supply in southwestern Asia during drier, warmer conditions and diffusion of such knowledge into Eastern Europe may have been accelerated by population pressure. The Asian connection in agricultural development is inferred by evidence suggesting that early farming cultures in Europe possessed barley and emmer wheat as well as cattle, goats, sheep and swine. And although there are some anomalies radio-carbon dates

Figure 1.1: Prehistoric sites in Eastern Europe

Source: Archaeological and historical atlases

suggest a diffusion across Europe from southeast to northwest. The earliest farming settlements in southeast Europe date to the sixth millennium BC and settlers from Anatolia and Greece were probably responsible. But a standard pattern throughout Eastern Europe can hardly be anticipated since the variations in physical potential would require significant adjustments. Rye and oats which might at first have been simply weeds associated with wheat and barley cultivation in the Mediterranean zone were eventually appreciated as crops in their own right, given hungry soils or particularly cool and damp conditions characteristic of parts of Eastern Europe. Also, while pigs were well-suited for grazing in woodland, sheep were generally preferred on grassland and heath.

In spite of these variations technology was too limited to cope with many areas, particularly the damp oak forest. Instead it was the loess soils that were clearly favoured by the pioneer farmers of Eastern Europe. Gradmann's Steppenheide thesis may now be rejected in the light of pollen analysis which shows that the loess lands were not naturally free of woodland, but the mixed oak forest on these light soils could quite easily be cleared with flint implements to accommodate a 'slash and burn' type of agriculture from which grasslands and heaths were eventually derived.[4] The Danubian peasant cultivated beans, flax, lentils and peas as well as barley and wheat but particular skills were shown in cattle breeeding and in the domestication of the wild auroch to yield strong but docile oxen. Cultural unity can be seen most obviously in the style of decorated pottery found over a wide belt of Eastern Europe from the upper Dniester valley westwards to Poland, Pannonia and Bohemia across whose loess lands settlement spread rapidly until c.4000 BC (the date for Magdeburg which lies close to the northwestern limit). There was also a spread of farming activity northwards across the boulder clay zone of the Urstromtaler/pradoliny, developing the old Mesolithic hunting and fishing traditions of the North European Plain. Indeed the Danubian culture is frequently labelled Linear Pottery or LBK (an abbreviation of Linearbandkeramik) because of the distinctive incised ware produced by the peasants. There is no need to invoke important migrations for these developments. Farming in these areas might have been a temperate European invention and a response to the deteriorating Atlantic climate which made the area marginal for foraging yet feasible for agriculture.[5]

On the boulder clay typical LBK settlements involved mixed farming in small clearings in a heavily-forested landscape. Shifting cultivation could well have meant periodic shifts in the sites on which large rectangular timber houses were erected, but cereal cultivation was limited and cattle were the key resource, at Brzesc-Kujawski for example (with game hunting and the collection of fish, molluscs and turtles from the nearby lake). But on the loess soils there was a much thinner woodland cover and villages were larger and more numerous. There was intensive garden cultivation around Krakow and evidence of considerable prosperity in the polished axes near the longhouse at Olszanica. There could have been some specialisation among the two categories of settlement with stock from the loess zone herded in the forests to the north.[6] Further expansion of agriculture into the third millennium is marked by a change in pottery style from LBK to Funnel Beaker (or Tricherbecher, abbreviated TRB), although this would seem to indicate an evolution process among the indigenous population and not a migration, or struggle for supremacy between two cultures. Forest clearance accelerated and Brzesc-Kujawski became a settlement of around a hundred people dwelling in longhouses all the year round in connection with agriculture and crafts. Grain cultivation and pig rearing supplemented cattle herding and foraging. Another consequence of a rising population was a shift to the coast. Settlements were now placed on patches of light soil at the contact between wet grazing lands and heavy but fertile soil immediately inland. Cattle were kept and this implies that the nearest wet grazings were reserved for hay making and the more distant pastures were used for summer grazing. Amber was being traded along the Baltic coast.

THE NEOLITHIC REVOLUTION IN PANNONIA AND THE BALKANS

From the very beginnings of human settlement man has been able to thrive in the Carpathian-Danubian territory because of the complementary resources of the different zones: 'the mountains contained iron, copper, gold, silver and even tin depositions. Vineyards could flourish on the slopes and hillsides; all types of cereals spread over the fields lower down, while in many cases the forest extended down to the banks of the Danube'.[7] It is also relevant to point out that numerous passes and defiles make the Carpathians a particularly accessible mountainous region while 'the numerous depressions within the Carpathians offer particularly favourable conditions for human life and accordingly have always been densely populated'.[8] The history of settlement began with the scattered Mesolithic hunter-fisher communities whose activities occupy a huge span of history from the tenth millennium down to the fifth or sixth. But it is quite impossible to offer a satisfactory historical narrative and few sites are well-known. Some evidence from the Ceahlau area of Moldavia ties in with a hunting culture embracing the Baltic-Black Sea zone but the best evidence is from the Danube gorges and the mountains of Banat and Oltenia: hunter-fisher settlement has been radiocarbon-dated as far back in time as the eleventh millennium when the forested environment supplied some sixteen species of mammals to complement the local resources in birds, fish, mussels and snails. Evidence from several caves in the area including Baia de Fier, Carasova, Cheia and Ohaba Ponor reveals a Mousterian hunting culture and a transition through a vegetational climax (early in the seventh millennium) to the beginnings of Neolithic settlement with its agricultural base. A Schela Cladovei culture replaced flint with quartzite and deer horn tools, secured more permanent dwellings and achieved primitive plant cultivation and animal domestication in addition to hunting and gathering.

J. Nandris emphasises the importance of the Lepenski Vir site (on the Yugoslav side of the Danube) in demonstrating 'that in favourable conditions in a hunter-fisher climax could rise to a settlement type which, if not a village, was at least a hamlet', to be succeeded on the same spot by a 'First Temperate Neolithic' settlement which may have been more permanent if not entirely perennial.[9] This latter occupation 'clearly took up and even extended the range of hunting exploitation of the forest environment, continued to emphasise fishing and adopted the dog from the hunter-fishers'.[10] The hunter-fisher culture thus overlaps with the Neolithic with its emphasis on the harvesting (rather than simple gathering) of plants and control of reproduction of certain animal species, allowing regular village settlements with substantial houses and allocation of effort to carpentry, ceramics and weaving. Evolving gradually out of hunting and gathering in the Middle East the new Neolithic model could be widely adopted wherever the

Figure 1.2: Prehistoric settlement in the Tiszazug, Pannonian Plain

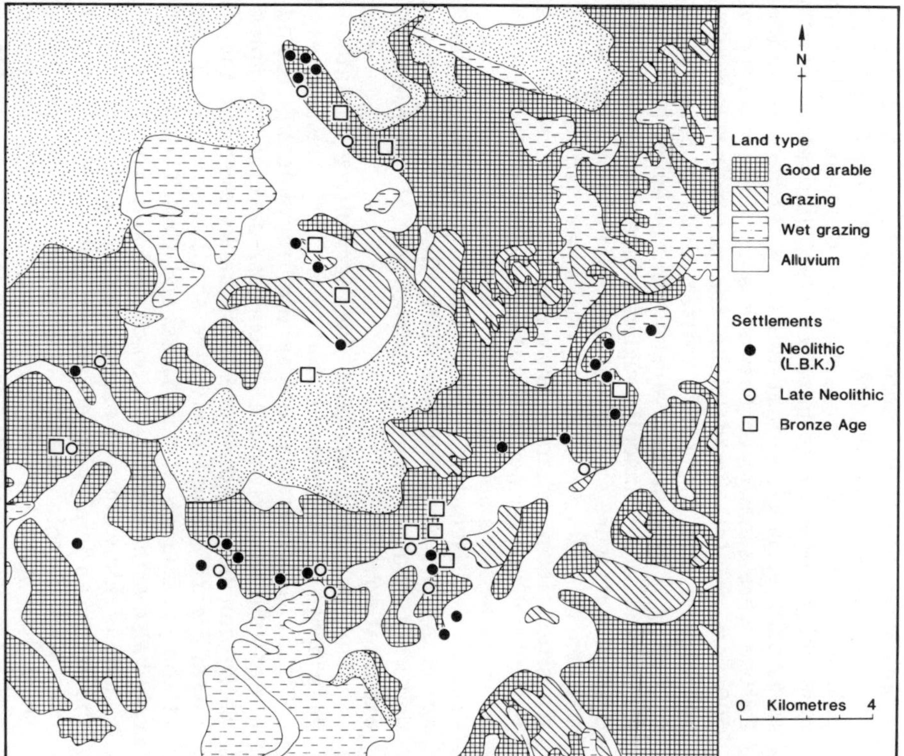

Source: M.J. Jarman et al. eds. 1982 (note 5) 182-3.

pressure of a growing population provided the stimulus.

The environment was at least permissive and probably stimulative. Sheep and goats were available as well as native European cattle, which remained common enough for a Moldavian bull to be incorporated in the arms of several of the principality's distinguished Medieval rulers. And while paleoenvironmental reconstruction does not yet allow convincing correlations between Neolithic settlements and loess soils it is clear that the early farmers in southeast Europe were sandwiched between a dry Pontic steppe with 500 mm rainfall (insufficient for prevailing agricultural techniques) and the much wetter lands of the Adriatic, exceeding 750 mm per annum. Micro-regional studies in Macedonia and Pannonia suggest furthermore that well-drained soils were sought and that part of the importance of southeastern Europe lies in the scope it offered for a transition from reliance on water-retentive soils (crucial to the Neolithic farmer in the Middle East and Mediterranean) to the well-drained soils which were essential for the extension of Neolithic culture to temperate latitudes. For above all 'the Neolithic was distinguished not by economic uniformity but by regional adaptation of its premises of exploitation'.[11]

The potential of land for agriculture dictated the geography of settlement but the very best sites for habitations occurred where fertile tractable soils could be integrated with riverside resources, several examples of which can be found where loess banks overlook the river Tisza. Figure 1.2 deals with the small area called Tiszazug at the confluence of the Tisza and Cris/Körös. Such sites could also offer a combination of freedom from flood on dry islands of alluvium and easy access to water supplies, with the latter an important advantage until wells were sunk in low water table areas. The river could also provide protection and facilitate movement. Cereals were grown on the loess soils, well able to stand long periods of cropping, while cattle grazed on the high-quality wet-land pasture created by the shifting river courses, though there may have been transhumance to exploit the grazing of the Tisza-Danube interfluve and the Bükk mountains.[12] In the Nova Zagora area of Bulgaria villages were placed at the contact between the limestone hills and the plains, convenient for the cultivation of sandy soils at the foot of the hills for cereals and fodder while the riverine soils and the waterlogged soils of the plains provided only grazing. Sheep and goats would be taken to the hills in summer.[13]

The farming population formed a large group traditionally labelled Starcevo, impinging on Pannonia and the Morava-Vardar corridor. Anza was a typical Starcevo settlement, comprising a small cluster of houses on the edge of a polje. Cropping concentrated on einkorn and millet, although the cereal harvest was supplemented by wild fruit, and while sheep and goats were kept, predominating over cattle and pigs, hunting was still widespread.[14] In other parts of the Balkans the prevailing culture was variously labelled Cris/Körös, Hamangia and Karanovo I. Settlements were usually dispersed and people lived in small rectangular one-roomed houses which were partly subterranean and built of timber and clay. There is no evidence of fortification. Considerable information is available from Asmaskamogila and Karanovo in Bulgaria on both houses and the wider settlement plan. Dwellings were far superior to their Mesolithic counterparts and almost resemble the accommodation used by some of the metal-using cultures such as the Cucuteni in Moldavia, Gumelnita in Bulgaria, Lengyel in Hungary and Vinca in Serbia. Kazanlik in Bulgaria reveals corduroy timber flooring while Ludvar near Szeged in Hungary shows a gabled roof with alternately interlocking rafters. On the other hand, equipment for fishing, hunting and wood-cutting is also commonplace and includes more than a hint of continuity with the Mesolithic. The same applies to pottery which reveals much about each local culture on account of the decoration and production methods. Wares were painted before firing (hence 'painted pottery') and in southern Hungary animal designs incised on the pottery recall Mesolithic art. Other important sites include Ciumesti near Satu Mare, Erbiceni near Iasi and Hamangia in Dobrogea: the latter area demonstrates early domestication of sheep and (in the Tîrgsor cave) continuity of settlement from the Mousterian period to the Neolithic.

New regional cultures have been identified for the Middle Neolithic, including Karanovo II and Veselinovo in Bulgaria, Hamangia and Vadastra in Romania and Vinca-Tordos/Turdas in Yugoslavia and Banat. They may result from further migration associated with the spread of linear pottery (i.e. pottery with linear decorations) from the north but the present consensus is that they developed out of the earlier cultures with subsistence economies now sufficiently advanced to allow permanent settlements. The more stable economy comprised cereal growing and stockrearing with some manufacturing indicated by finds of spindle whorls and loom weights. For example, settlement is reported in the fifth century B.C. at Tîrpesti on a terrace in the Topolita Valley of Moldavia, with potential for agriculture and hunting in adjacent woods.[15] Archaeologists still speak of a basic cultural unity in Eastern Europe but it is evident that the man-environment 'synthesis' in each area was generating contrasts which progressively eroded simplistic notions of uniformity. This applies in the case of defence for by the end of the Middle Neolithic some cultures were finding it necessary to fortify their settlements with defensive ditches.

A further phase of indigenous cultural development yields the various Late Neolithic cultures of the Balkans: Boian, Gumelnita and Maritsa in Bulgaria, Cucuteni-Tripolye and Salcuta in Romania and Vinca-Plocnik in Yugoslavia. There was considerable growth at existing settlements and many new settlements emerged. The growth of population may well have led to extensive woodland clearance to supplement the grazing for cattle and pigs and to allow renewed emphasis on hunting. But it is difficult to reconstruct the Neolithic environment with great accuracy and it is not clear for example to what extent the chernozem soils of the Lower Danube and Pannonia would have been available.[16] It is also uncertain how far changing sea and river levels affected the grazing available on the floodplains. Increased flooding of the lunci of the Lower Danube, along with rising population, could have instigated the search for new grazing areas as far afield as the Carpathians and so resulted in the long-wave transhumance systems which continued until modern times. This scenario could then be extended to envisage initial seasonal settlement in the intermontane depressions of the Carpathians. The bell-shaped pits found at Rotbay near Brasov could possibly be the food stores of migratory pastoralists. The Neolithic-Bronze transition brings the first evidence of cereal growing in this area of Transylvania, where millet and barley reflect adjustment to the rigorous climate, while the timber and daub buildings noted at Ariusd might be associated with the beginnings of permanent settlement in districts with particularly severe winter conditions. Evidence from Nova Zagora points to some abandonment of settlements during the third millennium. This may have arisen because population growth outstripped the limited potential for cropping and the necessary expansion of pastoralism may have resulted in serious erosion and necessitated radical economic and social change. It is also possible that a slight deterioration of climate could have increased liability to late frosts and reduced the agricultural potential considerably.

Although the plough was not fully introduced farming may now be described as prosperous and the development of copper metallurgy was a very significant achievement, allowing the production of various tools and weapons.[17] Hostilities between tribes increased and defence became quite general, either through simple ditches or by ditches and ramparts. With surpluses of metal, as well as grain and livestock, pillaging expeditions may well have become more frequent. Manufacturing was still more important for spindle whorls were now used, with either a distaff or upright loom, and the closed down-draught kiln gave rise to the magnificent painted pottery associated especially with the Cucuteni culture in Romania. This originated in southeastern Transylvania with the important site of Ariusd but several remarkable sites have been explored in Moldavia including Habasesti and Trusesti as well as Cucuteni itself. Considerable nucleations of settlement now existed with areas as large as 6.0 ha surrounded by double ditches. Houses were evidently packed closely together with a circular layout at Habasesti and parallel rows at Trusesti. The former settlement was based on a platform of tree trunks covered with several layers of clay burnt to produce a foundation with the colour and consistency of brick. The lower terraces of river valleys certainly appear to have been the most valuable settlement sites although caves were still used. Another important site more recently investigated is Nedeia at Ghelaiesti in the Moldova valley where twelve Cucuteni dwellings have been found. In addition to painted pottery interesting evidence was found of the spiritual life of the tribesmen and their primitive conception of certain natural phenomena.

Such was the distinction of this culture that, given favourable physical conditions and political unity 'it might have developed into a rival of the early civilisations of the Middle East and Egypt', with its access to forest, sea and steppe assuring a formidable combination of resources and considerable population movement which was important in stimulating trade and innovation.[18] However prosperity was affected by the deterioration of the Atlantic climate into a colder and wetter phase. The environmental change seems to have sparked off a great deal of population movement and given rise to the greatest 'migration period' of prehistory. Although complex the migrations will be treated below on a simplified basis with discrimination between the Battle Axe (metal) and Bell Beaker groups. The successful metal-working cultures seem to have come to an abrupt end and subsequent innovations emerged from other parts of Eastern Europe, although it may be argued that the net result of the upheavals was a sequence of technological developments working through to the Iron Age which were undoubtedly beneficial to the continent as a whole.

DIFFUSION OF TECHNOLOGY IN THE LATE NEOLITHIC AND BRONZE AGE

The Late Neolithic brought significant technological change with the use of the wheel in both pottery and transport, but above all wider knowledge of copper working. This was very significant for Eastern Europe in view of the generous mineral endowment. The earliest-known copper mines have been located at Aibunar near Stara Zagora in Bulgaria and Rudna Glava in the Majdanpek area of Yugoslavia. Some very early metal objects are of Anatolian origin but in the light of recent finds like the Varna treasure (dating to the fifth millennium) it is likely that metallurgy was invented independently in Eastern Europe.[19] For areas immediately to the east did not have copper when the first beginnings were made in the Balkans, an unlikely situation in the event of diffusion from Anatolia. And the industry in Europe also evolved its own style with emphasis on the manufacture of core-cast shaft-hole axes, probably the earliest of all metal shaft-hole tools. The technology could have emerged from the pottery industry which was achieving high kiln temperatures, while the social stimulus (creating a demand for metal ornaments) presumably arose through the emergence of a more highly stratified society headed by tribal chiefs. These technical and social developments seem to have been the work of two basic cultures: Battle Axe and Beaker, which incidentally shared a preference for burial in single graves, often under barrows. It is quite possible that there were metal prototypes for the polished stone axes (frequently found deposited with male skeletons) which are characteristic of the Battle Axe cultures. The latter embraced the river valleys of the North European Plain and the steppelands extending from the Crimea towards the middle Vistula, the river valleys of the North European Plain and the northern shores of the Baltic where the pastoral people settled for the most part on land not already occupied by the Beakers.

The idea of a cultural diffusion of Battle Axe peoples from the Black Sea is given substance by technological and cultural similarities with the Kurgan (Pit Grave) Culture of the Caucasus, and Russian steppes linked in turn with Mesopotamia, although it is not impossible that some elements of the Battle Axe culture could have evolved within Eastern Europe with population pressure the stimulus for secondary settlements, more sophisticated farming and herding skills (such as domestication of the horse) and production of war materials (including wheeled vehicles). Traces of a patriarchal society could be related to the enhanced status of the male population given the higher level of conflict. Nevertheless the possibility of local adaptation by the indigenous populations need not rule out all migration from the east while the correlation of archaelogical finds with the classic diffusion path makes a completely independent origin in Eastern Europe highly unlikely. A similar problem arises in those parts of the North European Plain and Pannonia where the Battle Axe folk evidently mingled with Bell Beakers, another group of warrior-pastoralists known from the shape of their drinking cups. These people, who may have migrated inland from Iberia, were traders as well as farmers; they could have started copper mining in the Carpathians and developed the amber trade from the shores of the Baltic south to the Aegean. However an alternative hypothesis which places the origin of the Beakers in the east can also find support, with westward migration arising from pressure by people lying further to the east such as the Kurgan folk. Many local beaker varieties suggest assimilation of the culture by established societies but the uniformity of the early style suggests an element of migration.

The same uncertainties continue into the Bronze Age. Long distance trade is manifested above all by the supply of amber to the Mediterranean by the Elbe-Danube and Saale-Main-Danube routes towards the Brenner Pass and Adriatic. It is also implied by the intensive working of Carpathian minerals for the copper and tin from which bronze is derived. One of the important trade routes made use of the Elbe-Vltava waterway and its importance is brought out by amber found in Early Bronze Age graves in Bohemia and by the assumption that Jutland amber would have been exchanged for Bohemian tin, quite apart from exchanges taking place over longer distances. An alternative route along the Saale is suggested by the Dieskau amber hoard (near Halle) and the amber found in burials at Apolda and Seebergen in Thuringia.[20] A more easterly trade seems to have operated from the Lower Vistula, Warta and Oder valleys to the Sudeten Mountains and thence through the Moravian Gate to the head of the Adriatic (though with some trade diverted down the Sava into Croatia and Bosnia). Amber found at Gorszewice near Oborniki in the Warta area and the beads from the Byciskala cave near Brno lend support to this idea, with activity persisting into the Iron Age. With the new metallurgical techniques used in Mycenaean Greece the bone, flint and wood which had continued to be used for most tools, due to the scarcity of copper, was gradually substituted and with the collapse of Mycenaean power c.1400 BC there was more metal available for use in Europe.

But there is also evidence to suggest that while knowledge of copper working came into Europe from the southeast, discovery of bronze is related to the minerals of Bohemia and the Alps: the classic site is Unetice (Ger. Aunjetitz) where metal working pre-dates the start of activities in Syria, once thought to have been the diffusion centre.[21] And certainly the burial customs of the Urnfield Culture evolved locally. From c.1200 BC cremation was preferred to burial and as the ashes were placed in urns the cemetery or urnfield replaced the tumulus of earlier times. However a more important contrast lies in the greater importance of agriculture thanks to the ard, a light wooden plough drawn by animal power, which gave rise not simply to further woodland clearance but a system of permanent fields and nucleated settlements. Although the relationship between the Urnfield Culture and the collapse of Mycenae is uncertain there is no doubt that settlement spread outwards from the centre of Europe in practically all directions. It was an essentially continental phenomenon, with the mainspring of expansion rooted in the Danube Valley at a time when Mediterranean trade was in decline. The continuing development of industry is evident in Austria and Bohemia. For instead of the early practice of collecting copper ore at the surface or in shallow opencast workings there was now deep mining, requiring the large-scale organisation and the permanent work force suggested by the

Mühlbach-Bischofshofen area of Austria. With this improved metal supply went improved skills in manufacturing and the range of products now included complicated core-cast tools and sheet-metal armour.

Meanwhile in the Baltic there was a lack of ore and hence the persistence of a Stone Age technology.[22] However amber could be traded in the south for bronze, so that metal appeared eventually, even though its use was not as widespread as it was in other parts of Eastern Europe. In the south material progress was much more evident. Well-known Early Bronze Age cultures include the Periam-Pecica Culture of Pannonia, the Cernavoda-Cotofeni-Glina, Monteoru-Weitenberg and associated cultures of Romania and the Nagyrév Culture of Pannonia and Slovakia.[23] Large cemeteries are typical of the period and help to indicate extension of settlement to new sites like Pecica and Toszeg while hoards of buried metal goods have been unearthed at Apa and Hajdusamson. The tribes in this area (which may be collectively labelled Thracian) were strategically situated between the metal-working centres on the northern side and the industrial/commercial complex of Mycenae to the south. Transit trade flourished, along with exchanges based on local minerals including copper, gold and salt. Increasing prosperity is evident. The tribal aristocracy could enjoy a life of luxury which is reflected in a taste for personal ornaments in bronze and gold, faience amber beads of Mycenaean origin and fine richly-ornamented pottery. Weapons were appreciated as symbols of wealth like the gold dagger and silver axes found at Persinari near Tîrgoviste or the Mycenaean sword from Rosiorii de Vede. It should not be supposed that all need for defence disappeared for settlement shows some tendency to use the higher ground.

The Monteoru culture, a refinement of the Cernavoda and Glina cultures of the Early Bronze Age, has left a legacy on a hill-top at Sarata Monteoru in the Subcarpathian zone near Buzau: this is Cetatuia which could be described as an acropolis and an important centre for the tribal community. In Transylvania the Weitenberg culture (a development of the Early Bronze Age Cotofeni culture) shows a preference for high ground close to rivers and similar trends are evident in the associated Tei and Verbicioara cultures. Caves were inhabited too at Baia de Fier and Baile Herculane. Mixed farming remained the norm (though with intensified stockrearing and some hunting) but transport was greatly eased by the introduction from the south of the four-wheeled cart which spread beyond the Carpathians during the Bronze Age. Weitenberg pottery found near Sighisoara in Transylvania shows remarkably elegant spiral and meander patterns and metal manufacturing was also of a high order. Trade, migration or war booty may account for the various hoards of Transylvanian origin found to the east, giving rise to considerable Late Bronze Age cultural uniformity (Noua culture) in Romania and adjacent areas of the USSR. In western Romania, extending into Hungary, another large cultural unit emerged - the Suciu, forming a transition through to the Hallstatt Iron Age. Contact with Mycenae should not however be exaggerated. At times the Morava-Vardar trade route fell into disuse, leaving the Stara Planina as a clear cultural boundary between the influences of Mycenae and Weitenberg. For if normal trade was always carried on then it is likely that Carpathian bronzesmiths would have adopted Mycenaean forging techniques (with heating and forging in contrast to northern methods of casting without subsequent forging): in fact only a few swords were manufactured in Transylvania in the Mycenaean style. However the external influence must have increased as a result of Macedonian conquest leading to the establishment of new cities in the Balkan interior like Beroe (near Stara Zagora), Kabyle (near Yambol) and Philippopolis (Plovdiv).

IRON AGE

The relationship between indigenous development and external stimuli is a little clearer from the Iron Age. The technology of iron smelting, for long a secret of the Hittite Empire, spread to Palestine in the twelfth century and on to Greece. But when iron became common in Eastern Europe in the seventh century the new Hallstatt Culture (named after the settlement of that name near Bad Ischl in Austria) was based essentially on Urnfield foundations and a similar diffusion from the middle and upper reaches of the Danube Valley can be traced. Mixed farming became more efficient with iron implements while trade in copper, tin and salt as well as the new metal contributed to prosperity. Larger settlements emerged, with signs of economic specialisation and social disparities - for the richest burials, presumably relating to the ruling families, contain a great many valuable items some of which were imported. But there must have been near-constant hostilities between tribes, judging by the prominence of fortified hill-top settlements doubtless conditioned by the great Celtic migrations extending from the fifth to the third century BC.[24]

However the Scythians have been considered an important factor in this explosion. These steppeland peoples based in southern Russia, and in contact with both China and Greece, moved westward by the usual route through southern Poland and into Germany as well as through the Carpathians and into Pannonia.[25] Scythian influence on the Urnfield Culture can be seen in the treatment of the dead (chieftains were buried with all their equipment, in wooden chambers over which tumuli were built) while Hallstatt swords and ornaments suggest that fairly small groups of horse-riding warriors acted as a new aristocracy in Eastern Europe ruling over the indigenous population. Specialist craftsmen in glass, metal and pottery were present and society became more clearly stratified with wealthy chieftains and slaves respectively occupying the top and bottom positions of the pyramid. It would be unreasonable to ignore the vitality of the Urnfield people in transforming their own way of life into the Hallstatt Culture with external influences (Greek and Scythian) perhaps more important by way of modifications to produce the La Tène Culture.[26]

Greek influence emerges in the greater importance of central places. The oppida were fortified townships (with towers and walls) acting as foci with political, cultural and economic significance: traders and artisans were present as well as soldiers, religious leaders and local chieftains. The Mediterranean civilisations provided luxury goods to the wealthy chieftains in return for amber, metal ores and other raw materials. Various examples have been investigated in Pannonia and adjacent areas. Thus Zemplin on the Bodrog comprises a fort above a hill-foot settlement of the first century BC, with massive earthworks surrounding the whole settlement. Other cases of urban complexes developing around small defended forts include Davin near Bratislava, Steinsburg bei Romhild in Thuringia, Stradonice on the Berounka in Bohemia, Taban-Gellerthegy in Budapest, Trisov in southern Bohemia and Zavist south of Prague. It seems that initial concern for defence was balanced, by late La Tène times, by convenience for trade when sites were being considered. Much of this trade would have been local. Thus Stradonice and Zavist, along with Cesky Lhotice, lie at the interface of the mineral rich highland zone of Bohemia and the zone of lowland agriculture. In Moravia again exchange centres lie at the contact between the high ground and the Moravian corridor, but long-distance trade is suggested by the discovery of coins and foreign wares at Stradonice, while the Hallstatt fort at Sticna in Slovenia demonstrates a perception of commerical opportunity as well as a knowledge of local iron resources.[27] Trade routes leading north from the head of the Adriatic were important at first but after the Greek colony of Massalia (Marseilles) was planted in c.600 BC the Rhône-Saone valley became more prominent. Hallstatt people were highly mobile and from a core area of settlement in the upper reaches of the Danube, Elbe and Vistula and the intervening Hercynian hill country (as well as the Rhineland and northern Gaul) migrations penetrated both the Balkans and Iberia. In the latter case there was some contact with Greek trading colonies planted on the Black Sea coast. Meanwhile there were some migrations taking place further north with a southward movement by Germanic tribes, possibly triggered by the deterioration in climate during the sub-Atlantic period. Their settlements seem to have impinged on the lower and middle sections of the Elbe and Vistula valleys. However they remained a minor force in East European affairs until the declining years of the Roman Empire.

On the whole Eastern Europe became somewhat peripheral during La Tène times for although this culture takes its name from a site in Switzerland the focus shifted westwards to the middle Rhine and beyond. The northern plain, especially in Poland, appears to have been remote in the context of both Hallstatt and La Tène and hence local Bronze Age culture persisted longer than in most other parts of the region. Knowledge of iron working spread to this area only during the second half of the first millennium BC. The Lusatian Culture is the chief proto-Slavic culture and covers the millennium 1300-300 BC. Farming extended into the forests using slash and burn techniques. Settlement focussed on small open communities but there were forts built in refuge situations, on islands or lake peninsulas: Izdebnik, Kamieniec and Sobiejuchy are known but the most remarkable example is Biskupin, excavated on the shores of a lake in the Znin district near Bydgoszcz. The two hectare settlement, first founded in Lower Palaeolithic times, consisted of a row of about one hundred homesteads aligned along streets and surrounded by a rampart of wood and earth as well as by a breakwater made of beams and poles.

Agriculture was probably complemented by handicrafts judging from pottery found in Kujawy (notably Kalisz and Łeczyca). The amazing island settlement of Biskupin was revealed by a fall in the level of the lake in 1933. Inside the stockade at Biskupin were log-built cabins providing animal stalls and dwelling accommodation for a population of several hundred. Analysis of a single 'household cluster' at Brzesc Kujaswki, not far from Biskupin, has revealed the multi-functional use of pits.[28] Dug initially for storage (including live storage of fish, molluscs and turtles and anticipating the *sadzy* used by Polish fishermen until quite recently, the pits were evidently used later on for both the dumping of rubbish and the burial of deceased members of the family. Was there continuity of settlement into the Dark Ages and the period of the Slav migrations? J. Czekanowski certainly hints at this through identification of Poland as an area of particularly impressive population growth: a 'human volcano which threw up waves of expansion in the early historical period' and one whose 'power presents us with one of our greatest demographic enigmas'.[29] On the other hand there were great problems resulting from the sub-Atlantic climatic deterioration, with great danger of flooding, so that the fortified centres (including Biskupin) were evidently abandoned in favour of settlement in hamlets and individual farmsteads.

THE IRON AGE IN THE BALKANS

Archaeological work provides some insights into the process of adaptation that enabled the well-developed Bronze Age cultures to assimilate the new technology developed to the northwest. It marks a very significant stage in the transfer of the technological diffusion 'centre' from Eastern Europe to Western Europe where (in a purely European context) it has tended to remain ever since. Stock breeding stands out as the predominant occupation with cultivation subsidiary. Settlements were usually fortified by banks and ditches. Knowledge of iron may have arrived first of all in Dobrogea as a result of the destruction of the Hittite Empire: diffusion could have occurred from the Caucasus through either Anatolia and Greece or the Black Sea steppes. A key site in Dobrogea is Babadag, fortified with ditches and ramparts and a veritable Thracian *oppidum*: the small iron finds probably originated in Anatolia. It is not clear just when Cimmerian and Scythian tribesmen arrived, or in what strength, but evidently the indigenous population was able to maintain itself, although names for individual groups are available by Roman times and the natives of the Carpathian-Danubian territory are referred to broadly as Geto-Dacians. Contacts with Scythians brought about a wider diffusion of iron and also introduced some new elements into Thracian art, but cultural development (especially of the Basarabi people) owes most to the Greeks who followed the Phoenicians and extended their activities from the Ionian city of Miletus across Pontus Euxinus (the hospitable sea) during the second half of the seventh century.[30] Pressure on their local hinterland may have triggered the search for Black Sea colonies to resolve the problem of food supply but 'that trade and not territory was the Miletan objective helped to establish relations with the native population and archaeological evidence suggests that usually this and even a degree of integration were quickly achieved'.[31] Many of their settlements, founded in the space of a few decades, lie outside the region in what is now Soviet territory: Olbia (Nikolayev), Panticapaeum (Kerch), and Tyras (Belgorod). A particular target of the Greek commercial assaults were the Scythian grain barons of the Crimea who were supplied with luxuries in return for food.[32] But Apollonia (near Burgas) and Odessus (Varna) relate to Bulgaria and Histria to Romania. Subsequent developments also affected the Romanian section of the Black Sea coast. Callatis (Mangalia) was settled from Heraclea Pontica very early in the sixth century and Tomis (Constanta) from Miletus in the fifth.

There was inevitable interaction between the settlers and the natives 'who by their very existence conditioned the economic and political climate to which the newcomers had to adapt themselves if they wished to settle down in their new home, establish friendly contacts with the local people and find markets for the goods which they imported or manufactured on the spot'.[33] The gold, silver and bronze coins of Callatis indicate trade in cereals with the Geto-Dacians. The natives evidently appreciated Greek luxuries (ornaments, pottery, weapons and wine) exchanged for gold, grain, honey and slaves. Greek wares have been found in the villages close to Histria and much further afield, as evidenced by the gold treasures of Panagjuriste in Bulgaria. Greek art can also be seen in the wall paintings of the Kazanlik royal tomb in Bulgaria. Greek influence seems to have been important in the introduction of La Tène culture and the relatively advanced Geto-Dacian peoples living close to the Black Sea depots contrast with neighbours who remained at the Hallstatt level. The diffusion of the potter's wheel is significant here. With a pronounced social hierarchy among the natives treasure continued to be valued by the elite. The Greek cities grew in consequence of the growth of trade but they had to defend themselves in view of the perpetual risk of hostilities breaking out, given the endemic conflict in Iron Age society. Walls had to be kept in repair and local tribal chiefs bought off where necessary, but only the Roman conquest could provide a longer-term solution to the security problem.

Part of the danger arose through the Scythians who are thought to have made a major violent incursion of Getic territory in the fourth century. Prior to this their occupation limits may have been in northern Moldavia as suggested by their fort of Stîncesti at Botosani commanding the Prut and Siret valleys. The defence line was gradually extended from the fifth into the fourth century with Arsura, Cotnari, Mosna - and even Poieni which lies south of the confluence of the Siret and Trotus. It is reasonable to suppose that Scythians maintained a peaceful and profitable tripartite association with the Greeks and Thracians, drawing luxuries from the former and primary produce (as well as some cloth and metal manufactures) from the latter. But for reasons possibly connected with developments in the east affecting Scythian relations with Persia there was an advance further south to the Danube and Arges and a creation of 'Little Scythia' which appears to have restricted the commercial activities of the Greeks until 339 when the Geto-Dacians were again able to cross the Danube and resettle both Hîrsova and Zimnicea as important crossing points.

The exchange of material and spiritual values with the Greek world was very important for the Dacians, enjoying direct contacts with the Greek colonies on the Black Sea and indirect links with the rest of the Greek world through the Thracians and Celts.[34] The evidence covers Greek pottery along with bronze vessels, helmets and objects in precious metals while amphorae indicate a trade in wine, oil, dyestuffs and resins on the Lower Danube where water transport for these fragile containers would have been available. Trade flourished for more than two centuries before the Roman conquest and had a bearing on the development of the main centres of population initially stimulated by the local economy and internal trade. However after the second century the Greek merchants began to lose their supremacy in the face of merchants from the Adriatic and Italy from whom the Roman military doubtless obtained considerable intelligence before mounting their attack against Dacia.

The link with the Greeks can also be seen in contemporary urban developments, including the Thracian city of Seuthopolis, discovered by the Tundza river some eight kilometres from Kazanlik when work started on the Georgi Dimitrov Dam in 1947.[35] Intense archaeological work between 1948 and 1954 revealed both the name of the city (mentioned in an inscription discovered in 1953) and its former importance. The newly-founded city was the work of Seuthes III, King of the Thracians, whose status derived from military successes against the Macedonians. Seuthes' capital was much influenced by the Hellenistic world and especially the Greek colonies on the Thracian shores. These are links with the Greek polis in terms of town planning, architecture, economy and culture, although the insulae (the plots demarcated by the grid-iron plan) were not densely built over and there were large spaces left between the detached houses. The five hectares of land within the walls were taken up by the royal family, with their fortified palace, representatives of the local tribal aristocracy and by merchants and craftsmen of local or Greek origin, while the common people lived outside the walls in mud huts. However the city which flourished after 323 BC was weakened by the process of political decentralisation among the Thracians after the death of Seuthes. It was burnt at the time of the Celtic invasion between 280 and 277 BC and the site then seems to have remained empty until Bulgarian settlement took place in the twelfth century AD.

The arrival of Celts in the Balkans constitutes a further significant exotic influence once credited with a southward diffusion of La Tène culture. For although modest in numbers the Celts came to settle and they may have introduced more advanced iron-working techniques and the potters wheel into Transylvania early in the third century BC, thereby complementing the role of Greeks further to the southeast. Both their technology and their readiness to integrate is suggested by the contents of Celtic tombs at Apahida (near Cluj), Ciumesti (near Satu Mare) and Medias. At this time Transylvania may have been part of an extensive Celtic territory, covering Illyria and Italy as well, with the native population obliged to pay tribute in goods and services. Also included in the migration patterns were the relatively backward Bastarnes, a people of German origin who arrived in the second and first centuries BC and left a legacy in such sites as the cremation cemetery at Poienesti near Iasi. 'After the violence of the first encounters a measure of coexistence seems to have been established as is shown by the finding of Bastarnian pottery in native settlements'.[36] But the traumatic changes associated with the contemporaneous retreat of the Scythians may have caused some redistribution of settlement and a greater emphasis on well-defined sites.

This was the time when the social and economic development of the Geto-Dacian people reached a peak. Substantial defended settlements (oppida) appeared, as indicated by excavations at Popesti (probably Argedava) on the Arges, where the local craftsmen had learnt to imitate the best Greek wares. Popesti has been described as a major tribal centre occupied in the late second century BC by a ruler who may well have exercised control over the whole of Muntenia. For the settlement enjoyed a central position in such a regional context (not far from Bucharest) and may have succeeded Zimnicea as the process of political consolidation advanced. Trade routes led to the various Black Sea settlements with Danube crossings at Calarasi and Ruse as well as Hîrsova and Zimnicea already mentioned. There was also a trade route into Transylvania connecting the fortified centres: from the Bran Pass the usual route ran south to Cetateni on the upper Dîmbovita with branches either to Popesti or to Hîrsova (for Histria) via Tinosu on the Prahova and Piscu Crasani on the Ialomita. All these places were well-defended and show elements of Greek culture. In Moldavia, Poiana (probably Piroboridava) near Tecuci re-emerged after the Scythian advance as an important tribal centre and staging point on the trade routes from Histria running north to the Prut Valley and northwest to the Bistrita and Trotus, tributaries of the Siret, where salt was found (at Tîrgu Ocna) and where access to Transylvania could be gained by the Oituz Pass. The large amount of Greek pottery indicates the great importance of these routes, justifying fortified settlements not only at Poiana but also at Brad and Racatau. The forts previously mentioned in connection with the Scythians in northern Moldavia (along with others between the Prut and Dniester) could at least have been reoccupied to give increased security for these routes and similar ones further east such as the trail from Tyras leading northwards through Bessarabia.

However a particularly important development in the settlement pattern involved the construction of hill forts in very commanding situations in the Carpathian zone: Bîtca Doamnei near Piatra Neamt, Covasna, Cetateni, Piatra Craivii near Alba Iulia and Tilisca near Sibiu. Whatever the stimulus for such impressive activity it seems clear that it was accompanied by a more effective unification of the Geto-Dacian tribes under the leadership of Burebista who selected Gradistea Muncelului as his base: a far more impregnable headquarters, on the high plateau surfaces of the Orastie Mountains, than the previous capital, presumed to have been at Popesti. A whole complex of citadels was built to defend Gradistea Muncelului: Banita for the south, Blidaru, Costesti and possibly Vîrful lui Hulpe as well, for the north, Capîlna for the eastern flank and Piatra Rosie to the west. With fortified houses for leading citizens and sohisticated water supply arrangements the forts show a dependence on Hellenistic military technique, but related to local traditions. Pressure was exerted on the Celts in 60/59 BC and the frontier advanced into Pannonia to complement the removal of the Scythian influence from the Pontic zone where tribute had previously been extracted from the Greek towns. The boundary in the vicinity of the Tisza/Tisa between Celts and Dacians is indicated by the second century BC pottery at Pecica, a prosperous trading centre at the contact between the two peoples. Although the Celts were not pursued to the point that would make a confrontation with Rome inevitable there was evidently sufficient risk of major hostilities to justify the development of the fortresses in the Orastie Mountains. Coins from Histria have been found at Costesti and Piatra Rosie and suggest that the builders may have received help from the Greeks.

The Dacians kenw about writing and they also devised a calendar, based on independent astronomical observations, though 'their particular achievement lay not in any inventions or discoveries of their own but in the blending of elements from other cultures into a new cultural amalgam which found expression in a variety of novel and typically Dacian forms'.[37] Small wonder therefore that the Dacians should pose as a threat to the Roman Empire, commemorated by the Roman monument of Tropaeum Traiani (Adamclisi) in Dobrogea. On the other hand it may have been the progressive Roman encirclement of Dacia, extending to Dobrogea in 28 BC and Muntenia in 11/12 AD (when many of the Getic people were moved south of the Danube) that completed the political unification of the Geto-Dacian tribes and so precipated the threat which the Romans were eventually obliged to overcome by the military conquest (in the campaigns of 101-2 and 105-6 AD) and its subsequent Romanisation. A renaissance might still have taken place, following the division of the empire and the establishment of a new imperial city at Constantinople but the stream of new invaders and settlers, culminating in the arrival of the Slavs, prevented such a revival until modern times.

NOTES

1. C.G. Childe 1929, 'The Danube in prehistory' (Oxford: Clarendon Press); C.G. Childe 1947, 'The dawn of European civilisation' (London: Kegan Paul); J.G.D. Clark 1952, 'Prehistoric Europe: the economic base' (London: Methuen); J.G.D. Clark 1961, 'World prehistory' (Cambridge: Cambridge University Press); K. Sklenar 1983

2. C.T. Smith 1967

3. A. Prinke 1973, 'A note on the Mesolithic of eastern Great Poland', S.K. Koslowski ed. 'The Mesolithic in Europe' (Warsaw: University Press) 477-83.

4. A.J. Ammerman and L.L. Cavalli-Sforza 1973, 'A population model for the diffusion of early farming in Europe', C. Renfrew ed. 'The explanation of culture change: models in prehistory' (London: Duckworth) 343-57; G. Clark 1947, 'Forest clearance and prehistoric farming' Economic History Review 17 (1), 45-51; G. Clark 1965, 'Radiocarbon dating and the spread of the farming economy' Antiquity 39, 45-8; P.M. Dolukhanov 1979, 'Economy and ecology in Neolithic Eastern Europe' (London: Duckworth); A. Garnett 1945, 'The loess regions of Central Europe in prehistoric times' Geographical Journal 106, 132-43; J. Murray 1970, 'The first European agriculture: a study of the osteological and botanical evidence until 2000 BC' (Edinburgh: Edinburgh University Press).

5. G. Barker 1985, 'Prehistoric farming in Europe' (Cambridge: Cambridge University Press); M.J. Jarman et al. eds. 1982, 'Early European agriculture: its foundations and development' (Cambridge: Cambridge University Press); R. Tringham 1971, 'Hunters fishers and farmers of Eastern

Europe 6000-3000 BC' (London: Hutchinson); A. Whittle 1985, 'Neolithic Europe: a survey' (Cambridge: Cambridge University Press) 132-83.

6. P.I. Bogucki 1982, 'Early Neolithic subsistence and settlement in the Polish lowlands' British Archaeological Reports International Series 150; P.I. Bogucki and R. Grygiel 1981, 'The household cluster at Brzesc Kujawski' World Archaeology 13, 59-72; R.W. Ehrich 1956, 'Homolka: a fortified Neolithic village in Bohemia' Archaeology 9, 233-40; J. Kruk 1980, 'The Neolithic settlement of southern Poland' British Archaeological Reports International Series 93; S. Milisauskas 1976, 'Olszanica: an early farming village in Poland' Archaeology 29, 31-41.

7. D. Berciu 1967, 'Romania before Burebista' (London: Thames & Hudson) 16.

8. A. Bolomey 1973, 'An outline of the late epipapaeolithic economy at the Iron Gates' Dacia 17, 41-52; E. Condurachi and C. Daicoviciu 1971, 'Romania' (London: Barrie & Jackson) 23-4.

9. J.G. Nadris 1977, 'The perspective of long-term change in southeast Europe', F.W. Carter ed. 25-57 (quote p.48). See also J.G. Nandris 1970, 'Ground water as a factor in the first temperate Neolithic settlements of the Koros region' Zbornik Narodog Muzeja (Belgrade) 6, 59-71; D. Strejovic 1972, 'New discoveries at Lepenski Vir' (London: Thames & Hudson).

10. J.G. Nandris 1977, op.cit 48.

11. Ibid. 50.

12. M.J. Jarman et al. eds. 1982 op.cit. (note 5).

13. E. Bozhilova 1975, 'Changes of vegetation belts in the Rila mountains during late and post-glacial time' Biuletyn Geologiczny 19, 93-9; R.W. Dennell 1974, 'Neolithic flax in Bulgaria' Antiquity 48, 220-2; R.W. Dennell 1978, 'Early farming in south Bulgaria' British Archaeological Reports International Series 45.

14. G. Barker 1975, 'Early Neolithic land use in Yugoslavia' Proceedings of the Prehistoric Society 41, 85-104; J.L. Bintliff 1976, 'The plain of western Macedonia and the Neolithic site of Nea Nikomedeia' Proceedings of the Prehistoric Society 41, 78-84; S. Bottema and B.S. Ottaway 1982, 'Botanical malacological and archaeological zonation of settlement deposits at Gomolava' Journal of Archaeological Science 2, 315-25; A.T. Clasen 1982, 'Padina and Starcevo: game fish and cattle' Palaeohistorica 22, 141-73; M. Gimbutas 1970, 'Ohre, Yugoslavia: two Neolithic sites'

Archaeology 23, 287-97; M. Gimbutas 1972, 'Excavations at Anza, Macedonia' Archaeology 25, 112-23; M. Gimbutas 1974, 'Anza c.6500-5000 BC' Journal of Field Archaeology 1, 25-66; M. Gimbutas ed. 1976, 'Neolithic Macedonia' (Los Angeles: University of California Institute of Archaeology); R. Tringham 1980, 'The early agricultural site of Selovac, Yugoslavia' Archaeology 33, 24-32; W. Van Zeist 1975, 'Preliminary report on the botany of Gomolava' Journal of Archaeological Science 2, 315-25.

15. V. Dumitrescu 1965, 'Casciorarele: a Late Neolithic settlement in the Lower Danube' Archaeology 18, 34-40; V. Dumitrescu 1980, 'The Neolithic settlement of Rast, southwest Oltenia' British Archaeological Reports International Series 72; S. Marinescu-Bîlcu 1981, 'Tirpesti: from prehistory to history in eastern Romania' British Archaeological Reports International Series 107; C.N. Mateescu 1975, 'Remarks on cattle breeding and agriculture in the Middle and Late Neolithic on the Danube' Dacia 19, 13-8.

16. M. Gimbutas ed. 1976, op.cit. (note 14).

17. B. Jovanovic and B.S. Ottaway 1976, 'Copper mining and metallurgy in the Vinca group' Antiquity 50, 104-13; A.G. Sherratt 1982-3, 'Neolithic and Copper Age settlement on the Great Hungarian Plain' Oxford Journal of Archaeology 1, 287-316.

18. R.F. Hoddinott 1981, 20; A. Fol and I. Marazov 1977, 'Thrace and the Thracians' (London: Cassell).

19. J. Briard 1979, 'The Bronze Age in barbarian Europe from the Megaliths to the Celts' (London: Routledge & Kegan Paul); J.M. Coles and A.F. Harding 1979, 'The Bronze Age in Europe: an introduction to the prehistory of Europe c2000-700 BC' (London: Methuen); I. Ecsedy 1979, 'The people of the pit-grave Kurgans in eastern Hungary' (Budapest: Hungarian Academy of Sciences); C. Renfrew 1969, 'The autonomy of the southeast Europe Copper Age' Proceedings of the Prehistoric Society 36, 12-47; C. Renfrew 1978, 'Varna and the social context of early metallurgy' Antiquity 52, 199-203.

20. J.M. de Navarro 1925, 'Prehistoric routes between northern Europe and Italy defined by the amber trade' Geographical Journal 66, 481-507.

21. E. Neustupny and J. Neustupny 1961, 'Czechoslovakia before the Slavs' (London: Thames & Hudson).

22. K. Jazdzewski 1965, 'Poland' (London: Thames & Hudson).

23. M. Gimbutas 1965; P. Roman 1977, 'The late Copper

Age Cotofeni Culture of South East Europe' British Archaeological Reports Supplementary Series 32.

24. T.G.E. Powell 1958, 'The Celts' (London: Thames & Hudson); H.D. Rankin 1987, 'The Celts and the Classical world' (London: Croom Helm).

25. T.T. Rice 1957, 'The Scythians' (London: Thames & Hudson); D. Gabler et al. eds. 1982, 'Studies in the Iron Age of Hungary' British Archaeological Reports International Series 144; F. Trippett 1974, 'The first horsemen' (Amsterdam: Time Life International).

26. P.S. Wells 1985, 'Medieval trade and cultural change in Early Iron Age Central Europe', T.C. Champion and J.V.S. Megaw eds. 'Settlement and society' (Leicester: Leicester University Press) 69-89.

27. J. Collis 1984, 'Oppida: earliest towns north of the Alps' (Sheffield: University Department of Prehistory and Archaeology); D. Gabler et al. 1982, 'Studies in the Iron Age of Hungary' British Archaeological Reports International Series 93; P.S. Wells 1984, 'Farms villages and cities: commerce and urban origins in Late Prehistoric Europe' (Ithaca, N.Y.: Cornell University Press) 79-101.

28. P.I. Bogucki and R. Grygiel 1981, 'The household cluster at Brzesc Kujawski' World Archaeology 13, 59-72. See also P.I. Bogucki 1979, 'Tactical and strategic settlements in the Early Neolithic of lowland Poland' Journal of Archaeological Research 35, 238-46.

29. J. Czekanowski 1946-7, 'The ancient home of the Slavs' Slavonic & East European Review 25, 356-72 (quote p. 370).

30. M.E. White 1961, 'Greek colonisation' Journal of European History 21, 443-54. See also J. Alexander 1972, 'Yugoslavia before the Roman conquest' (London: Thames & Hudson); S. Pribichevich 1982, 'Macedonia: its history and people' (London: Pennsylvania State University).

31. R.F. Hoddinott 1981, 88.

32. E.C. Semple 1921, 'Geographic factors in the ancient Mediterranean grain trade' Annals Association of American Geographers 11, 47-74.

33. E. Condurachi and C. Daicoviciu 1971, op.cit. (note 8) 74.

34. I. Glodariu 1976, 'Dacian trade with the Hellenistic and Roman world' British Archaeological Reports Supplementary Series 8.

35. D.P. Dimitrov and M. Cicikova 1978, 'The Thracian city of Seuthopolis' British Archaeological Reports Supple-

mentary Series 38.

36. E. Condurachi and C. Daicoviciu 1971, op.cit. (note 8) 83.

37. Ibid. 110. See also J.G. Nandris 1981, 'Aspects of Dacian economy and Highland zone exploitation, Dacia 25, 231-54.

2

The Roman Empire in Eastern Europe

The triumph of Roman power over the Balkan tribes must be regarded as the outstanding development of the pre-Medieval period: a traumatic event unprecedented for its efficiency and for its immediate impact in terms of economic development and the improvement of the infrastructure, leaving an ample legacy in the landscape. Even more important however was the cultural impact over the longer term. This effectively guaranteed that the empire would exert a powerful influence on the subsequent political development of Europe, demonstrating the essential complementarity of cultural, economic and military elements (or as T. Parsons puts it, directions of differentiation, each yielding their own functions, organisations and elites).[1] The cultural drive came through Christianity as the empire became the vehicle for the diffusion of this major script religion. The economic power came through control of a great network of cities around the Mediterranean and military success was based on the establishment of an effective centre acting as a base for the conquest of new territories. By combining a powerful core with an economically prosperous heartland the Romans in effect brought together the two established traditions of empire-building: the Mesopotamian tradition, exemplified by the Greek city states (and later by the Hanseatic League), resting on co-ordination of a network of basically autonomous cities, and the Egyptian tradition, with its parallels in China and Russia, resting on a major centre of administration and military control over a predominantly rural area. For a time the different elements were mutually reinforcing despite their separate organisations and elites. Eventually stability was lost, but it is nevertheless significant that while the empire collapsed as a military unit maintaining control of extensive territories a great deal of the cultural and economic infrastructure was left intact (Figure 2.1). Subsequent political developments may therefore be seen one way or another as a process of reorganisation.

According to S. Rokkan 'the system of states emerging in Europe from the twelfth to the twentieth century can only be understood against the background of the Roman inheritance and the reduction in the range and scope of cross-territorial communications which gradually took place in the wake of the fall of Rome'.[2] Feudal structures, amounting to a parochialisation of economic and political power, became the basic units in a process of developing new relationships with urban commercial-industrial communities and with military establishments of central governments. But constraints were imposed on the cultural front as the Roman Church, maintained in two languages (Greek and Latin), was undermined by the establishment of various national systems of communication as the printing press was invented and the Reformation swept Europe. So the Roman Empire was recreated as a 'necklace' of nation states surrounding the city-rich 'trade route belt' of Europe where it was difficult for any one centre to gain the ascendancy and become a core area controlling an extensive periphery. Not that the nation states were necessarily well-endowed for long-term stability, for Eastern Europe in particular shows the debilitating effects of economic weakness and ethnic-cultural divisions which frustrated any lasting congruence between states and nations.

The main concern here is to consider the impact of the Romans on the various Balkan tribes whose lands were progressively incorporated into the empire. In view of the emphasis in previous discussion it is appropriate to begin with the Thracians whose enormous capabilities were freely acknowledged in Herodotus' assertion that 'the race of the Thracians is the greatest, after the Indians, of all mankind'.[3] But they were destined to be politically weak because of the failure to unite under a single leader. They shared a common language and culture 'but politically they had not risen above the tribal stage and in cases had not even attained it'; some village groups comprised territories ruled by kings but there were also settlements of free Thracians in the Rhodope who acknowledged no overlord.[4] However the Geto-Dacians must be considered an important exception and their assertive disposition made Roman conquest virtually inevitable. In contrast, to the south of the Danube

Figure 2.1: The development of the Roman Empire in Eastern Europe

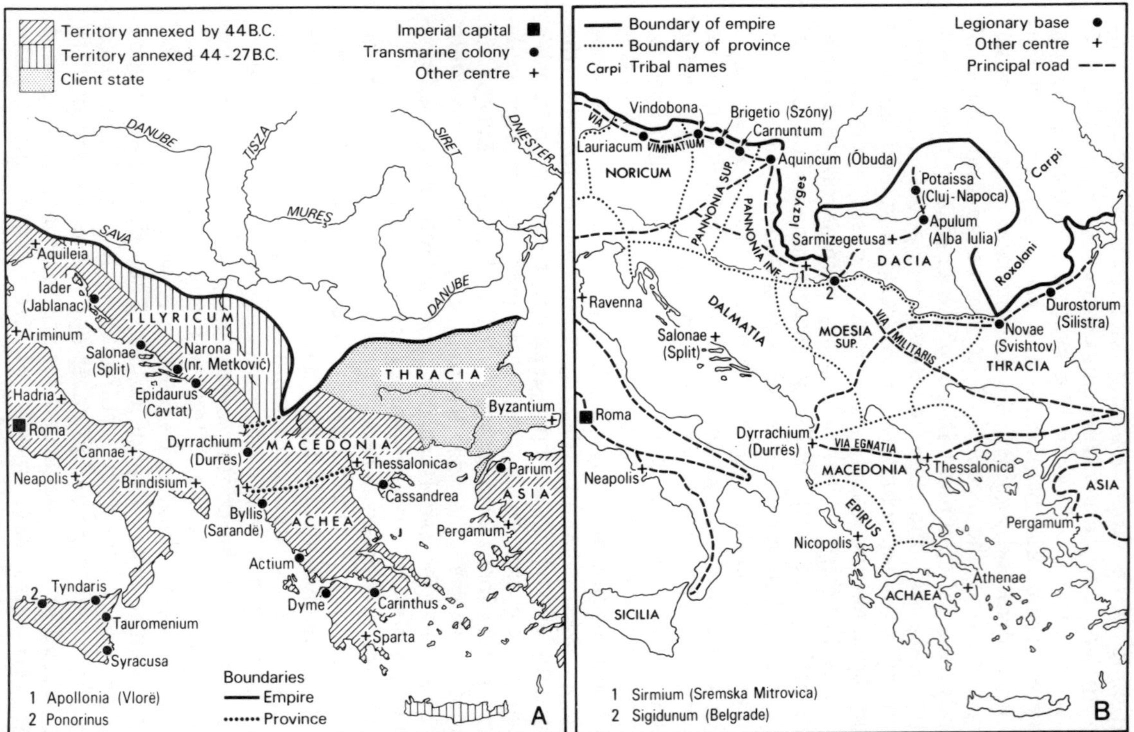

Source: Historical atlases.

the Romans entered into alliances with Thracian tribes against the Macedonians and worked through the Thracian kings despite the fact that they did not rule over effectively centralised states.[5] The division of the province into strategiae was based on tribal lines although the administration was altered from time to time and there appears to have been a distinct shift of emphasis under Trajan and Hadrian with the rise of local authorities based on the towns in preference to the decaying tribal organisation.

A somewhat higher level of political consolidation is evident among the Illyrians whose state was an early target of Roman expansionism. D. Garasanin examines the achievements of the Illyrians and sees an evolution process stretching forwards from the disintegration of the late Neolithic cultures under the pressure of Indo-Europeans arriving from the steppes, but with contacts with Greek civilisation as a critical influence.[6] Major fortresses were built and according to Polybius it was to one of these, Rhison, that Queen Teuta retreated during the First Illyrian War. Medun near Titograd is another example. Roman control of both Illyria and Dacia was evidently consolidated through the wholesale resettlement of population, resulting in the arrival of Illyrian miners in the Apuseni Mountains of Romania while migrations of Dacians penetrated the eastern edge of classical Illyrian territory, with evidence from sites like Gomolava near Sremska Motrovica and Velika Trnja near Leskovac. Such 'divide and rule' tactics were to be employed later by the Byzantines and constitute an early example of organised colonisation which has been a persistent feature of Eastern Europe's historical geography.

The road system was an essential infrastructure for the empire.[7] Highways already existed in many of the territories. Some of them were built by Celts, Illyrians and Thracians, who the Romans defeated during their military campaigns, but others probably originated back in Neolithic times. However the inherited system of roads was adapted by the Romans to their specific military and political needs. It was also extended where necessary to produce a specifically Roman network and at the same time the first 'planned' system in Eastern Europe. Three roads may be singled out as having particular importance. Roman rule over the Balkans was secured above all by the Via Militaris from Singidunum (Belgrade) to Byzantium. The origins of this route probably lie in prehistory. The Danube road (Via Viminatium) was also of great importance, part of a system of border fortifications and military routes known as the limes. Then thirdly the Via Egnatia offered the shortest route between Rome, Byzantium and the east. From this basic system various secondary roads were added to facilitate the conquest of recalcitrant tribes, the exploitation of gold and silver ores and allow colonisation. Roads were endowed with inns (tabernae), some of them offering sleeping accommodation (mansiones) and stations where horses could be changed (mutationes). Fortifications graded upwards from simple towers (turres) and small forts (castella) to the military camp (castrum) and fortified city (castellum). The essential complementarity of road and military stronghold meant that Roman forts were always readily accessible, unlike their Illyrian and Thracian counterparts which were situated on hill tops. An additional feature of the limes was the valum (wall) consisting of moat and embankment. The Roman roads were normally straight and in consequence were often steeply graded. Width varied (between as much as two and nine metres) and roads might be covered in sand, cut in stone or paved depending on local conditions, but bridges were almost always built in stone.

The road network conditioned town development which could take the form of colonies (coloniae), municipalities (municipii) and cities (civitates).[8] These might comprise pre-existing Greek towns like Appolonia and Dyrrhachium (Durrës) conquered by the Romans in the third century BC, important tribal settlements, spontaneous developments around military camps or planned veteran communities. Of the Adriatic ports Salona (Split) was probably most important, furnishing the earliest evidence of Christianity in the Balkans (by 290 AD) but Narona near Metkovic was an outlet for the mining in Bosnia and Serbia while Aquileia at the head of the Adriatic gave access to Noricum and Pannonia. Dyrrhachium (with the short sea crossing to Italy) controlled the most direct route between the two halves of the empire. On the whole the area was relatively weakly urbanised compared with other parts of the empire, reflecting perhaps the lack of political development among the Thracian tribes and also the Romans' initial preference to work through indigenous institutions. The only early towns in the interior of what is now Bulgaria were the Greek city of Philippopolis, the Roman colony of Deultum (near Burgas) and the short-lived Thracian capital of Seuthopolis (near Kazanlik), described in the previous chapter. It was only in the time of Trajan and Hadrian that city-based administrative units emerged. Trajan founded Pautalia (Kyustendil), Ulpia Marcianopolis (near Varna), Ulpia Nicopolis ad Istrum (Nikyup near Resen) and Serdica (Sofia), while Hadrian was responsible for Hadrianopolis (Edirne). Eventually there seems to have been one city for each *strategiae*. The new towns were generally old tribal capitals which had not previously been recognised as towns because of the desire to govern through the tribal system. Many of the urban centres must have been very small with a purely village economy, otherwise more towns would surely have been recognised by Trajan and Hadrian. However the security of the *limes* eventually required a measure of economic development and the urban growth policy then involved the transfer of people from other provinces, especially Asia Minor, to provide those commercial and industrial skills which the indigenous population could not offer.

Under the circumstances it is hardly surprising to find that many of these towns failed to survive as urban units. The port cities later enjoyed quite effective Byzantine protection and considerable monuments survive, like the arena at Pola (Pula). But in much of the interior the legacy is less compelling despite some substantial fortification (as in Justinian's time), although the gridiron plan typical of the *coloniae* can be picked up in the present layout of Ljubljana. One town on a road in Macedonia parallel to the *Via Egnatia* has the rare distinction of losing its urban status due to environmental change. It has been demonstrated that the town of Bokeria (presumed to be close to Kelemesh) lost its nodality as a result in the rise in the level of Lake Ostrovo which destroyed its road link with Novigrad. As the economy was now restricted to agriculture, goat herding and fishing the settlement became essentially rural. Evidence from cemeteries confirms the view that lake levels have risen steadily from classical times to the present.[9]

Although the Roman Empire did not impinge directly on the northern part of Eastern Europe its influence was felt through the consolidation of German tribes, present in the Elbe, Oder and Vistula valleys. Numerous German groups are mentioned by ancient writers, but it still remains unclear how these tribal labels can be related to particular territories and archaeological finds. Hence this discussion will concentrate on generalities. The cultural homogeneity is arguably the result of the Roman impact, beginning with Maroboduus, the Marcomannic king whose political activity prepared the ground for greater uniformity. A distinctive culture arose in Bohemia, where Germanic peoples had come to rule over a Celtic population, and spread occurred northwards across the North European Plain. The unity should not be exaggerated, for perhaps the Romans did nothing more than present the Germans with a common interest in reacting to the empire's territorial development and the trade opportunities that were available: the uniformity evident in the diffusion of costly Roman imports should not obscure important local variations in tribal economy and society. Yet there was a growing differentiation in social structure which can be ascribed partly to the arrival of leading figures of different ethnic origin, like Maroboduus in Bohemia, but also to contacts with Rome. For it was customary for German noblemen to serve in the Roman armies and then to return home with their earnings to set up house in a manner befitting their status and fortune. Inter-marriage would then consolidate an administrative and military elite living in mansion-style houses which now introduced the same differentiation into rural settlement patterns as did the lavish grave-gifts to funerary ritual.

As F. Millar explains 'in barbarian societies leading families have often been raised to positions of still greater eminence as a result of contact with highly developed civilisations; and in both settlement and funerary ritual the barbaric nobility of this period has left material proof of that desire for outward distinction'.[10] It is reflected in cultural forms which have extended across tribal boundaries. In the marshland Wurten it appears that during the second century these communities of some thirty households were structured into groups of prosperous farmers, poor farmers and craftsmen all of which lived under a starosta (administrator or elder), living in a particularly well-appointed farm house.[11] Such developments in long-settled coastal marshes seem to have been taking place throughout Germany and while they may reflect a logical development process, with small homogenous hamlet settlements coalescing into larger units that could support a range of local industries (and at the same time demand more sophisticated administration), they also provided opportunities for the more talented and acquisitive to project themselves, especially when there were models to be emulated. In such a way links may be forged between the Roman Empire and Medieval feudalism.

THE ROMAN IMPACT IN PANNONIA

Pannonia appears to have been an area of great ethnic complexity lying in the heart of Europe at a major crossroads of migration routes.[12] The thorough mixing of Celtic peoples with Illyrians and Thracians makes it difficult to ascribe many specific characteristics to groups like the Dardanians (of Illyrian or Thracian descent) or the Celtic Scordisci. La Tène culture was evident, though with variations that have been tentatively ascribed to the degree of Celtisation.[13] The Romans advanced only gradually into this territory having initially established themselves at Aquileia. This was an important port and military centre at the head of the Amber Route which negotiated the edge of Pannonia by way of Savaria (Szombathely) and Scarbantia (Sopron), on its way towards the Baltic. The Roman advance was first pressed in the south among the Dalmatian tribes of the Sava Valley. North of the Drava the Romans were first content with an alliance although under Tiberius settlements for veterans were founded near Lake Balaton and around Savaria and Scarbantia. Roman policy was for a time based on a system of 'client states', including the Sarmatians-Iazyges who occupied the area between Danube and Tisza in agreement with the Romans around 50 AD and acted in effect as a buffer state separating the Dacians of Transylvania from the Moesia and Pannonia. The settlement of large numbers of barbarians south of the Danube in Moesia is another expression of this strategy. It was not entirely successful and the rising power of Dacia (raiding into Moesia), along with the wars by Germanic and Sarmatian tribes (in which the Sarmatian-Iazyges turned against the Romans), preoccupied the Romans in the years 85-89 AD and resulted in a Roman <u>limes</u> along the Danube. Further reaction followed through Trajan's campaigns (101-2 and 105-6) against the Dacians leading to the incorporation of the province into the empire along with territory occupied by Sarmatians between the Danube and Transylvania which was necessary to connect Dacia with Moesia.[14]

Sarmatians still lived freely in eastern Pannonia, in the Tisza Valley, although this territory was important to the Romans for communication between Dacia and Pannonia. Guarded by watchtowers the routes led eastwards from such frontier towns as Aquincum (Obuda) and Dugio (Dunaszekcsö). It was probably this hemming in of the Sarmatians that led to further wars between 107 and 124 AD. For the nomadic Sarmatians, originating in the Crimea, were outstandingly successful in their dealings with the Romans: periods of peaceful coexistence were punctuated by determined attacks of mounted archers whose Hunnic crossbows (strengthened by a bone inlay to cope with heavy arrowheads) could be devastatingly effective against Roman cavalry. The Danube limes was further strengthened as Trajan's wooden camps were rebuilt in stone. But this system only allowed for the policing of the border and Rome's security had to rest largely on further understandings with client peoples like the Sarmatians.

The balance was next disturbed by the arrival of the Goths, leading to a general barbarian attack on Pannonia which engulfed the province for a decade between 164 and 175: in the end the Sarmatians were made to supply cavalry to the Romans and prevented from settling within fifteen kilometers of the Danube. Marcus Aurelius even contemplated the occupation of barbarian territories (Marcomannia and Sarmatia) after 179, but his successor quickly reverted to the old frontier policy and re-established the client relationship. The scene then shifted to the outer limits of Dacia where increasing pressure associated with Gothic migrations led to the consolidation of the frontier along the Olt in 196: some groups broke through the passes of the eastern Carpathians and created a disturbed situation in Dacia and Pannonia during the reign of Septimus Severus. Considerable reconstruction was carried out along the limes but evidently war damage did not prevent a measure of prosperity as places like Aquincum, Brigetio (Szony), and Siscia (Sisak) increased their status. Native communities disintegrated and Roman cities became dominant, as agents of Romanisation both culturally (through the adoption of Roman names) and materially (through the distribution of Roman manufactures). However the military cities developing near the legionary camps were far larger than the other towns.

The onslaughts reached a climax in 269-70 when an attack by Goths on Dacia coincided with the arrival of Gepids and Vandals on the borders of Pannonia. Under this pressure Aurelianus was forced to abandon Dacia in 271 and resettle part of the population south of the Danube. This may have allowed a breathing space as invaders allied themselves with the natives to frustrate later arrivals. Further reorganisations under Diocletian kept Germanic and Sarmatian tribes clear of the border while Pannonia was grouped in with Dalmatia and Noricum to comprise a single province administered from Sirmium (Sremska Mitrovica). Some defeated barbarians were taken into the empire, as was the case with the remnants of Carpians who were settled in Sopianis (Pécs) by Diocletian: 'the new settlements not only supplemented manpower but also enlarged areas with agricultural potential in order to increase the economic power of the empire'.[15] Another important development was a strengthening of the limes with counter fortifications at Aquincum, Bononia (Banostor) and Lugio (Mohacs) between 289 and 293 with the aim of giving better protection to the clients of the empire against outside enemies. Military expeditions were also undertaken to take stock of the constant population movements in the barbarian world. The work was continued under Constantine and involved not only the construction of new camps for the limes but a fence and palisade system in Oltenia running from Drobeta (Drobeta-Turnu Severin) for about 700 km. to meet the Danube again near Braila. Similar fences were built during the fourth century further east in Bessarabia, Dobrogea and Moldavia. In the Pannonian Plain a system of earthworks surrounded the Sarmatian homeland which had become more vulnerable since the evacuation of Dacia. However the Sarmatians remained ambivalent allies and revolts were put down in 356-7 and 358-9, while Gothic attacks on the Sarmatians in 332 are thought to have led to extensive resettlement in the Balkans and more distant parts of the empire. There was also a movement of Gepids in 340 which has given rise to the suggestion that they took over from Sarmatians the defence of the earthworks system, subsequently extended to comprise inner and outer trenches by 374. The fourth century was a time of considerable economic progress with an increase in the number of villas and in their level of occupation. The estates were generating significant exports of cereals, livestock and wine and there was an increase in agricultural land with the extension of vineyards in place of forest and moorland. And in addition to the villae rusticae were the towns, essentially military strongholds developing contemporaneously with Constantine's work on the limes but with a significant commercial function in the case of Valcum (Keszthely-Fenékpuszta) which may have originated as a refuge for population of an imperial estate and blossomed into a market centre.

The limes

As a frontier province of the empire Pannonia is a useful example to take with regard to the consolidation of the border. Indeed life throughout Pannonia was closely bound up with the limes: it was the army stationed along the border which was largely responsible for the Romanising of Pannonia and for the development of the economic and cultural life, while equally the later incorporation of alien groups with feoderati status led to the demise of the Roman tradition. As Rome was forced to modify its pretensions to mastery over all the known world, frontier demarcation became an important preoccupation throughout the empire. The Pannonian limes however has its own characteristics, partly because the natural frontier line of the Danube restricted building to military camps (without walls and ditches) and partly because the intense barbarian pressure after the withdrawal from Dacia required progressive rebuilding and elaboration of the system right up to its abandonment at the turn of the fourth century. In the first place fortifications and garrisons were intended to support Roman expansion. Temporary camps were built of earth with palisades, as were the route camps like Bassiana (Sarvar) and Gorsium (Tac) which led up to the Danube, but they were subsequently rebuilt in stone as the frontier became a permanent feature of the political geography. The first permanent camp was Carnuntum (Altenburg), built where the Amber Route crossed the Danube, and it is possible that under Claudius there were also important garrisons at crossing points like Aquincum, Arrabona (Györ) and Brigetio, representing a trend towards a more forward deployment of troops away from the initial concentration in the Emona (Ljublaina)-Poetovio (Ptuj)-Siscia triangle. Domitian increased the number of palisaded camps through the founding of Ad Flexum (Magyarovar), Lugio, Vetus Salina (Adony) and others, but Trajan brought about the greatest development with the addition of Azaum (Almasfüzitö), Cirpi (Dunabogdany), Salva (Esztergom), Ulcisia (Szentendre) and others to finish up with thirty-seven units of which four were now legionary camps (Aquincum, Brigetio, Carnuntum and Vindobona).[16]

Hadrian consolidated the defence system with the reconstruction of camps in stone. Nevertheless the frontier was not stout enough to withstand the heavy pressure to which it was subjected during the second century and the enemy easily broke through the simple one-line system. Some of the stone forts near Aquincum had to be rebuilt after Sarmatian raids in 136-8 but burnt layers show that every camp in the chain was severely damaged by the invasions of Marcomannians and Sarmatians during the reign of Marcus Aurelius. The limes now began to assume a defensive role, calling for changes in the ground plans and the laying out of additional defensive lines. Marcus Aurelius ordered a general rebuilding, with the addition of stone watchtowers (burgi) and watch stations (praesidia), while corner towers were added to several camps. Further Sarmatian raids in 259-60 and again in 270 brought another wave of reconstruction under Diocletian (and also the complete abandonment of Alberfalva, whose Roman name is not known). A feature of the limes was now the counter fortess (Contra Bononiam and Contra Acumincum), but several new camps appeared on the right bank of the Danube like Rakovac which defended Sirmium. Under Constantine the army was reorganised and military service became hereditary but defence of the limes was entrusted to mercenaries. Earthworks provided additional lines of defence, and several new camps were built where the Danube frontier connected with these walls, as at Pone Navata (Visegrad) which strengthened defences in the vicinity of the Danube bend. An important merit of this integrated system was that the earth walls tended to guide barbarian attacks to places on the Danube that were well defended by the Romans. Increased emphasis was given to bridgeheads and also to towns like Tricciana (Sagvar) and Valcum which formed an inner defensive line. Villas were invariably fortified at this time. The limes remained an important preoccupation for Valentinian ordered both rebuilding, new camp construction and watch towers along the most vulnerable sections (such as the Brigetio area which was liable to assault along the Vag valley). There were forward camps such as the one discovered at Hatvan some 60 km. away from the Danube. Yet even with this enlarged programme, which endowed the frontier with a total of fifty camps and almost a hundred smaller installations (minor camps, bridgeheads and watch towers), there could be no really effective solution as barbarian pressure became overwhelming. With the expansion of the Huns and a new balance of power the defence function of limes collapsed. Small watch towers were given up before the end of the fourth century but even the major camps were abandoned by 440.

Valentinian established more new camps and built a particularly elaborate chain of watchtowers along the Aquincum-Brigetio limes, though this was not enough to prevent further invasions and eventually Valeria, the eastern part of Pannonia, may have been handed over to the Huns. Certainly Huns, along with Alani and Goths, were settled as feoderati and kept to separate areas because of their violent history. The Goths had three kings at this time (Valamer, Vidimer and Thiudimer) and each king settled in a different area: Valamer's people occupied the area between the Lajta and Raba rivers, with Vidimer's territory in northern Valeria (between the Raba and Bakony Mountains) and Thiudimer's lands to the southeast. Feoderati gave rise to some barbarisation of the military population of the limes and people may well have fled from Pannonia because of the unsettled conditions. On the other hand the new troops helped to pacify the neighbouring peoples and the Danube frontier remained in force, certainly until 433 when a new agreement brought the Great Huns (under Rua, Uptar and subsequently Attila) into the province. But as more of the original inhabitants fell before the advancing Huns the cultural replacement process was complete. Pannonia remained nominally Roman however and in 455 Emperor Avitus paid a visit, while the Byzantine Empire subsequently maintained a presence in Sirmium and the road to Scarbantia as late as the sixth century. Yet by this time the Lombards had arrived and Justinian had not only to acknowledge their occupation of Pannonia but their demand for other territories as well (Savia and the eastern part of Noricum Mediterraneum). They did not remain long, departing for Italy in 568, but they were immediately replaced by their allies the Avars. Under Khagan Bajan, whose ascendancy was as pronounced as Attila's had been, the Avars took over Sirmium as an important power base and pressed westwards towards the Alps and southwards into Dalmatia and Thrace.

The feoderati system had now reached an extreme form where barbarian culture was now ascendant: 'basic differences had ceased to exist between Romans and barbarians in culture, in attitude to life and in living standards, by contrast with the second and third centuries when the dividing line had stretched as between two different worlds'.[17] Before the arrival of the Huns there had been important colonising movements but this particular alien element finally destroyed the Roman ethos of the province and completed a process which had begun in the Severan period, after the Marcomannic Wars, when the depradations of the Sarmatians resulted in the introduction of exotic oriental elements (mainly from Syria) through the new military formations sent into the province. Considerable evidence has recently come to light through the outstanding archaeological find unearthed at Pécsüszög which includes gold plates worn as a belt harness and sword decorations, while bone plates found at Vindobona (Vienna) are evidently bow fittings and relate to the typical Hunnic weapon found over the whole area between Pannonia and Mongolia. Cauldrons used for sacrifice have been found at Brigetio and Intercisa (near Dunaujvaros) as well as in areas outside the empire (Moravia and Silesia), while skulls from the family burial at Mozs show signs of deformation, a deliberate practice imposed on children, which was introduced in Pannonia in the fifth century following the arrival of the Huns. Information is accumulating on the Avars who also evolved an equestrian nomadic culture. They were buried along with horses, fully harnessed. Harness was decorated with metal while the bow, also a frequent find in Avar graves, was strengthened by bone plates at each end. A variety of pots, both hand-made and wheel-turned, has come to light while the rich decoration and ornamentation associated with Avar belts has given rise to a 'Keszthely Culture' in the area of Lake Balaton.

Communications and urban development

The Danube was an essential part of the transport system, supplying the various frontier garrisons and cities. The Pannonian fleet (Flavia Pannonica), consisting mainly of oar-driven craft, was based at Aquincum, Carnuntum and Sirmium but it operated on the tributary streams and could reach some places well away from the Danube, that were consequently able to grow as part of the water transport system. A good example is Savaria on a terrace above the Gyöngyös river accessible for barges and small craft, although this town was also an important nodal point on the road system. During the first century AD a main road was driven eastwards to Poetovio at the crossing of the Drava (the capital of Pannonia when it existed as one province, a legionary headquarters and colonia) and on to Savaria (Figure 2.2). From Savaria roads led north to Carnuntum and

Vindobona as well as northeastwards along the Gyönygös to Arrabona, Brigetio and Aquincum. From Aquincum a road continued along the west bank of the Danube as far south as Mursa (Osijek) and there was also the riverside road from Arrabona to Vindobona. Such a system was appropriate to the initial military entry into Pannonia and provided a basic link between the major Danube garrisons and the imperial capital. During the second and third centuries commercial interests grew in the shape of manufactures moving into Pannonia from Gaul and the Rhineland through Vindobona and precious metals transported westwards out of Dacia from the colonia municipium of Napoca (Cluj-Napoca) towards the Danube at Aquincum or further south in the Mursa area. Thus new roads were needed to provide a direct link from Vindobona to Mursa and two routes appeared extending the existing roads from Vindobona to Arrabona and Savaria southeastwards to Mursa with a convergence point at the new town of Sopianis some seventy kilometres short of Mursa. The two roads passed Lake Balaton at its eastern and western extremities, creating growth at Cimbrianae (near Balatonfüzfö) and Mogentianis (near Keszthely) respectively. Finally the further growth of the empire in the east during the third and fourth centuries and the rise of Constantinople gave rise to a major impulse affecting Pannonia from the south through Sirmium and Mursa. This confirmed the importance of the roads from Mursa and Sopianis to Aquincum, Arrabona and Savaria and led to further road construction between Lake Balaton and the Danube: notably Aquincum to Sopianis and Arrabona to Intercisa as well as the short link from Cimbrianae on Lake Balaton to the Danube at Intercisa. All three roads crossed at Herculia (near Sarosd) which thus became an important road centre, though one which emerged simply through the development of a transport system rooted on the key points which had emerged during the first century.[18]

The Romans obviously had a central place system in mind for Pannonia and various settlements and road links emerged in consequence, but the foundation of the system was not laid out in model form on a featureless plain. Rather it emerged through the need to connect the Danube frontier (particularly certain individual sites along the river) with Rome. The Romans created an urban network from scratch with town development probably beginning in the lands between the Drava and Sava (Sirmium and Siscia for

Figure 2.2: Roman roads and settlements in Pannonia

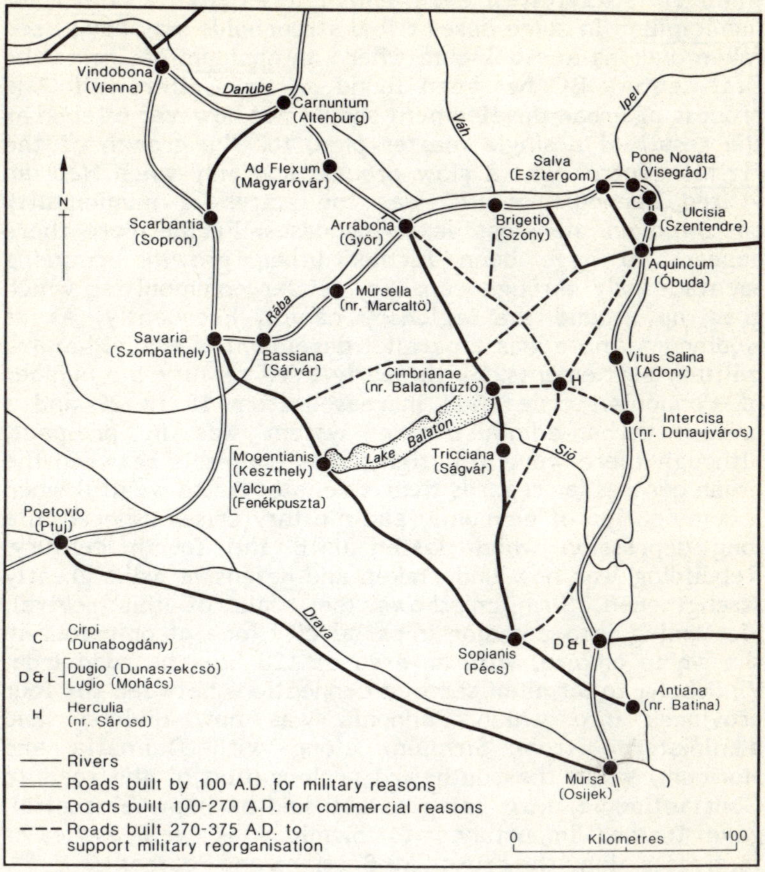

Source: A.F. Burghardt 1979 (note 18).

example). It seems that tribal territories were split into small units (civitates) each administered from a colonia or municipium. In some cases tribal strongholds may have been taken over as at Aquincum where an oppidum dating to the first century BC has been found on the Gellért hill. The process of urban development should not however be seen as the result of a single master plan, for the growth of the civitas centres was a slow process and only when Hadrian visited Pannonia in 124 was the status of municipality bestowed on the most deserving cases. Furthermore there appears to have been further urban growth occurring spontaneously through canabae, settler communities which grew up around the legionary camps. Frequently, as at Aquincum, there was a parallel development of civilian and military settlements. By the early third century the number of Pannonian cities had increased from 18 to 26 and a uniform urban-administrative system was in prospect, although there were still significant contrasts between the urban centres (as regards their size, status and wealth) when a combination of economic and military crises ushered in a long depression which lasted until the fourth century. Rebuilding was now undertaken and defensive walls greatly strengthened. Sirmium shows the scale of this revival, blossoming into a major imperial city (one of only four in the whole empire) with an area of 120 ha. The road from Vindobona to Sirmium secured connections between the four provinces into which Pannonia was now divided (and administered from Sirmium along with Dalmatia and Noricum) while the southward prolongation of the road to Constantinople, now being established as imperial capital, gave further importance to Sirmium as well as lesser fortresses along the route like Bassiana and Scarbantia.

At the other end of the scale there were now fortified agricultural settlements with modest industrial functions, like Tricciana and Valcum already mentioned. Industrial production did not feature prominently in Pannonian exports: rather there was an import of manufactures, initially from Italy but diversified by the second and third century by goods from other western provinces. Some Pannonian goods were sold to barbarians (slaves, raw materials and livestock) but many of the manufactures involved originated in other parts of the empire. Little is known of the other rural settlements, but there were clearly certain concentrations of villa (villa rustica) settlements, notably around Lake Balaton where the road network was well-developed and where climatic conditions were very similar to those prevailing in Italy. Settlement related to the large estate (latifundium) therefore became an important point of origin for the diffusion of Romanism among the native population. Of course pre-conquest practices were not displaced immediately and this is evident from such archaeological finds as grind stones. Villas were also established in considerable numbers west of Lake Fertö (in what is now Austria) and on the hills behind the Danube limes where there were strategic advantages. There may well have been a connection between villas and watchtowers to say nothing of the important service role that many villas may have performed through changing horses and accommodating travellers. The agricultural potential was considerable and the villas were able to supply not only the frontier garrison but generate further surpluses for export to Italy. In addition to arable farming there was stockrearing (supported by an abundance of pasture and forest land) and wine production (with Pannonia excelling here, along with Gallia and Hispania), while larger estates may well have maintained fish ponds and hunted game in the forests. The villas were also industrial centres for excavations have uncovered pottery workshops, weaving mills, foundries and smithies, while it is likely that the skills of carpenters, masons and glassblowers were also represented. With labour shortages slavery evidently gave way to the hiring of coloni or agricultural workers. Maybe the degeneration of freemen to servile status, through entering into contracts with landowners (perhaps in part to guarantee their security), provided a precedent for medieval serfdom. The smallholders' village, the most frequent form of villa settlement in Pannonia, is thus a prototype for the feudal settlement.

THE ROMAN IMPACT ON DACIA

In this section Rome's relations with two closely-related Thracian peoples will be considered: the Dacian and Getic tribes who inhabited the Carpathian and lower Danubian territories respectively. They reached a new stage of development in the first century AD with more effective political unity and the more advanced technical level of the final La Tène era. 'Burebista and Decebalus creatively assimilated the technological achievements of Greek and Roman cultures out of which Decebalus was in the process of making a Dacian classical age when Trajan's legions struck the final blow'.[19] Agriculture was a dominant occupation, with particular emphasis on cattle breeding in the mountains, but the Dacians were also skilled craftsmen in silver and iron and hence were well-supplied with tools and fearsome weapons like curved daggers, swords and lances. The principal stronghold lay quite close to the Danube in the Banat Mountains south of Orastie, but throughout Dacian territory fortified centres emerged with economic, military and religious significance. This oppidan culture no doubt depended on slave labour controlled by the state and also by aristocratic families (tarabostea) who were now distancing themselves more emphatically from the commoners (comati). Tilisca was surrounded by two outer walls, one of earth and another of stone, the material also used for the foundations of watchtowers. It is quite characteristic to find the outer earthen wall, with moat, complementing the murus dacicus with freestone walls joined together by beams wedged into the masonry. Such a structure, which contrasts strongly with practice in neighbouring Celtic lands, has been identified at Piatra Craivii, overlooking the Transylvanian Plain at a height of over 1000m. There is a complex terrace system here and occupation may well have commenced in the second century BC.

Established in the mountains of Orastie were the royal residences and a number of rectangular and circular sanctuaries open to the sky. The latter may have served a urano-solar cult which tied up with a Dacian calendar of sixty six-day weeks grouped into twelve months. The principal sanctuaries were associated with Gradistea Muncelului set out on a terraced hill-top with a large refuge area (a fortified enclosure of 3.5 ha.) and some industrial zones concerned with metalworking and pottery. As already noted defence was provided by a constellation of forts which evolved over a considerable period of time: the time of construction as well as the local terrain conditions determine the precise nature of the building. Costesti for example is considered a tribal settlement inhabited in the late second century BC and fortified by Burebista while Blidaru was built subsequently in the region of Decebalus to reinforce Costesti: its walls are a fine example of murus dacicus showing inner and outer drystone faces linked with thick horizontal beams laid in swallowtail grooves which helped to withstand lateral pressure until the earth and stone fill had solidified.

The threat from Dacia however lay not simply in its advanced technology, spirited belligerence and strategic situation (with a mountainous heartland which provided a base for attack in either Moesia or Pannonia), but also in the possibility that a grouping of barbarian tribes might crystallise and threaten the whole empire. The Marcomanni and Sarmatians were obvious potential allies and when Trajan started his Dacian campaign in 101-2 he faced a combined force of Dacians, Germans and Sarmatians. The first campaign was indecisive and the peace terms produced nothing more than an armed truce. It required a further campaign in 105-6 supported now by a bridge over the Danube at Drobeta, to complete the conquest. The Romans followed up their advance into the Orastie Mountains with a deliberate policy of destroying the native religion.[20] As elsewhere the tribal territory and its capital was transformed by the Romans into a basic unit of administration (civitas), although new sites for oppida might be found if the native settlements were badly located in relation to the main transport routes. The centre of the Roman administration was at Ulpia Traiana near the modern market town of Hateg and its position on the low ground convenient for the road to Drobeta by way of the Iron Gate Pass stands in sharpest contrast to the main Dacian refuge.

Dacia's significant permanent population was enslaved by the Romans to maximise the agricultural and mineral output. The effort in stockrearing is indicated by the villa rustica complex of Hobita near Ulpia Traiana which includes storerooms and workshops. The gold of the western Carpathians was greatly prized and work was administered by an imperial officer with headquarters at Ampelum (Zlatna): copper and iron were also worked in this district which extended to Baia de Aries, Baia de Cris, Brad and Rosia Montana. There was a considerable loss of population through plague and the export of slaves, but some Thracians achieved high office and the prospect of advancement in the imperial system seems to have rendered desirable not only Roman citizenship but the adoption of Latin or Greek names. Equally however these accommodations may well have been made in order to avoid prejudice, for in Dacia the adoption of imperial family names did not mean a complete switch to Roman cultural practices. Local rites remained prominent in burial ritual and cremation continued as the almost universal Dacian custom. At Cincis near Hunedoara cremation burials in stone-covered pits lie near the brick sarcophagus of the Roman or Romanised proprietor.

R.F. Hoddinott has argued for a major displacement of the Dacian population from the low ground: 'they were dispossessed of the fertile Danubian plain and pushed into the forests and hills in the north' while in Transylvania 'they were mainly driven into the eastern areas where the land was poor and a string of forts guarded the frontier'.[21] Other Dacians must have fled after Trajan's victory to join the free tribes beyond the Carpathians. Yet such evidence of a major redistribution of settlement triggered by Roman ambivalence towards the native population must be set against the continuity evident at Slimnic near Sibiu where a Dacian village has been traced from the third century BC to the third century AD without any change in buildings (rectangular semi-dugout wattle and daub huts): the only developments are in grain storage and pottery, with the latter reflecting the tremendous increase in wheel-made pottery in both city workshops and rural centres where Dacians worked along with immigrant craftsmen using Roman techniques. Since archaeological research in Moldavia shows that the fortresses there did not remain in use after the Dacian Wars it seems that the Romans were active beyond the borders of the new province and prevailed upon the natives to settle in open and unfortified places. No doubt there was an element of force used in establishing alliances with local leaders but the large amount of Roman coinage found in Moldavia indicates that a substantial *subsidium* was paid and, insofar as the coinage was counterfeited, shows that the free Dacians were happy to accommodate the Romans.[22] Cultural influence was extended partly through the intercourse between Dacians on both sides of the Roman frontier and partly by the *castellum* at Barbosi, near Galati, which boasted a large military and civilian population. And with the growing menace of barbarian raids a significant Romanised population arose in Moldavia through the settlement of prisoners of war: the fourth century incursions of the Goths were very important in this respect. Discoveries made in Bessarabia at Komarovo near Hotin and Sobari near Soroca indicate the presence of Roman craftsmen.

There was a particularly powerful Roman presence in Dobrogea in connection with the *limes*. The army played a large part in the Romanisation process as many natives were recruited.[23] Troesmis (near Tutrakan) was the chief military stronghold but there were other important settlements at Capidava (near Seimeni), Carsium (near Hîrsova), Dinogetia (near Luncavita), Ibida (near Stejaru), Noviodunum (near Isaccea) and Tropaeum Traiani. After the withdrawal from Muntenia and southern Moldavia in 119 the Danube became the frontier as far upstream as the Olt confluence. But in the time of Septimus Severus and Alexander Severus the natural defence lines were supplemented by continuous earthworks which ran in an east-west direction across the plain from Drobeta to Dobrogea and further north from the lower Siret across Bessarabia. There were also north-south running dykes east of the Olt, related to a line of camps on both sides of the river.[24] Recent work has however raised the possibility that some of the dykes may be the work of the Byzantine Empire in the tenth century. After the evacuation of Dacia the Danube became all the more critical and a girdle of forts along the lower river protected the Dobrogea salient, including Arrubium (Macin), Axiopolis (near Cernavoda) and Durostorum (near Ostrov). Development also went ahead on some earlier fortifications like Capidava and Dinogetia. The old Greek towns were still inhabited but Ovid's poems vividly reflect the harsh and insecure life of the Black Sea townspeople and the threat posed to Histria and Tomis by Getians and Sarmatians who would cross the frozen Danube in winter and carry off both prisoners and livestock. Yet the exiled Ovid was to some extent seeking pity and urban life did prove quite durable. With the revival of the empire in the east the old Greek Black Sea trading bases were reactivated and the rebuilding of walls at Callatis, Histria and Tomis can be traced through to the sixth century. Although the Avars were a great threat, disrupting trade and laying siege to the towns, as at Tomis in 599, it was the emergence of states in Bulgaria in the seventh century that introduced a major hiatus into urban life in Dobrogea.

It is however possible that the Romans did not abandon Dacia from a legal standpoint and the the inhabitants accepted the status of _foederati_. Continuity in Daco-Roman life has been revealed by excavations not only in Transylvania (the _vici_ of Noslac, Obreja and Soporu de Cimpie) but also on the Romanian Plain at Olteni and Tîrgsor, as well as Spantov where there is evidence of Dacian settlement in an area once thought to have been purely Gothic. The migrating peoples, including Gepids, Avars and Slavs, inevitably influenced the native population and harassment may have led to more emphasis on stock-rearing in remoter areas. Further fragments of evidence have been presented by the Romanian historian C.C. Giurescu.[25] The late fourth century burial at Brateiu in the valley of the Tîrnave Mare indicates the survival of a funerary ritual which was adopted in Dacia during Roman rule. And a fourth century Latin inscription at Biertan discovered in 1775 is also significant. More ingeniously Giurescu cites the Romanian word pacura (meaning crude oil) which is derived from the Latin picula: 'this word which does not exist in the other Romance languages could only have come into being and been preserved on the left bank of the Danube, where crude oil was known and exploited since ancient times, and not on the right bank where neither the Romans nor the medieval peoples had such exploitations'.[26]

Thracian culture in general was much enriched by Roman influence and hence the idea of Romanitatea as an ethnic-cultural force in southeastern Europe in the Dark Ages with the Dacians as merely one of several related elements. However although the first Romanian state was established in Thessaly in the tenth century under the Byzantine Empire the most persistent political entities have been those on the territory of the present Romanian state. Slav influences became powerful of course but it is remarkable how strongly the people inhabiting the Carpathian-Danubian territory followed up their stubborn defence of Dacia with an equally determined defence of their Roman heritage. J.C. Dragan explains the paradox of a 'miraculous ethnic continuity' in the Carpathian-Danubian zone alongside a distinctly restrained development of urban centres through the lack of stability in an area that was basically very attractive for settlement: 'an urban civilisation did not exist here: it took shape every time there was a moment of respite but it was soon destroyed by the nomads coming from the eastern steppes or by the conquerers coming from the south or from the west'.[27] It seems that the Romanians organised themselves at the level of the village community (obstea taraneasca) based on agriculture, fishing, hunting and small-scale manufacture. The need for defence seems to have brought together groups of villages along particular route ways under a single jurisdiction and the fact that the Romanian name for such a wider unity (judet) is derived from the Slavonic sudet suggests that pressure may have come from the Bulgarians who temporarily extended their influence northwards across the Danube to Transylvania.

The Dacian and Greco-Roman monuments have therefore drawn attention from archaeologists for political as well as academic reasons, although for a long time foreigners were responsible for the collection of information. For example the Italian A.F. Marsigli, a military engineer in the service of the Habsburg emperor at the end of the seventeenth century who travelled through the Carpathian-Danubian lands examining and sometimes excavating Roman remains. The eighteenth century saw several publications like F. Fasching's work on Dacia in 1725 and the first native efforts at collecting ancient remains; most importantly S. Brukenthal of Sibiu (1721-1803), who was followed in the nineteenth century by M. Ghika in Bucharest and J. Kemény in Kolozsvar (Cluj). These collections have formed the basis of the archaeological museums of the three cities. Further momentum arose from the foundation of universities in Bucharest and Cluj, with particular importance attaching to the work of Grigore Tocilescu on Dacia Inferior in Roman times and in particular the triumphal monument of Tropaeum Traiani which marked the defeat of the Dacian challenge to the Roman position in Dobrogea. Archaeological excavation was expanded by Vasile Pârvan (Tocilescu's successor at Bucharest University) who started digging at Histria in 1914 and had his celebrated work on Dacia translated into English after his lectures at St John's College, Cambridge in 1926. After his untimely death in 1927 the work at Histria was continued by S. Lambrino. Meanwhile Constantin Daicoviciu was writing on the Dacian forts and sanctuaries in the Orastie Mountains in the inter-war period, but the work has expanded since through other researchers such as I.H. Crisan, H. Daicoviciu and N. Lupu. The important lowland settlements of Pioana and Popesti have been investigated by I. Andriesescu, R. Vulpe and others.

NOTES

1. T. Parsons 1966, 'Societies: comparative revolutionary perspectives' (Englewood Cliffs, N.J.: Prentice Hall), 208-17; S.P. Savage 1981, 'The theories of Talcott Parsons: the social relations of action' (London: Macmillan) 179-86. See also T. Cornell and J. Matthews 1982, 'Atlas of the Roman world' (Oxford: Phaidon); M.I. Finley 1973, 'The ancient economy' (London: Chatto & Windus); A.H.M. Jones

1974, 'The Roman economy: studies in ancient economic and administrative history' (Oxford: Blackwell); F. Miller 1981, 'The Roman Empire and its neighbours' (London: Duckworth); R. Syme 1971, 'Danube papers' (Bucharest: Association Internationale d'Etudes du Sud Est Europe).

2. S. Rokkan 1973, 'Cities states and nations: a dimensional model for the study of contrasts in development', S. Eisenstadt and S. Rokkan eds. 'Building states and nations' (Beverly Hills: Sage Publications) I 73-97 (quote p.77).

3. A.H.M. Jones 1971, 'The cities of the eastern Roman provinces' (Oxford: Clarendon Press) 1.

4. Ibid. 2; F. Marazov and I. Marazov 1977, 'Thrace and Thracians' (London: Cassell).

5. N.G.I. Hammond and G.T. Griffith 1972-9, 'History of Macedonia' (Oxford: Clarendon Press).

6. D. Garasanin et al. 1971, 'The Illyrians and Dacians' (Belgrade: National Museum). See also J.J. Wilkes 1969, 'Dalmatia' (London: Routledge & Kegan Paul).

7. G. Skrivanic 1977, 'Roman roads and settlements in the Balkans', F.W. Carter ed. pp. 115-45.

8. V.J. Velkov 1977, 'Cities in Thrace and Dacia in late antiquity' (Amsterdam: Hakkert). See also N.J.G. Pounds 1969, 'Urbanization in the classical world' Annals Association of American Geographers 59, 135-57.

9. M. Hushick 1936-7, 'Archaeological history of Lake Ostrovo in western Macedonia' Geographical Journal 87, 118-47; 89, 448-56; 90, 446-57.

10. F. Millar 1981 p. 311.

11. E.A. Gutkind 1964 pp. 439-46.

12. A. Lengyel and G.T.B. Radan eds. 1980. See also A. Mocsy 1974, 'Pannonia and Upper Moesia: a history of the middle Danube provinces of the Roman Empire' (London: Routledge & Kegan Paul); P. Oliva 1962, 'Pannonia and the onset of crisis in the Roman Empire' (Prague: Czechoslovak Academy of Sciences).

13. M. Szabo 1971, 'The celtic heritage of Hungary' (Budapest: Corvina).

14. J.J. Wilkes 1983, 'Romans Dacians and Sarmatians in the first and second centuries', B. Hartley and J. Wacher eds. 'Rome and her northern provinces' (Gloucester: Alan Sutton) 255-89.

15. A. Lengyel and G.T.B. Radan eds. 1980 p. 110.

16. W.G. East 1966, 'The European frontier regions of the Roman Empire', W.G. East pp. 28-47. See also G. Alföldy

1974, 'Noricum' (London: Routledge & Kegan Paul).

17. A. Lengyel and G.T.B. Radan eds. 1980 p. 157.

18. A.F. Burghardt 1979, 'The origin of the road and city network of Roman Pannonia' Journal of Historical Geography 5, 1-20.

19. P. MacKendrick 1975, 'The Dacian stones speak' (Chapel Hill: University of North Carolina Press) 66.

20. L. Rossi 1971, 'Trajan's column and the Dacian wars' (London: Thames & Hudson).

21. R.F. Hoddinott 1981 p. 164.

22. D. Garasanin et al. 1971, op.cit. (note 35); see also M. Chitescu 1981, 'Numismatic aspects of the history of the Dacian state: the Roman Republic coinage in Dacia and Geto-Dacian coinage of Roman type' British Archaeological Reports International Series 112; N. Gostar 1980, 'The ancient character of the Roman element in the east of the Carpathians' Anuarul Institutului de Istorie si Arheologie A.D. Xenopol (Iasi) 17, 1-9; G.D. Teodor 1980, 'The east Carpathian area of Romania V-XI centuries AD' British Archaeological Reports International Series 81.

23. A. Aricescu 1980, 'The army in Roman Dobrogea' British Archaeological Reports International Series 86.

24. I.B. Cataniciu 1981, 'Evolution of the system of defence works in Roman Dacia' British Archaeological Reports International Series 116; C. Scorpan 1980, 'Limes Scythiae: topographical and stratigraphical research on the late Roman fortifications on the Lower Danube' British Archaeological Reports International Series 88.

25. C.C. Giurescu n.d., 'Transylvania in the history of Romania' (London: Garnstone Press).

26. Ibid. p. 39.

27. J.C. Dragan 1976, 'We the Thracians and our multimillenary history' (Milan: Nagard) I 250.

3

Dark Age Colonisation and Trade

The review of a complex settlement history leading up to the emergence of Medieval nation states is completed by the Dark Age colonisation of Eastern Europe. Settlers from the east created a new political geography which maintained some slender continuity with the Roman period. Such themes as feudal relations and ideology, within clearly defined territories, link the Roman Empire forwards in time to the necklace of nation states encountered in the Medieval period. And in view of the persistence of Rome's cultural influence the military defeat of the empire may appear enigmatic. There appears to have been conflict on the frontiers and the priority inevitably given to defence could have increased the power of the bureaucracy, strengthened control over the provinces and reduced social mobility. A decline in population from the second century AD is frequently postulated and this arguably led to some dependence on barbarians (especially Germans) and _feoderati_, serving under their own leaders, in military campaigns. The shortage of rural labour should have acted as stimulus to technical innovations in agriculture but evidently the owners, dismissed by N.J.G. Pounds as 'playboys of the ancient world', did not get involved in such mundane matters as agricultural methods, while the heavy burden of heavy land taxes tended to drive talented farmers away from the countryside.[1] Taxation was levied in a discriminatory fashion which allowed the wealthy to enlarge their estates while urban craftsmen and peasant farmers were tightly bound to their humble occupations. For example, free peasants degenerated in status to the level of _coloni_ (estate labourers) and under Diocletian were forbidden to change tenancies or abandon agriculture: this step towards Medieval serfdom was taken in the interest of securing

Figure 3.1: The transition from Rome to Byzantium (A) The Roman Empire divided 395 AD (B) The empire of Justinian 526 AD

Source: Historical atlases.

capitation taxes and maintaining land in cultivation. Although supported by agriculture the towns never generated industries and commerce on a major scale. Excessive spending went on public buildings whose maintenance was a great burden under conditions of a falling population. Decay however was a very long-term process and the final collapse of imperial rule did not mean a revolutionary change, as the urbanised society was only gradually transformed into the predominantly land-based society of the Dark Ages. For the whole scenario has been reduced to the simple matter of technological diffusion from centre to periphery, surging through the provincial towns and passing beyond the limits of the empire with the effect of increasing pressure from barbarians. 'When the initial relative advantage of technology was lost the costs of maintaining such a large political entity as the Roman Empire began to outweigh its advantages'.[2]

FROM ROME TO BYZANTIUM

Decline was not equally evident in all parts of the empire and in much of Eastern Europe the imperial structure survived for another thousand years with its base at Constantinople. This contrast arises because of a dramatic reversal in the status of east and west compared with Medieval and modern times. With greater population and wealth the east could better support the administrative and military burdens imposed, while both grain and manufactured goods were in surplus. Furthermore the eastern provinces were on the whole less exposed to attack: the Persians were much less troublesome than the Germans and Mongols who pressed up against the Danube and Rhine frontiers. Although evidence is not conclusive it has been suggested that the eastern half of the empire was less plagued by corruption and class antagonisms than the western portion. Free peasants remained quite numerous in the Balkans, particularly in Macedonia and Thrace: 'in this small difference in the course of social development may lie in some degree the reason for the survival of the Eastern Empire'.[3] There was considerable introduction of new blood. Settlement of barbarians on the south side of the Danube occurred in Moesia even in the first century AD and the assimilation process must have continued on a growing scale. Visigoths and Ostrogoths both moved into the Balkans and in many cases served to swell the ranks of the Roman military.[4] They seemed to have acquitted themselves well and if there were revolts, as at Adrianople (Edirne) in 378, they arose out of a cruelly ambivalent attitude towards them by the Roman government. There were also important trade contacts across the Danube, following the broad alignment of the Amber Route, for archaeological finds have produced a convincing picture of Roman exports to all northern parts of Eastern Europe. Evidently the strength of the eastern half of the empire was more pronounced east of Constantinople rather than in the Balkans, where population was probably quite sparse, but for the most part the Roman Empire in Eastern Europe proved to be remarkably durable.

The (eastern) Byzantine Empire with its central organisation at Constantinople did not maintain its territorial integrity exactly according to Diocletian's boundary running from Sirmium on the Danube to Epidaurus (Cavtat) on the Adriatic. Some western lands were regained under Justinian in the sixth century (Italy and even southern Spain) but in the seventh century the process was dramatically reversed by the advances of the Arabs and Visigoths, and in Eastern Europe the Bulgarians and Slavs. The great migrations of Slavs and later Bulgarians constituted grave challenges to central authority and its armies could not always prevent the emergence of independent barbarian kingdoms (Bulgaria and Serbia) within the historic limits of the empire. The Romanised native population was able to survive in many parts of the Balkan mountains and, despite considerable assimilation of alien elements, the Albanians and Romanians of today claim a cultural and ethnic continuity extending back to the days of the empire. Yet these people had little option but react passively to the great migrations and in many of the more accessible areas replacement rather than assimilation was the rule. Justinian tried to hold the southern Balkans through a chain of fortress towns while ecclesiastical organisation also helped to generate central places. The lost town of Stobi (near Titov Veles) is a particularly remarkable Balkan city, situated at the Vardar-Crna confluence not far from the Via Egnatia. Although developed under Hadrian in the first half of the second century (when the theatre was erected) it experienced considerable expansion and rebuilding (along the lines of the inherited Roman street plan) during the fourth-fifth century 'period of the great palaces' when Stobi was capital of Macedonia Secunda and also an important religious centre. There is no building later than the sixth century with stagnation presumably responsible for the headlong dive into architectural obscurity. But the town plainly flourished in early Byzantine times and the monuments are a great source of information on contemporary art. Early churches are complemented by magnificent secular architecture, both exhibiting fine mosaic floors. And with indications that Romanisation never went very deep there may be new insights available on the integrity of the Greek lands and the transmission of cultural impulses westwards to Rome.[5]

The decline of town life was a depressing reality throughout the Balkans. The breakdown of any remaining long-distance trade and military withdrawal from frontier districts eliminated any need for towns, while the depradations of the invaders probably put many of the surviving townspeople to flight: the citizens of Salona (Solin) sought refuge nearby in Diocletian's palace while the inhabitants of Epidaurus fled to the offshore island of Ragusa where the city of Dubrovnik stands today. The nature of rural society is still more enigmatic and it is a matter of conjecture how far a system of estates, using slave labour, was complemented by a free peasant society based on village communities. Arguably there was a prototype of Medieval feudalism in force with peasant farmers cooperating in the working of a primitive field system of the infield-outfield type, but owing certain obligations to manorial estates and their lordly owners. The weakness of the Byzantine Empire was manifest between 600 and 800 when its territory was reduced by two thirds and when regular raids by Arabs and Bulgarians threatened Constantinople itself. Yet thanks to a major cultural and political revival half the lost territory was to be regained and the economy rebuilt. It seems that during the eighth century there was an increase in scholarly activity among the ruling class and this created the prospect of better administration. The realisation of this potential may be attributed to Emperor Nicephorus I who was successful in improving the efficiency of the civil service. 'Thus in the ninth century the empire's diplomacy was more effective, its taxes were more equitably assessed and more efficiently collected, its army functioned better and its whole administration was tightened and improved'.[6]

The Byzantines did not share the good fortune of Rome in enjoying a solid peace in the core of the empire with wars restricted to the border regions. The challenge from militarily-gifted immigrant peoples was an almost perpetual one and for long periods imperial rule was restricted to Asia Minor and Thrace. The civilian population was reluctant to accept the necessity for permanent activity on a war footing, although the emperors were not for the most part beguiled by the Christian view of military hostilities however much they might seek to avoid such action by skillful diplomacy. Ultimately the empire collapsed both as a cohesive social unit and as an expanding economy. Yet its achievements should not be too hastily belittled. Perhaps first and foremost it demonstrated the potency of faith in the divinely decreed destiny of the empire: empire and church were welded together into a single unity to the point where separation seemed quite impossible. In the words of R. Jenkins, 'to pretend to be a Christian without loyalty to Christ's representatives at Constantinople is rank hypocrisy, heresy and blasphemy'.[7] It was through missionary activity inspired by this ideology as much as by war that the barbarians were pacified in the ninth century. Of course the formula was not foolproof as the attacks on the empire by Bulgarians and Serbs testify, but Jenkins would argue that the Orthodox faith injected an element of uneasiness into such hostilities because of 'the feeling that brother was murdering brother and that the angels looked on with sad and wondering eyes to see the children of Christ shedding one another's blood'.[8] Also it is clear that the Byzantine model was widely copied by the nation states of the Balkans in Medieval times, with tremendous importance attached to the establishment of an autonomous ecclesiastical hierarchy to back up the emperor and his ministers. Westerners would no doubt have reservations about the culture which developed on such rigid ideological foundations, yet there can be no doubt that the faith of the Byzantines could inspire great energy and inventiveness in peacetime as well as courage in war. And it is perhaps not too much of an exaggeration to see the Byzantine outlook living on in communist regimes of Eastern Europe, so that the sense of mutual incomprehension which often pervades discussions between present-day inhabitants of the two halves of the Roman world (through failure to understand each other's moral and cultural environment) may not be entirely different from the gulf that formerly separated Byzantines and Franks.

DARK AGE MIGRATION AND STATE DEVELOPMENT: THE GERMANS

This section attempts a summary of the major migrations which exerted a powerful impact on the Roman and Byzantine empires and laid the ethnic foundations for the political geography of the Medieval period. Mention must be made of Huns who were nomadic livestock herders and masters of cavalry warfare. These Mongoloid peoples were repelled from China and made an impact in Europe in the third and fourth centuries when they broke through the Danube frontier and went on to establish an extensive empire in Central Europe. But the Huns made no significant long-term contribution to the peopling of Eastern Europe and their influence may best be seen through disturbance of the German peoples who are first reported as making inroads into Celtic territory in the Oder and Vistula valleys. As opportunity arose the Germans advanced south into the more civilised and physically more congenial lands comprising the börde country and further loess lands beyond the Hercynian forest. For as W.G. East has explained 'the alternative was to push into the well-wooded plains of Poland or Russia where there was no highly developed civilisation to plunder or inherit, where the winters were long and hard, where the naturally defensive frameworks for state building were lacking and finally where nomad populations then roamed'.[9] Although urban developments were restricted to rudimentary forms the Germans nevertheless established permanent settlements as bases for a primitive agriculture that involved the ploughing of different sections of grassland each year. It may be supposed that groups of villages comprised tribal territories, each surrounded by its Mark, a fringe of woodland and waste that served both economic and strategic purposes. Yet the extensive agriculture of the Germans required large areas of land and since much of the North European Plain was unsuitable because of forest, marsh or moor it is understandable that there was a degree of overpopulation, relative to their technology, that stimulated penetration of the more densely settled lands of the Roman Empire. The people were highly mobile and quite small in numbers: 'it was perhaps because of these characteristics that they tended to constitute a minority among the populations they invaded, establishing new kingdoms, laws and lordships but making relatively little permanent impression on rural settlement and customs or on language'.[10]

The principal trade routes were taken over, with the Moravian Gate appreciated as a particularly easy route through the Hercynian lands from the upper reaches of the Oder and Vistula to the Morava and Danube. Not surprisingly great importance attached to the Roman fortresses of Carnuntum and Vindobona since they guarded the routes leading on into Pannonia and across the eastern Alps into Italy. Penetration would also have occurred from the upper Saale Valley through the Bohemian Forest in the direction of Regensburg. But the easiest route was the one used by the amber traders from the Vistula southeastwards to the Dniester and Prut with Carpathian passes like to Oituz offering access to Pannonia and Transylvania. Pressure along these lines of approach required the Roman withdrawal from Dacia and the consolidation of the Danube frontier, including the earthworks across the Dobrogea peninsula and a bridge over the river near the modern town of Nikopol to extend the road from Serdica (Sofia) into hostile territory. But the precautions were in vain as the Goths repeatedly overran the frontier in the third century forcing the Romans back on their key bases of Adrianople, Constantinople and Thessalonica. For example in 250-1 a major Gothic raid reached the Thracian Plain. Philippopolis was sacked, many people were taken captive and the Emperor Decius killed. As a result of this setback it became more difficult for the native Thracian population to produce the cereals required by Rome and additional people had to be settled towards the end of the third century. Some of the new arrivals may have been Dacians from Transylvania, resettled after Aurelian's withdrawal from that province, but the majority were probably aliens whose arrival must have permanently affected the ethnic composition of the rural population. The economic importance of the newcomers is underlined by their exemption from many military and civil duties. 'In the following century more Gothic invasions, even a Gothic civil war which devastated Thracia, and a major Gothic immigration further impoverished and diluted the Thracian element'.[11] Eventually in 380 the Goths were allowed to settle south of the Danube on the northern slopes of the Balkan mountains.

However the Goths, with feoderati status within the Roman Empire, were merely one of a number of German tribes. Lombards and Vandals were also active in the east while J. Fleckenstein describes a complementary movement southwards from western bases against Celtic and Illyrian peoples.[12] In this theatre we hear of the Alamanni, Bavarians, Burgundians, Franks, Saxons and Thuringians. Evidently there were significant changes in organisation occurring during the Dark Ages and these became significant for the development of the whole of Eastern Europe during the Medieval period, substantiating the long-held proposition that German history provides the main-stream of European history. By the tenth century the German tribes were very different from those described by Tacitus, for some tribes were enlarged at the expense of others while further growth would have arisen through the absorption of foreign populations. Effective leadership must have played a major role in this process so 'the belief that the German tribe started off as a unified mass of freemen has long since been exposed as romantic wishful thinking'.[13] 'The Germanic nobles were there as soon as German history began ... deriving their primacy from the gods and displaying their prosperity as a sign of divine powers'.[14] Marked differences in the ownership of property were evident even in the Iron Age: thus tribal elite held most of the land, necessitating a predominantly servile population. It would appear that the leadership initially involved a nobility which derived authority from the gods and enjoyed a priestly prerogative to represent the tribe in worship and legal proceedings as well as warfare. But successful campaigning required continuity in leadership and produced a more elaborate hierarchy which culminated in the formation of a military monarchy; for the occupation of new territories could only be accomplished if the strongest leader among a group of chieftains could persuade the others to join him. Such tribes thereby achieved greater size and strength at the expense of others which failed to consolidate. Only a few of the fifty or so tribes known to Tacitus survived the great migrations.

However it is worth adding that these tribes, with specific settlement areas to ensure cohesion in later times, have continued to exist to the present within the wider framework of the German nation. This introduces a further stage of political consolidation which had much to do with the empire created by one of the tribes, the Franks. A half-historical and half-legendary lineage boosted the capacity of the Merovingian monarchy to inspire allegiance and the subsequent ninth century division of Charlemagne's empire provided the territorial basis for the Holy Roman Empire. It is very noticeable that these further political developments occurred in the western area of German settlement. The king of the Franks (rex Francorum) posed as the head of an association of nobles, embracing the ideology of Christianity to hasten the fusion of Frankish and Gallo-Roman elements. The classical legacy was assimilated through religion, although centuries of effort were needed before the northern peoples could regard it as an essential ingredient of their own past. In the east however the sovereign monarchies established by the Germans after feoderati status was thrown off did not prove durable. They lost contact with the regions of their origin and failed to maintain effective leadership, partly at least because of the lack of an ideology to assimilate the classical tradition and attract allegiance from non-German peoples. They were overcome by the Avars, Bulgarians and others. In Medieval times therefore Eastern Europe reacted to economic and social developments occurring in the west and showed little capacity for independent innovation.

The Avars

The power of the Avars in Pannonia was maintained for some two hundred and fifty years.[15] Their pressure on the Byzantine Empire was eased through a sharp defeat outside Constantinople in 626, but in reaction to this they made stronger efforts in the west against Slav tribes in Slovenia. Their border then lay against the Bavarians and it was Frankish annexation of Bavaria in 788 that created the major political problem for Charlemagne of settling the Frankish-Avar frontier. No agreement could be reached and the issue was resolved militarily through a Frankish victory over the Avars in 803. The Franks now established a prefecture in the east, covering Pannonia. But it is probable that the Avar chiefs remained in power for some time, as in the Carantanian area where Slav chiefs continued to govern. A Frankish administration may have been imposed around 828 through uprisings (certainly on the part of the Slav prince Liudevit) combined with a Bulgarian attack on Pannonia which placed Sirmium and part of the territory between the Drava and Sava rivers in their hands. An interesting detail at this time is a reference to a Slav chief Pribina who received lands from the Franks in the Zalavar area of Pannonia. But the reference also makes it clear that the Franks were very much in control and there is no evidence to suppose that Pribina was the head of a Slav state in Pannonia. His castle of Mosaburg, while being a typical Slav stronghold (continuously fortified until the sixteenth century) sheltered an important religious settlement subordinate to the church of Salzburg which was already carrying out its missionary work at the time of Pribina's arrival. Salzburg consecrated many churches in Pannonia and some of these have been located: Betthobia (Ptuj), Durnauua (Somlovasarhely), Ortahu (Veszprém) and Quinque Basilicae (Pécs). However Slav pressure increased and the Moravians under Svatopluk were certainly out raiding in Pannonia in 883-4. It was very much a mixed Avar-Slav population that the Magyars subsequently assimilated. The Frankish administration remained in force until the arrival of Hungarians in Transdanubia (Dunantul) in 896 but in that year Emperor Arnulf handed over the defence of Pannonia (including Mosaburg) to a Slav chief, Brazlav and this gives some ground for supposing that the Frankish Empire instinctively carried on the concept of feoderati from the Roman period using alien groups (whose leaders like Pribina were endowed with estates on the medieval feudal principle) to help consolidate a frontier region.

Armenians, Magyars and Scandinavians

The Armenians constituted another ethnic element introduced into the Balkans during Byzantine times. These people from Eastern Anatolia were resettled in Thrace by emperors Justinian and Maurice during the sixth century as part of what has been described as a 'divide and rule' policy. Religious ferment in the seventh century associated with the Paulician heresy brought more Armenians into the empire and eighth century raids by the Byzantine armies yielded still more colonists. Dispersal from Thrace has been attributed to the Bulgarian leader Khan Krum who forced many Armenians to move northwards towards the Danube valley in northern Bulgaria (where they were later to play an important role in propagating the Bogomil heresy). It also seems that some Armenians were settled in Macedonia in the late tenth century by Basil II to consolidate the area against further Bulgarian expansion. But the Armenians were already associated with commerce and trade so it is not unlikely that economic development was also a motive for this further redistribution. More importantly however there were challenges to the empire arising from a spate of invasions in the ninth century. The Muslim grip on the Mediterranean islands further reduced Byzantine authority, but did not directly affect any part of Eastern Europe. By contrast the arrival of Magyars in Pannonia created a major upheaval since this talented people reacted to their repulse from German lands (at Augsburg in 955 at the hands of Otto I) by consolidating their hold over the Pannonian Plain, which they have dominated ever since. They constituted a powerful neighbour for the Byzantine Empire and also drove a wedge between the Slavs, separating the Southern Slavs (Yugoslavs) from the northern groups (Czechs, Poles and Slovaks). The third major migration flow, that of Scandinavians, had a more positive significance for the empire since the colonisation of the Dneiper valley led to formation of the state (rus) of Kiev and a growth of trade between Constantinople and the Baltic. Of course the Vikings also settled on the Baltic coast around the estuary of the Oder and along with other colonies outside the limits of Eastern Europe (like Hedeby or Haithabu, which can be regarded as a precursor of Lübeck) created a trading system that was to reach its fullest extent centuries later under the Hanseatic League.

The Slavs

The record of political development in Dark Age Eastern Europe rests very heavily on the Slavs whose original homeland extended from the Vistula eastwards and southwards to the Bug, Dneiper and Pripet.[16] For centuries the Slavs were restricted to a small territory by the presence of Goths, Sarmatians and Scythians but the advance of the Huns and Avars prepared the ground for a wider spread of Slavic settlement. Whereas the invading nomads returned home after their campaigns the Slavs were an agricultural people constantly seeking outlets for their population surplus. They first moved southwards to the lower Danube (c.500) and then followed the river upstream towards the Alps before dispersing further afield into upland country under pressure from the nomadic, cattle-breeding Avars. There was also some considerable penetration south of the Danube. Early sixth century references to Slav mercenaries in the Byzantine army suggest important advantages to the empire in assimilating these sedentary settlers. However the Emperor Justinian made a curious decision in 565 by encouraging the nomadic Avars to attack the Slavs in the rear. The results were disastrous, for the provincial capital of Sirmium was destroyed and territories immediately south of the Danube were lost. It was therefore as an essentially hostile force that the Slavs established themselves in the Balkans, going so far as to lay siege to Thessalonica with Avar assistance. However the more serious threat posed by the Arabs stimulated a resolution of Byzantine ambivalence towards the Slavs who were now welcomed as settlers to devastated areas where they might be Hellenised and exploited for military manpower. This policy was pursued during the later part of the seventh century and was extended, with less satisfactory results, to the Bulgarians in Dobrogea. Where Hellenisation, and conversion to Christianity, was accomplished Slavs could take up an imperial career but it was only in peninsula Greece where they were effectively assimilated.

Archaeological evidence shows a certain uniformity of Slav settlement with villages on river terraces comprising small semi-subterranean dwellings three to four metres square with simple hand-made or wheel-made pottery, rough and undecorated, in everyday use. One such village in Suceava-Sipot with more than twenty square-shaped dwellings sunk 1.3m into the ground: it has close parallels with villages in Bulgaria (such as Popin in the northeast) inhabited from the eighth to the eleventh centuries) and the Ukraine (Luka-Rajkovetska complex). Good evidence of agriculture comes from sites in the Presov area where settlements dating from the third to the fifth centuries may represent the earliest Slavic occupation of Slovakia: mill-stones, fragments of iron sickles, storage pits and many bones of domesticated animals (mainly cattle, but also goats, horses, pigs and sheep) were found. Early Slav settlement sites in Czechoslovakia are also interesting in showing contact with Germanic peoples: a meeting of the two elements has been noted at Brezno near Prague where one third of the thirty or so houses are long and rectangular. This may indicate the residue of a Germanic population present when the Slavs arrived. Both were farming communities and may well have lived together for some time until the Germans were fully assimilated. Again on the lowlands of Poland between the Elbe and Oder rivers the arrival of Slavs in the fifth and sixth centuries led to domination of the formerly substantial German population. This contrasted initially with experience in the south where many Slavs were Hellenised, but of course a later German resurgence was to roll the western limit of Slav culture beyond the Oder apart from the islands of Bautzen and Cottbus where some 150,000 Sorbs still use a Slav language. K. Bosl has suggested two alternative incipient state forms for the Slavs: well-defined tribal groups in the north, like the Sorbs or Vilzi, and lordships in the south 'in which one leader united different tribal elements with the aid of a group of warriors who secured him control of market places and highways of traffic'.[17] But political developments in this area must be seen in the context of a reciprocal relationship between the various Slav groups and the Byzantine and Carolingian empires against which they came into contact. These rival pressures are most clearly seen in Moravia, where a very substantial buffer state (Great Moravian Empire) developed after Charlemagne's defeat of the Avars.

Territorial organisation: Great Moravia[18]

The Moravians are first mentioned (as the Marvani) in documents in 822 when Slav ambassadors attended a parliament in Frankfurt am Main convened by Charlemagne's son Louis the Pious. The state grew far beyond the limits of present-day Moravia to embrace the whole of Czechoslovakia as well as the southern parts of the GDR and Poland and Hungary as far southeast as the Tisza. It appears that the expansion began in the 830s under Mojmir I when he drove the 'Slovene' leader Pribina from his hill fort near the modern town of Nitra and forced him to retreat to a new stronghold south of Lake Balaton. This aggression by Mojmir is interpreted as a bid to remove Frankish influence from Pribina's principality (evidenced by the consecration of a church at Nitra in the early 830s by the Archbishop of Salzburg) which could have been a preliminary to the seizure of Moravia itself. Mojmir's successors Rastislav and Svatopluk continued the struggle through the ninth century and extended the boundaries northwards to the upper reaches of the Oder and Vistula rivers as well as southwards to the Danube where contact was made with the Bulgarian Empire. The power behind this formidable barrier to Frankish expansion was based on a cluster of hill forts with an urban character. Most finds come from the Morava and Svitava valleys of Moravia and the adjacent Nitra and Vah valleys of Slovakia. At Mikulcic near Hodonin on the Morava a seventh or eighth century acropolis (detinec) with wooden ramparts, represents the early tribal stage of political development. It was evidently replaced by a larger acropolis with stone walls and around this a bailey of a hundred hectares developed by the early ninth century. Within it lies a seven hectare palace complex, a total of six churches (including a basilica) and workshops producing glass, iron and jewellery.

Timber and clay ramparts are found at various other sites such as Pohansko near Breclav where the settlement (dating back to the sixth and seventh centuries) was eventually enlarged to cover 28 ha. with ramparts not only palisaded in wood but faced in stone. These defences, along with a prominence of male burials, suggests a border stronghold at this point. A ten hectare stronghold has been excavated at Zobor on a hill top at the approach to Nitra and another defended enclosure has been found in the centre of the town. At Knourin in the Labe valley east of Prague another Slav settlement of sixth-seventh century date was defended first with a single mound, enclosing a five hectare site, and later with intermediate and outer mounds which extended the security zone to forty hectares. It seems that particularly substantial fortification at Mikulcice enjoyed the highest status as the princely seat with Staré Mesto and other forts comprising the feudal centres. Workshops making articles from antler, bone and horn were common, since these commodities were readily available to farming and hunting communities. Wooden objects were used extensively and some items including dug-out boats have been found preserved in water-logged ground such as the sediment of old river beds. Stone was used in churches but had to be brought in from outside. Moravian resistance crumbled after the Magyars defeated the Bavarians at Bratislava in 907. The fortified sites were destroyed in the course of the tenth century and also many of the churches as the Slavs reverted to paganism: a community may have persisted at Nitra but when a bishop is next mentioned Olomouc is given as the residence. Industry however continued and a hybrid Belo-Brdo culture emerged.

The rival Byzantine and Carolingian influences on the Moravian state are seen most effectively in religious affairs.[19] A primitive form of Christianity was embraced by 852 and missionaries were present from both east and west, each trying to organise a church in its own tradition. There was also an Irish mission in the eighth century but this had no political implications. It seems that Prince Rastislav was particularly suspicious of Frankish ambitions and was consequently disposed to turn a sympathetic ear to

Byzantium. This could have arisen partly from the strong support from the Franks sought by his rival Pribina for whom the Archbishop of Salzburg consecrated the church at Nitra (about thirty years after the foundation of the first church in Moravia at Modra near Staré Mesto). Pribina's lands extended into Pannonia (with administration at Mosaburg at the southern end of Lake Balaton) and more than a dozen churches were established in cooperation with the Salzburg authorities. The result was the arrival of two Orthodox missionaries from Thessalonica: Cyril (Constantine) and Methodius, both great Christians and intellectuals (credited with the invention of the Cyrillic script) who were able to translate liturgical texts into Slavonic and so allow the scriptures to become more widely known.

The Byzantine government saw the mission as a mainly religious operation, but there was also a political aspect in view of the ecclesiastical and political overtures which the Franks were making towards Bulgaria.[20] And it was with a view to Byzantine influence on the Moravian church that the missionaries were called to report on the general ecclesiastical situation in the country. However after completing their mission in 867 Cyril and Methodius began their homeward journey with a visit to Rome at the invitation of Pope Nicholas. It says much for the mutually conciliatory attitudes of the two churches that such an itinerary could be entertained. But Nicholas and his successor Hadrian II were sympathetic to the idea of a Slav church which would be distinct from both the Latin and Byzantine churches and could potentially be a buffer between them. Hadrian appointed Methodius as bishop of a large Slav diocese, doubtless with Byzantine acquiescence if not outright approval. That the name of the bishopric was Sirmium, once capital of Illyricum Occidentale but far to the southeast of the new political centres, is a further indication of the rather speculative nature of this papal initiative. A Slavonic liturgy, allowing people to praise God in their native language, would make the Catholic Church more acceptable and provide an effective alternative to Orthodoxy while the diocese might be seen as a basis for uniting all the Slavs in Eastern Europe and bringing them together under papal authority. However this imaginative strategy did not succeed. Frankish control of Pannonia in 874 brought that area under the ecclesiastical authority of Salzburg, while Svatopluk (who had regained power in Moravia in 872) accepted Frankish suzerainty in return for a guarantee of autonomy. The pope still favoured a Slavonic liturgy but the Salzburg authorities were insistent that the Latin language should prevail in all parts of the Frankish Empire. In 880 a bishop sympathetic to Latin rites was appointed to Nitra (Svatopluk's capital) and subsequently all priests using the Slavonic liturgy were expelled. Soon after this Moravia was further weakened by the secession of Bohemia in 895 while the empire was destroyed completely by the Magyar onslaught of 907. However the work of Cyril and Methodius was of long-term significance in one respect, namely that Constantinople realised the significance of the Slav language in church and concluded that Bulgaria could be held more effectively if the use of the Slav language was allowed to prevail there.

Croatia

The development of a Slav state can be seen again in Croatia which was able to maintain its independence until 1091 thanks to capable rulers like Ljudevit and Borna. In this case the Slavs arrived amongst a native population that was already Christian. However while there was no destruction on a vast scale (markets and ports probably paid protection money to the barbarians) the conversion of the Slavs did not proceed far beyond the limits of main towns in the early years and was probably delayed until the tenth century even on parts of the Dalmatian coast. Again the situation was complicated by conflicting external forces: Frankish suzerainty was imposed over the Pannonian Croats at the end of the eighth century, while Byzantine interests extended along the Dalmatian coast northwards from the important ecclesiastical centre of Dyrrachium. But she found a rival in Bulgaria when seeking to exert control over the Slavs inland, to say nothing of Venice - that Latin-Byzantine hybrid prepared to pay tribute to the Slavs until the very end of the tenth century in order to navigate the Adriatic unhindered. In 811 the Franks and Byzantines adopted the river Cetina, just south of Split, as the limit to their respective spheres of influence but Constantinople retained suzerainty over coastal settlements to the north and when missionary work by the Frankish Patriarchate of Aquileia gave rise to a missionary bishopric at Nin (one of the residences of Croatian princes) it 'looked alternately more towards Frankish Aquileia or towards Byzantine Split as politics determined'.[21] Once Nin was established however it began to develop pretensions and claimed all territory under Croatian rule, which embraced Tomislav in the first quarter of the tenth century. His power was also recognised in the coastal towns of Dalmatia (including Split and Zadar) because of military support to the Byzantine Empire against the Bulgarians and Serbs.

The Croats' position was simplified by the simultaneous renunciation by the patriarch of any ecclesiastical jurisdiction over them. However the Croats were now to experience the same papal ambivalence as had been evident in Moravia for severe checks were placed on the use of the Slav language, tolerated through the tenth century over a gradually shrinking area. More significantly Latin supremacy was underlined by the reassertion of the control of the Archbishop of Split over Croatian bishops in 928 and resistance to the idea of an independent hierarchy equivalent to the Bulgarian patriarchate. Even the See of Nin was suppressed for a time in favour of a new centre of Latin influence further down the coast. While a papal desire to enforce uniformity is understandable it raises a fundamental question about the importance of territorial organisation and liturgical language as ecclesiastical factors in the consolidation of independent states. Although Croatia was still powerful under Stephen Drzislav in the late tenth century she declined into anarchy in the eleventh century and had to look for Hungarian support against Venice, now the dominant influence in the Dalmatian cities to underpin the Latin archbishoprics for the north, based on Split, and the south (Dioclea), then disputed between Bar and Ragusa (Dyrrachium remaining a Byzantine fortress). Ultimately the whole of Croatia was integrated into Hungary through a personal union under a single crown. Thus not only does the Dalmatian saga show a gradual changeover from the eastern to the western world, leaving monuments like the church at Porec on the Istrian coast to symbolise a Byzantine past - it provides a hint of the potency of ecclesiastical forces in moulding the political geography. This is not to suggest any inherent perversity over the treatment of the Croatian church in the tenth century, for there was no particular logic attached to unity among Southern Slavs as a whole. But the events mark a stage in the process of separation which was not vigorously reversed until the twentieth century.

Poland

Finally what of the geography of the northern Slav lands where the tribal organisation seems to have been more durable? Rural settlement for Dark Age Poland is conventionally studied in the context of opola: small ecological units ranging in area from fifty to three hundred square kilometres and usually restricted to areas of good agricultural potential separated by forest and swamp. Combination of units would build up into tribal territories perhaps covering as much as 1500 square kilometres, and at a still higher level the Polish state (with its name derived from the opola) can eventually be seen as a product of the socio-economic evolution of a cluster of these Slav tribes. The basic units typically comprised a scatter of villages all tributary to a central stronghold. The villages were open, apart from a surrounding fence and tended to transfer from one site to another within the communally-owned estate: hence no deep occupation layers are normally available to archaeologists. The impermanence of individual agricultural settlements arose from the shifting cultivation of the time. Evidence from Szeligi near Płock suggests that the open settlements were quite dispersed with many of the houses wholly or partially subterranean. Fortified settlements, perhaps dating to the sixth or seventh centuries, were being replaced in some areas by the middle of the ninth century by new, stronger establishments which became the seats of a noble class (primores). These settlements were often quite large, covering several dozen hectares and capable of containing a great number of people. For example Chodlik in the Vistula valley west of Lublin has three oval concentric embankments. And it is quite probable that there has been continuity of settlement in some cases, perhaps with origins in prehistory. There is also archaeological evidence to link some Dark Age forts with the oval-shaped settlements of the Rundling type which offered some security for the centrally placed common grazing. As already noted the morphology sometimes survived the introduction of the three field system and was adopted for new settlements as colonisation struck into the forested morainic country in the twelfth century. Defence from bandits and wild animals was still an important consideration. There is also a link forwards with some market towns, like Kwieciszewo where the earthwork of this eighth century fort on the frontier of Great Poland is still a prominent feature: the market here dates to the eleventh century. But equally the encroachments of the Piast dynasty led to the abandonment of some fortified centres, as in the upper Vistula valley where only Krakow survived to represent the old settlement pattern by the eleventh century.[22]

TRADE AND URBAN DEVELOPMENT

During the migrations there was little scope for East European involvement in commerce. Around 300 AD the Vistula-Pripet-Dniester and Dvina-Dneiper amber routes were being used to link the Scandinavians with the Goths, but it was the Atlantic-North Europe commercial axis that became all-important as the Slavs cut the amber routes. Trade between Scandinavia and the east then involved the Varangian route focussing on the Volga valley, reflecting the Byzantine interest in the Crimea in the sixth century. The Slavs were concerned above all with subsistence farming on their new lands but, like the Germans immediately to the west of them (with an economy scarcely more advanced than their own) they were cut off from the Mediterranean-Byzantine world by the Avars and Bulgarians. There were only limited exchanges through Moravia, bringing Avar goods into southern Poland. On the Baltic shores the Slavs were in contact with the more economically advanced Danes and Swedes but they found that the Scandinavians had little use for their agricultural products. Eastern Europe was still a commercial backwater in the ninth century though there were some exchanges with the Germans involving control points at Erfurt and Magdeburg (for the Slavs) and at Linz and Regensburg (for the Avars). But it was only after the passing of Great Moravia and the achievement of stability in Pannonia, following the Magyar incursions, that there was a commercial upsurge underpinned by the close political links of the Ottonian period between the Germans and their neighbours (Boleslas' Bohemia and Mieszko's Poland). 'By 911 this area was still relatively untouched by economic growth and change' but as the century progressed Slav traders began to work through from Krakow and Prague to German towns on the Danube. There were also contacts overland with Kiev and, through the Baltic ports, with Scandinavia providing alternative outlets for the products of farm and forest (along with minerals and slaves) which found their way as far as the Byzantine and Moslem lands.[23] And by 985 settled conditions in Hungary allowed the first tentative links with the Germans to be extended to contacts with Kiev and with Poland, to the point where trade between the Baltic and Byzantium could once again use the direct route by the Danube with the Hungarians playing the role of intermediary. 'The northern European trading area of the Carolingian and Viking times had expanded as better agrarian production and new urban centres appeared everywhere'.[24]

This interaction between north and south brought into being the system of European states, closely integrated by ideology and trade, that is investigated in the next chapter. However the relatively modest commercial tempo prior to the late tenth century brought a measure of urban development as the grody fortresses, to which the population could retire in the event of attack, took on economic functions. The tribal aristocracy controlled modest food surpluses, so artisans and merchants might settle beside the forts or a new commercial centre might develop some distance away, as at Kedrzyne which lies close to an early tribal stronghold. The Baltic coast provides evidence of bartering dating back to the sixth and seventh centuries at Kołobrzeg.[25] It is fortunate for modern research that eustatic movements along the Baltic have created long-term problems of submergence and hence the tendency for the level of buildings to be raised during each reconstruction by leaving the foundation of the old structures in place. This has greatly facilitated research since very deep layers (sometimes as much as ten metres in thickness) containing organic and structural material are available to archaeologists. The geography of trading stations is plainly related to the political geography of the Slav tribes.[26] Mecklenburg near Wismar in the GDR has seventh century origins as the centre of the Obodvites, who were in conflict with the Danes in the ninth century, while Ralswiek on Rügen is closely related to the centre of the Ranian tribe six kilometres to the south and Menzlin on the Peene near Anklam combined administrative and commercial functions for the Wilzians with the military stronghold in the Gorke district on the south bank contrasting with the commercial and industrial quarter on the opposite side. Menzlin was well placed for access by both road and sea, with the road from the middle Elbe to the Peene and the Oder mouth perhaps dating back to the sixth or seventh century. Burials at Menzlin show that the Scandinavians were the driving force in trade over the amber routes between the Baltic and

Byzantium but the presence of foreigners close to the tribal centre indicates cordial and mutually-profitable relations, with Slavic craftsmen adapting their production to imported goods during the eighth and ninth centuries. For amber collected on the Pomeranian coast would have been worked locally and traded through Novgorod and Pskov in return for the products of Russian craftsmen and oriental silver. Meanwhile contacts with Western Europe, handled for the most part by Frisian merchant ships, involved the exchange of raw materials for weaponry and luxuries.

For the inland areas there is evidence of proto-urban development in the Slav lands while for the Germans there are the notable cases of Erfurt, Halberstadt, Magdeburg and Quedlinburg.[27] The most impressive evidence comes from Magdeburg where merchants were trading with Slav tribes early in the ninth century, judging by the fortified trading post which has been traced on the site of the present cathedral. Development continued into the tenth century with particular importance attaching to consolidation by Henry I and Otto I at a time of German penetration into Slav territory during the second and third decades. The result was a defended trading settlement to the north of the cathedral precinct (near the later Johanniskirche). Documentary evidence suggests a Jewish settlement to the south and a further suburb (Sudenburg) nearby, but there is no archaeological or topographical evidence to support this. Meanwhile the German advance gave rise to town developments further east, for example the four towns which acquired bishoprics (Brandenburg and Havelburg in 948; Odenburg and Zeitz in 968), all of them developed on existing Slav settlements. Brandenburg was the centre of the Havelian Slavs and after the revolt of 983 became for a time the centre of a large Slav lordship between the Elbe and Oder. In the same area Köpenick stands as an early Slav commercial centre with a distinct artisan quarter evolving in the tenth century. This provided the base for Medieval growth, impeded however since the thirteenth century by the rise of Berlin in which city Köpenick now lies. But despite these commercial beginnings the scale of growth should not be exaggerated. M.M. Postan doubts that the Slavs were very active in trade with the west before the eleventh century. 'We must therefore assume that for all the romance clinging to trade routes and trading societies, so remote in place and time, commercial exchanges they supported were not and could not have been of very great importance to either Western or Eastern Europe and did very little to make them economically interdependent'.[28]

NOTES

1. N.J.G. Pounds 1974 p.46.
2. G. Gunderson 1976, 'Economic changes and the demise of the Roman Empire', Explorations in Entrepreneurial History 13, 43-68. See also W.I. Davidson and J.E. Harper 1972, 'European economic history: the ancient world' (New York: Meredith Corporation); H. Duncan-Jones 1974, 'Economics of the Roman Empire' (Cambridge: Cambridge University Press); E. Gibbon 1982, 'The decline and fall of the Roman Empire' (London: Penguin); D. Kagan ed. 1962, 'Decline and fall of the Roman Empire' (Lexington, Mass: Heath); M.S.L.B. Moss 1936-7, 'The economic consequences of the barbarian invasions', Economic History Review 7, 209-16; M. Rostovtzeff 1957, 'Social and economic history of the Roman Empire' (London: Oxford University Press); W.L. Westerman 1915, 'Economic basis of the decline of ancient cultures', American History Review 20, 723-43.
3. N.J.G. Pounds 1974 p.19.
4. J.B. Bury 1966, 'A history of the later Roman Empire' (Amsterdam: Hakkert) 2 vols.; J.B. Bury 1928, 'The invasion of Europe by the barbarians' (London: Macmillan). See also G. Laszlo 1974, 'The art of the migration period' (London: Allen Lane).
5. E. Kitzinger 1946, 'A survey of the early Christian town of Stobi', Dumbarton Oaks Paper 3, 82-162. See also H. Goldman 1933, 'Excavations at Stobi in Jugoslavia', American Journal of Archaeology 37, 297-300.
6. W.T. Treadgold 1979, 'The revival of Byzantine learning and the revival of the Byzantine state', American Historical Review 84, 1245-66 (quote p. 1266). See also H.W. Haussig 1971, 'A history of Byzantine civilisation' (London: Thames & Hudson); D. Obolonsky 1971, 'The Byzantine commonwealth: Eastern Europe 500-1453' (London: Weidenfeld & Nicolson); G. Ostrogorsky 1968, 'History of the Byzantine state' (Oxford: Blackwell); A.A. Vasiliev 1961, 'History of the Byzantine Empire' (Madison: University of Wisconsin Press).
7. R. Jenkins 1966, 'Byzantium: the imperial centuries 610-1071' (London: Weidenfeld & Nicolson) 380.
8. Ibid. 384.
9. W.G. East 1966, 'The barbarian invasions and

settlement', W.G. East pp. 48-70 (quote p. 51); G. Barraclough 1976.

10. C.T. Smith 1967, p. 125.

11. R.F. Hoddinott 1981, p. 159.

12. J. Fleckenstein 1978; K.J. Leyser 1982, 'Medieval Germany and its neighbours 900-1250' (London: Hambledon Press).

13. J. Fleckenstein 1978, 15.

14. Ibid. 15-6.

15. E. Garam et al. 1975, 'Avar finds in the Hungarian National Museum' (Budapest: Hungarian Academy of Sciences); E. Garam et al. 1975-7, 'Cemeteries of the Avar period (567-829) in Hungary' (Budapest: Hungarian Academy of Sciences) 2 vols; P. Liptak 1983, 'Avars and the ancient Hungarians' (Budapest: Hungarian Academy of Sciences).

16. M. Gimbutas 1971. See also S.H. Cross 1948, 'Slavic civilisation through the ages' (Cambridge, Mass.: Harvard University Press); F. Dvornik 1962, 'The Slavs: their early history and civilisation' (Boston: American Academy of Arts & Sciences); R. Portal 1969, 'The Slavs: a cultural and historical survey of the Slavonic peoples' (London: Weidenfeld & Nicolson).

17. K. Bosl 1970, 'Political relations between East and West', G. Barraclough ed. 43-82 (quote p. 46).

18. S. Beeby et al. 1982, 'Great Moravia: the archaeology of ninth century Czechoslovakia' (London: British Museum Publications); I. Boba 1971, 'Moravian history reconsidered: a reinterpretation of Medieval sources' (The Hague: Nijhoff); J. Poulik 1959, 'The latest archaeological discoveries from the period of Great Moravia' Historica (Prague) 1, 7-70.

19. Z.R. Dittrich 1960-1, 'The beginning of Christianity in Great Moravia', Slavonic & East European Review 39, 164-73.

20. F. Dvornik 1970, 'Byzantine missions among the Slavs' (New Brunswick, N.J.: Rutgers University Press).

21. A.P. Vlasto 1970, p. 192. See also S.W. Gould 1964, 'History of Medieval Croatia' (The Hague: Mouton).

22. T. Dunin-Wasowicz and Z. Podwinska 1978, 'Changes in the rural landscape of Poland till 1200 in the light of archaeological evidences', Geographia Polonica 38, 81-2; L. Leciejewicz 1976, 'Medieval archaeology in Poland: current problems and research methods', Medieval Archaeology 20, 1-15.

23. A.R. Lewis 1958, 312.

24. Ibid. 454.

25. K. Slaski 1979, 'Northwestern Slavs in Baltic Sea trade from the eighth to the thirteenth century' Journal of European Economic History 8, 83-107.

26. J. Herrmann 1985, 'Hinterland trade and craft-working of the early trading stations of the northwestern Slavs', H.B. Clarke and A. Simms eds. 249-66.

27. J. Herrmann 1977, 'Research into the early history of towns in the territory of the GDR', M.W. Barley ed. 243-59.

28. M.M. Postan 1970, 'Economic relations between Eastern and Western Europe', G. Barraclough ed. pp. 125-74. See also P.H. Sawyer 1981, 'Kings and Vikings: Scandinavia and Europe 700-1100' (London: Methuen).

Medieval Eastern Europe

c.1000-1648

4

Political Geography

The much reduced tempo of east-west migration at the end of the Dark Ages left Eastern Europe with an opportunity for consolidation. The following centuries brought about the crystallisation of a new political geography (Figure 4.1). It was not a durable scheme but, since the ethnic quilt of the region experienced relatively little change, the Medieval legacy exerted a strong influence on the moulding of the modern structures which, in broad outline, survive at the present time. Whereas early societies were essentially tribal, without clearly established boundaries or formal constitutions and legal codes, there was now an emergence of gentes or nationes, each with a sense of solidarity arising from personal links with the fighting nobility and the agricultural community. Subsequent consolidation went on to produce various larger groupings from clusters of nationes and some of these were disposed to embrace imperial pretensions, on the Roman model, and exert influence on neighbouring peoples. This is seen most clearly in the unity displayed by the German people when the Franks established an empire that enjoyed great power and prestige under the Carolingians, symbolising (for Western Europe) the transfer of Roman rule to the Frankish king in a new Christian form. Thus the evolution of the Medieval political geography was conditioned in part by spontaneous developments in different parts of the region but also by the imperialist forces expressed through military might in addition to economic and ideological offensives. The record is certainly complicated in the extreme but some order can perhaps be found in the struggle to maintain a sense of nationhood (often projected by distinctly impermanent royal houses) against urges for dynastic aggrandisement and the perceived threat of German imperialism in its secular and

Figure 4.1: States of Medieval Eastern Europe, c.1400

Sources: Historical atlases and N.J.G. Pounds and S.S. Ball 1964 (note 2).

ecclesiastical forms.

TERRITORIAL MILITARY AND SOCIAL CONSIDERATIONS

It is much easier to describe the emergence of nation states with their feudal systems than it is to account for this trend. Some interpretations may however be put forward. Geographers consider the physical basis of political systems and stress the connection between a nation state and its territory. The homeland must clearly offer physical resources conducive to economic development, integration and security. But additional significance may arise through emotional ties as definite territorial limits are established, to the point where a nation becomes quite inseparable from the land on which it is based. Thus, as D.S. Rugg argues, 'one cannot for example really understand Polish perception of space without taking into account Poland's long association with the Vistula river'.[1] Perceptions are also coloured by the cultural expression of the character of the motherland through literature and music: thus the link between Bohemia and the Vltava river is immortalised by the music of Smetana. The most useful discussion of these matters on a generalised basis is provided by N.J.G. Pounds and S.S. Ball who demonstrate that the prospects for the development of a nation state are bolstered when there is a fertile core area or ecumene which offers resources for agriculture and industry and combines accessibility to international trade routes with potential for defence and security.[2] However the political geography of Eastern Europe cannot be deduced simply from a knowledge of the physical resources, topographical and otherwise. The record shows that the present nation states established Medieval roots under a variety of circumstances, with an element of fluctuation in the location of the capital city during the evolution process in order to secure the best combination of advantages and opportunities. Berlin in Brandenburg became the capital of Prussia and subsequently the German Empire, yet Brandenburg was originally a <u>Mark</u> or frontier province of the Holy Roman Empire established as a defence against Slavs to the east. And Berlin's primacy within the province (in succession to Brandenburg) emerged only in the context of a modified transport system which followed the colonisation of the interfluvial areas above the Spree valleys and the provision of political support by the local feudal authorities.

The historian's perspective, tracing the development of

culture and ideology under charismatic leadership, is therefore highly relevant. But such national consciousness could not emerge very suddenly and so the nation state might be seen fundamentally as a response to changing military technology.[3] With the dominance of cavalry over infantry in the Dark Ages there was less demand for a centralised state, with its capacity to train large numbers of soldiers, while the change in the quality of castle building after c.900 reduced the disadvantages of decentralisation. Yet there was a revival in the fortunes of a professional infantry as an important military force in the fourteenth century, followed in the fifteenth century by the maturation of the cannon. Heavy pressures for increased defence spending by a centralised government then meant that the nobility had to be coerced into accepting the state's right to levy taxes. And furthermore the economies of scale involved in training infantry and equipping armies suggested not only a centralised state but one of considerable size. Hence in the Medieval period 'the first generation of European nation states coalesced under the control of central authority'.[4] Once the norm was established other states would have to face conquest or do likewise. Through this ability to control the aristocracy, raise revenue and equip a substantial army, a new equilibrium was established and it was to survive without fundamental change until the Napoleonic Wars. While this pattern was widespread in Europe there was no certainty that similar forces would control every state and here Eastern Europe appears in a distinctive light through the considerable power retained by the great feudal landowners.

On this question of feudalism and the institution of serfdom it seems appropriate to think of a monopoly system whereby the various members of the serf-owning class were given the ownership of both land and people within defined areas. There was no competition for labour and no labour market could develop. The monopoly might well be consolidated by judicial powers and by various economic privileges such as control of alcohol sales on the estate and of the marketing of cereals and livestock. Such a monopoly would clearly be dependent on the interest of the central authority to both create it and then to maintain it, with or without modifications: the 'monopolistic discipline' had to be enforced by a powerful authority and the relations between the supreme authority and the prospective or actual serf owners were therefore crucial.[5] For the institution of serfdom it may be helpful to think of the state's preference to obtain military service indirectly rather than by the direct formation of a standing army. But the state did not create the feudal system de novo: rather it formalised a social structure inspired by the Roman villa and fashioned in the atmosphere of the last barbarian raids with circulation both economically and socially restricted to the local area.

THE IMPERIAL CONTEXT: HOLY ROMAN EMPIRE

Despite subsequent vicissitudes, involving decentralisation, contraction and replacement, the development of states in Eastern Europe was closely conditioned by the power of the Holy Roman, Byzantine and Venetian empires. In north-western Europe the Carolingian empire of the Franks survived a ninth century division into eastern and western sections. For the eastern portion anticipated the formation of a German nation and 'clearly expressed the prevailing will of those noble leaders of the Bavarians, Swabians, East Franks and Saxons who met for the election of the kings in 887, 911 and 919'.[6] The power of the elected kings was sufficient to maintain cohesion among the community of nobles and a considerable measure of stability was reached by 1000. Language may well have played an important part in this remarkable process of unification, for although there was no single German language the various dialects were clearly distinct from the 'French' languages spoken further west and it seems that church writings provided an opportunity for some standardisation. The colonisation of the land east of Elbe by Franks, Saxons and Thuringians, complementing the Bavarian drive down the Danube valley, may also have contributed to unity by emphasising the difference between Germans and Slavs. Yet the success of this amazing political experiment depended mainly on the commitment of the nobility, and while some may have favoured an independent existence for the various tribes others were prepared to press the ideal of unity beyond the confines of the German lands in order to establish the universal empire: such ambitions were clearly indicated in 961 when Otto the Great took his German army over the Brenner Pass to intervene in Italy. But with support limited to the German nobility this programme could not succeed and it eventually became common practice to qualify the pretentious title 'Holy Roman Empire' with the words 'of the German Nation'.

The instinct for expansion arising from the Roman legacy is most relevantly manifested in the German colonisation of the eastern parts of the North European Plain and it provides an essential context for the political evolution of this part of Eastern Europe. It is also one of the great imponderables of German history. Was the imperial strategy a source of strength and inspiration or was it a great error which diverted resources away from the consolidation of a German nation state? The authority of the emperor in relation to the rulers of the various principalities was always a matter of dispute and the princes showed a distinct ambivalence towards the empire. While conscious of a wider unity that could not be destroyed by any formal act they nevertheless wanted a redefinition of functions to accommodate their own interests. In this respect the present chapter is well defined because it leads through to the Thirty Years War which was extremely significant for Germany. The war may be seen as an expression of diplomatic and ideological conflict between Bourbons and Habsburgs as France sought to break her encirclement by the Habsburg powers of Austria and Spain. But in Germany there were important constitutional issues at stake 'on the one hand by the attempt of the emperor to transform the loose confederation of several hundreds of principalities and free cities into a homogenous unit under his effective authority and, on the other, by the efforts of most rulers, including the emperor in his capacity as Archduke of Austria and King of Bohemia, to crush their medieval estates and establish monarchical absolutism'.[7] Religion was hardly an independent factor in the struggles although different spiritual affiliations might certainly help clarify the aspirations of the rival parties over which the Peace of Westphalia legislated in 1648. The treaty 'put the constitutional seal on the centrifugal political developments which had plagued the ideal of imperial unity for so long'.[8] The states could now keep their own armies and negotiate independently with foreign powers. Such is the constitutional basis for the later history of the empire.

Byzantium and Venice

The Byzantine Empire served as the counterweight to the Holy Roman Empire, beaming a largely conflicting influence across Eastern Europe. A distinguished early history (discussed in the previous chapter) led on to a Medieval record of cultural and ecclesiastical eminence contrasting with economic failure. The power of the state rested on its financial resources and as long as there was a substantial inflow of taxation revenue from private citizens (and in particular from strict controls on commerce and industry) the empire survived. But later this source was 'seriously compromised by the disappearance of the free peasantry and the increase in the wealthy privileges and power of the aristocracy, and was reduced almost to the vanishing point by the commercial privileges granted to the Italian republic and the consequent loss by Byzantium of control over its urban economy'.[9] The economic stranglehold by the Genoese and Venetians meant the permanent liability of an unfavourable balance of trade. The resulting inflation was demoralising and the negative demographic consequences of increased civil strife were exacerbated by the effects of plague. And in the background was the constant risk of barbarian raids as the Turks, 'having inherited the doctrine of holy war from the faltering Arabs, were to carry the centuries-old conflict between Byzantine Christendom and Islam to a conclusion'.[10] Curiously Constantinople was assailed in no small measure by the crusades in 1203-4: sacking by Latin soldiery certainly accelerated the process of political degeneration and contributed to the victory of Islam in the Balkans, the exact opposite of the real intention of the crusading movement. There was little scope for urban development across the empire and most of the European towns lay on the Aegean coast and the Sea of Marmara. The Roman towns of Pautalia (Kyustendil) and Serdica (Sofia), along with the new city of Germana (Samokov), belonged to the province of Inland Dacia while Thrace was dominated by Augusta Trajana (Stara Zagora) and Philippopolis (Plovdiv). The cities played only a small part in economic and social life: 'they were artificial creations superimposed on the village system native to the country and were too sparsely scattered to serve as centres of trade'.[11] Defence rested primarily on the forts scattered through the country with twenty in the territories of Germana Pautalia and Serdica and more than fifty in Thrace.

Closely associated with Byzantium was the trading empire of Venice, the successor to the late Roman ports of Aquileia and Ravenna.[12] The Byzantine connection helped to develop long-distance trade with the mineral wealth of the Carpathians (including Bohemia) exchanged for oriental spices and textiles. The trading advantages arose from the provision of transport for the Fourth Crusade given by the doge Enrico Dandalo and the prominent part played by the Venetians in the capture of Constantinople: these circumstances made it difficult for other Italian trading cities to win comparable advantage. As the original 'new Rome' Constantinople was an inspiration to the Venetians and a model that was widely copied, all the more so since the lagoon settlement had been part of the Byzantine Empire for several centuries. North of Corfu the Adriatic was known as the Venetian Gulf and the need for security for Venetian ships in safe anchorages and islands of the eastern coast led to the subjection of the mainly Slavic population of the Dalmatian ports or at least the negotiation of preferential treaties. Venice therefore controlled a succession of important towns on the Adriatic coast from Fiume (Rijeka) to Zara (Zadar), Sebenico (Sibenik), Spalato (Split), Cattaro (Kotor), Antivari (Bar), Scutari (Shkodër) and Durazzo (Durrës). To some extent the Turks provided a further stimulus to Venice and, while the territorial pattern throughout the eastern Mediterranean shows frequent change without any clear pattern, the overseas dominions (stato da mar) as a whole continued to grow until the early sixteenth century.

The Venetians suffered some initial losses through the Ottoman conquest (such as Valona (Vlorë) in 1414 and Scutari in 1479) but their Genoese rivals encountered greater setbacks. Provided that tribute was paid the Venetian trading system was not fundamentally harmed: Turkish possession of major seaports did not curtail commerce except in war. The eventual demise of Venice was due to a growth of competition not only by other Mediterranean ports, Ragusa (Dubrovnik) along with Leghorn and Marseilles, but by English companies who entered the Levantine trade in the late sixteenth century. During the next century the Dutch and English used the Cape route to the Indian Ocean to capture the spice trade and so induce both a further decline in the Venetian navy, already demoralised by plague and a growth of piracy in the Adriatic, and a transfer of capital by the wealthy to land development schemes on terraferma in Italy. The failure of Venice to adapt to changing trade conditions in the sixteenth century allowed Ragusa to expand its role as intermediary between Christian and Moslem Europe, extending its sphere of operations from the Levant to Western Europe through an expanding fleet of nave ragusea with greatly increased tonnage. Despite the development of Spalato as a more convenient port for Bosnia than Ragusa the latter attracted many more ships in the seventeenth century. And the failure to make adequate accommodations with the Ottoman Empire guaranteed sustained Turkish opposition to Spalato, continuing into the eighteenth century as British and French competition intensified.[13]

THE RELIGIOUS CONTRIBUTION

Imperialist pressures from both Byzantium and the Holy Roman Empire involved ecclesiastical as well as secular elements. The situation is complex in the extreme for although the gravity principle tended to operate, with the rival powers extending influence to the lands immediately across their borders, receptivity to external influences has tended to be greatest 'when they respond to the requirements of the milieu that is absorbing them'.[14] The Byzantine Empire with its Orthodox Christian ideology could pose as a legitimate force building the fortunes of the continent and it was only at the beginning of the ninth century that Charlemagne was treated as an equal by the Byzantine emperors. But the Frankish Empire was able to expand with the support of the Catholic Church which became in fact the 'imperial church': 'the Merovingian and Carolingian kings claimed its allegiance; the aristocracy had laid its hands on it, providing bishops and abbots, founding monasteries for its kin and seeking to adapt Christian values to its own social ideas. Christianity had thus become in many respects a political creed'.[15] It would be an exaggeration to say that all missionary activity amounted to political pressure, but it was often the case and these overtones created difficulties for the spread of the Catholic Church despite its clear superiority to the various heathen cults manifest through noble architecture, splendid liturgy and moving scriptures.

The Archbishopric of Salzburg was founded in 805 as a missionary centre for the east and along with its suffragan bishoprics of Passau and Regensburg was active in the Great Moravian Empire where plans for the establishment of an independent archdiocese with a Slavonic liturgy were effectively countered. However, German ecclesiastical interest in the east is most clearly seen in Otto I's efforts against the Slavs beyond the Elbe: both politics and religion were covered by a missionary programme that for a time became the conventional means of developing links between peoples and consolidating 'empire'. Missionary work in Bohemia, Hungary and Poland rested on the Frankish archbishops at Bremen and Salzburg (and also Magdeburg where an archbishopric was established in 968). The Slavonic liturgy was still opposed at first, although this did not prove damaging to the Catholic Church in the long run. Despite Slav suspicions of the Franks there was the economic factor of trade that made close ties with the west eminently logical. And conversely it cannot be thought certain that the Catholic Church would have captured the Balkans had a Slav liturgy been permitted since the cultural and military force of Byzantium could not be ignored.

The Slavs were duly sensitive and while capable of outright rebellion against aggressive policies nevertheless saw Christianity as a potentially effective instrument for combining the desired level of political independence with a regime of civilised behaviour between the various powers of Europe. 'By adopting the progressive institutions of the greater powers and by imitating their standards of civilisation and accepting the Christian faith the Slav princes built up their reputation at home, reinforced their power abroad and secured their political independence'.[16] Very simply, by embracing Christianity the states of Eastern Europe became autonomous members of a wider community and prevented any risk of war being waged against them under the guise of a missionary war or crusade. The bishopric of Prague became an independent diocese in 973, an independent Polish church dates back to the monastic missionary bishopric set up at Poznan in 966 (in the teeth of fierce opposition from Magdeburg) while the Hungarian archbishopric of Esztergom freed itself from the influence of Salzburg. With independent hierarchies and organisation of a territorial basis, coinciding with state boundaries, the church could identify itself closely with the state and the bishops were invariably champions of national unity, like J. Drazic of Prague and J. Swinka of Gniezno. Canonisation created saints of national importance, like Stanislav in Poland, Istvan (Stephen) in Hungary and Vaclav (Wenceslaus) in Bohemia, and places of pilgrimage were again of national interest, like Czestochowa for Poland and Prague for Bohemia. Hence, under the guise of a competition for religious enthusiasm a sense of nationhood was further inculcated. The ecclesiastical hierarchy offered the advantage of a 'commonwealth' subscribing to certain norms of civilised behaviour without any great risk of the structure being projected onto a secular plane by an acquisitive leader who aspired to empire. The German emperor Otto III did initiate a policy of Renovatio at the turn of the tenth century, with the eastern states accepting his suzerainty, but the idea collapsed with Otto's death in 1002.

It was precisely because the eastern states felt secure under the prevailing ecclesiastical structure that German colonisation was so successful in the thirteenth and fourteenth centuries. At a time of population growth and significant improvements in material prosperity it was appropriate to value German technology and German settlers who could apply it. Thus Polish rulers, seeking new land and more effective agricultural methods, welcomed German settlers to help diffuse a more advanced technology and legal system. Germans could have pressed eastwards as conquerors but progress would arguably have been more limited for 'reluctant, hostile and pagan barbarians would not have been able or willing to accept the new progressive way of life'.[17] Indeed the peaceful accomplishment of the conversion exercise seems to have depended very heavily on effective leadership among the Slavs. The Wendish tribes had no conception of themselves as a single people and 'the fact that no supra-tribal sovereignty existed at the time of the first important Christian impact upon them answers for much in their subsequent history'.[18] For Charlemagne's crusading zeal against the Saxons was now applied in even more extreme form by the Saxons against the Wends who were in no position to do other than cling vigorously to their traditional religious and social structures. Progress against the Wends was marked most dramatically by the creation of a bishopric at Magdeburg in 962 and its elevation to a metropolis five years later: Brandenburg and Havelburg (both established in 948) were transferred from Mainz and new bishoprics created for Meissen, Merseburg and Zeitz. The Slav reaction in 983 then cleared all the conquered lands, except the Lusatian territory in the Elbe-Saale triangle which was now firmly under German rule, and it was not until after 1125 that the Christians regained the upper hand, this time with Danes, Germans and Poles acting in concert and with a powerful economic motive to complete the trading network along the Baltic coast. The last pagan strongholds were on the Baltic coast and in 1160 Henry the Lion made an alliance with Waldemar of Denmark to control the Oder ports. Rügen was the last bastion and held out until

1168. While the Wends may be accused of a lack of realism in failing to react positively to the external stimulus (partly due to an embryonic city-state organisation on the Baltic coast and the absence of an overall leader capable of decision) it is hard to see how the episode reflects well on the Christian powers who in this case were too preoccupied with their own political and economic ambitions to countenance a civilising mission through steady infiltration.

Non-German rulers had to maintain vigilance to ensure that the German economic and technological advance did not acquire such cultural and political overtones as to subvert the ethos of the independent state. In much of Eastern Europe the threat was not great because German settlement was checked to the southeast by the highlands of Bohemia and Moravia but the North European Plain was an obvious line of advance. In the east Baltic lands German effort faded for lack of settlers, but in Poland the clergy and nobility played an important role in resisting assimilation by the German incomers and in fact reversing the process so that the advanced technology was practised by a basically 'Polish' population. The settlement of the Teutonic Knights, however, reveals the underlying pressures in sharpest focus. The project illustrates the more aggressive side of German colonisation with great headway made east of the Vistula where some slackening of effort might have been anticipated. The Teutonic Order was invited to settle in 1225 by the ruler of Masovia who had experienced a great deal of trouble through the depradations of pagan Prussians (Pruzzi). Colonists were attracted overland via Cottbus, Posen (Poznan) and Thorn (Torun), or else by sea to Elbing (Elblag) and Königsberg (Kaliningrad). Defence was provided by a chain of fortresses on the Vistula at Thorn (1231), Kulm (Chełmno) (1232) and Marienwerder (Kwidzyn).

The knights were immediately successful in pacifying the Prussians and converting them to Christianity, much to the relief of the Masovians. But the backing which the Order received from the emperor and the pope meant that their territory became in effect a separate state. 'Towns were founded, German peasants settled on the land and the knights soon built up a very progressive territorial state independent of the Polish king'.[19] Indeed this area drew ahead of the rest of Poland not only in administration and finance but also in agriculture, commerce and above all in military power. The situation changed only when the conversion of the Lithuanians (the last pagans in Europe) brought the missionary role of the Order to a conclusion and a dynastic union between Lithuania and Poland in 1387 created a barrier to further expansion by the knights. By the turn of the fourteenth century moreover the flow of settlers from the west was beginning to dry up while the population subject to the knights was beginning to tire of clerical domination. In 1410 the Order suffered a military defeat at Tannenberg (Stebark), in 1466 the western portion of its territory including Danzig (Gdansk) passed to Poland and half a century later the remainder was made subject to the Polish king whose vassal the grand master of the Order now became. Interestingly however the Thirteen Years War ending in 1466 was waged against the knights by a Prussian Union, comprising a force of German laymen from the rural districts and from the cities of Danzig and Thorn. In retrospect the political enterprise of the Teutonic Knights has rightly drawn censure from Polish writers who see the Order as 'a glaring example of the abuse of religious principles for purely secular aims conditioned by class and ethnic considerations'.[20] But the colonising effort in what were often unpromising conditions did reach quite heroic proportions, as testified by the placename elements of which brand (burning), hagen (fence), rode/roth (rooting up) and ried (marsh) represent a small selection.

Not that there was necessarily any great single-mindedness of purpose by the non-German states of Eastern Europe to resist the embrace of the empire. This can be seen in the attempts by the Premyslids in Bohemia to extend their power in the east while making use of their close ties with the empire. Otakar II was elected king of Bohemia in 1253 having previously secured the Austrian throne when the Babenberg dynasty died out in 1246. He went on to profit from the Mongol assaults and the defeat of King Bela IV of Hungary and occupied Carinthia, Carniola, Slovenia and Styria. A union of all Slav peoples now seemed possible but there was no conscious idea of an association with an ethnic basis and Otakar's encouragement of German settlers in agriculture, commerce, industry and mining stimulated some reaction from the Poles as well as from the Czechs. Otakar's ambitions were doomed to disappointment for his quest for the imperial crown ended with his death in battle against Rudolf of Habsburg in 1278. It was the latter dynasty which now embraced the policy of expansion beyond the empire and into Danubia, leaving the western Slavs free of the closer ties with Germany which Otakar would have sought. An alternative pattern of consolidation emerged when Otakar's son not only ascended the Bohemian throne as Wenceslaus II but found himself elected also to the thrones of Poland in 1300 (with the end of the Arpad dynasty) and Hungary in 1301. But the union did not last and in 1306 the Premyslid dynasty died out. The Piasts resumed their rule in Poland and consolidated their independence after years of pressure from the Czechs while foreign rulers appeared elsewhere: The Angevin house was favoured in Hungary (Charles Robert 1308) and the Luxembourgs in Bohemia (John 1310). French and Italian culture now penetrated on a greater scale than before, but the question of contact with the empire remained an imponderable.

While Hungary and Poland cooperated closely, culminating in a Luxembourg ascension to the Polish throne in 1370 on the death of the last of the Piasts, there was a strong orientation towards the empire in Bohemia where John's son, Charles, became German emperor as well as king of Bohemia. This had a cultural impact for, as imperial capital, Prague was endowed in 1348 with the first university in Eastern Europe (though followed shortly afterwards by Krakow for Poland and Pécs for Hungary as well as Vienna for Austria). But it also brought a return to Otakar's illusions of further grandeur as Charles cooperated with the Teutonic Order to embarrass the Polish king and edged towards the Hungarian throne through the dynastic marriage between his son and the daughter of the last Angevin king of Hungary, Louis the Great. Although Charles made the Bohemian church autonomous, through the formation of a single independent archbishopric in 1344, his policies sowed the seeds of reaction which were to ferment the Hussite revolution. Persecution of Czech reformer Jan Hus by Charles' son Sigismund brought rejection of imperial supremacy and demands for fundamental social change as the Hussites resisted all counter-attacks and became an impressive military power (based at Tabor) with which Sigismund was eventually obliged to negotiate. In 1433 the moderates signed the Compacts of Prague while the radical wing was defeated in battle the following year. Sigismund was then able to enjoy the thrones of Bohemia and Hungary to which his father's diplomacy had offered access, although the lack of an heir ushered in another period of instability. Even though some strong monarchs emerged such as Matthias Corvinus in Hungary (son of the heroic J. Hunyadi) the instability remained since the idea of national rulers was undermined by the precedents for dynastic unions. The Jagiellons provided a lengthy succession in the commonwealth of Poland and Lithuania but in Bohemia and Hungary there was no lasting stability until the Habsburgs gained the thrones of both St. Stephen and St. Wenceslaus during the sixteenth century.

NATIONAL STATES IN EASTERN EUROPE

The northern countries: Bohemia

Bohemia is one of the most rewarding studies for devotees of the concept of core areas for the territory embraces the drainage basin of the Elbe/Labe and its major tributary, the Moldau/Vltava, with Prague standing on the latter but only thirty kilometres from the confluence. The fertile heart of the region stands in contrast to the surrounding hill country with its four distinct elements together forming the 'Bohemian Diamond'.[21] Despite the historic links with the German people, continuing into the nineteenth century by the political ties with the Habsburg Empire and the economic links through the Labe waterway with Prussia and Germany, Bohemia continued to be first and foremost the core of the Czech nation. And although the present union with Slovakia has destroyed Bohemia's geographical centrality, Prague's historic role as a Slav capital has not been seriously challenged. An embryonic Bohemian state dates back to the early ninth century and even at this time there appear to have been some desires by the Slavs to enter into closer relations with Christendom, judging by the arrival of fourteen Bohemian chiefs at Regensburg in 845, asking for religious instruction. There was a close association with Moravia, a relatively advanced state which the Bohemians assisted against Frankish pressure. But after the death of its great leader, Svatopluk, Moravia went into decline and it therefore became appropriate to develop political as well as ecclesiastical contact with Regensburg in Bavaria. In some respects Saxony vied with Bavaria for influence over Bohemia, but although entry into Bohemia was easier from the north along the Elbe valley Saxony did not have any cultural centre at the time to rival Regensburg. Nevertheless this alternative link proved useful in c.924 when Wenceslaus assumed power and accepted the overlordship of Saxony (in the person of Henry the Fowler, King of Germany) no doubt as a reaction to the oppressiveness of

Bavarian influence. Unfortunately Wenceslas tried to create a Christian society too quickly and without a sufficient willingness to compromise. The result of the inevitable friction was the assassination of Wenceslas in 929 and the assumption of leadership by his brother Boleslav. However Henry's overlordship continued and when a bishopric was formally constituted in Prague in 967 this was not independent of the Germans but subordinate to the Archbishop of Mainz.

In sympathy with political trends the diocese fluctuated in its territorial extent during the tenth and eleventh centuries, at times embracing Moravia and Silesia, although the original intention was to restrict it to Bohemia. Certainly Bohemian princes seeking a permanent enlargement and the creation of an archbishopric on the precedent of the Moravian metropolis were disappointed, for a separate bishopric of Olomouc was fully established by the end of the eleventh century. Slav clergy were present but the question of a Slav liturgy in preference to Latin never appears to have been a real issue: the last stand was made by the monks at Sazava monastery at the end of the eleventh century when the reigning prince, a staunch Latinist, expelled the monks and installed a German abbot. 'The triumph of the Latinists, perhaps inevitable in a country more and more firmly attached to the western world, in whose capital a large German colony by now dominated trade and politics, is symbolised in the work of Cosmas of Prague who died in 1125 aged at least eighty: his Chronicle written at the end of his long life makes no mention whatever of the existence of a Slav language church in Bohemia at any time'.[22] Although Charles IV later founded a monastery in Prague for Slav Benedictines (1346) this was short-lived and the Czech language was never considered for liturgical use until the Reformation.

As Holy Roman Emperor and King of Bohemia Charles IV may be more significantly remembered for his action in elevating Prague to the status of independent archbishopric which was retained for a century and a half. And again, despite its ecclesiastical objectives expressed in a desire to return to the purity of the original church, the Hussite movement may be interpreted as a nationalist manifestation. The execution of J. Hus was taken as a national affront in Bohemia and there was a violent reaction through the expulsion of Germans from Prague in 1420.[23] Socially, however, the revolutionaries did not maintain their initial standards: at Tabor where a new town emerged out of the ruins of Usti Sezimovo, destroyed as a result of violent conflict between burghers and ecclesiastics, the ideal of common property as a basis for social and economic quality was undermined within a year. And in Prague too it was evident that individuals within the movement regarded the confiscation of church lands and German properties as a means to their own enrichment. Despite the best efforts of the radical faction therefore the Hussites did not in the end prevent a worsening in the position of the peasants and the poorer urban dwellers. The landlords continued to maximise opportunities to produce for the market and used their feudal privileges to exploit the peasantry to the utmost.

Poland

In the late tenth century Mieszko I brought together a number of Slav tribes east of the Oder under his rule and founded the first Polish state, centering on Gniezno, Kruszwica and Poznan where the nuclear area was defended by the forests and marshes associated with the Notec and Warta rivers. German pressure to the west may well have instigated or at least accelerated the process. Mieszko's power gradually extended eastwards over Pomerania and Silesia (and for a time Bohemia also). Despite initial acknowledgement of the supremacy of German kings completely independent policies were aided by a dynastic alliance arising out of marriage to the daughter of Bolesław. Mieszko received his Christianity from the Bohemians and his baptism in 966 is thus the conventional date for the conversion of Poland. When an ecclesiastical hierarchy was established Gniezno was given the status of archbishopric (1000) embracing an independent metropolitan province. This caused considerable resentment in Germany where it was considered that any new Slav bishopric should come under the new metropolis of Magdeburg. For it was through the interest of the Archbishop of Mainz and of Otto III that one Adalbert had gone as a missionary to Poland and met his death among the Prussians in 997: his remains were taken to Gniezno and, just one year after his canonisation in 999, this was the place selected as the seat of a Polish archbishop. Of course Poland could not be too dismissive of German contacts as conflict arose with Bohemia over possession of Krakow (a key point on the great continental trade route) and the Wendish revolt broke out in 983. Otto III made a pilgrimage to St. Adalbert's shrine and clearly regarded the development as part of his imperial conception, Renovatio imperii romanorum, based on the Byzantine notion of universal empire harmonising territorially with a universal church. A.P. Vlasto sees an act of great statesmanship involving the pope, Otto III and the Polish ruler Bolesław who now built a stone cathedral at Gniezno.[24] Magdeburg's pretensions were finally abandoned as the missionary bishopric of Poznan (initially subordinate directly to Rome) was brought under Gniezno's authority in 1012 and new bishoprics were created for Kołobrzeg, Krakow and Wrocław.

Poland was weakened by the death of Bolsław in 1025 and after the Bohemians had invaded and destroyed both Gniezno and Poznan (1039) it was Krakow that acquired both ecclesiastical and political primacy. The core area of Poland therefore shifted southwards from Great Poland (Wielkopolska) to Little Poland (Małopolska). But only for a further shift to occur, through the union between Poland and Lithuania as Warsaw was chosen as a compromise capital between Krakow and Vilna. It is interesting to reflect that the three political centres can be drawn together through the concept of a unified Vistula-Warta river system, for although there is no physical connection between the two the east-west trending glacial meltwater channels (pradoliny) provide easy routeways which have been exploited by canal, road and railway builders. And there has been some tendency to idealise the Slav state of Poland through the ideas of freedom (wolnosc) and citizenship (obywatelstwo) which contributed to the Polish commonwealth (Rzeczpospolita) a democratic character considered lacking in the state of southeast Europe which developed on the foundations of the despotic Roman Empire. Such romantic nationalism was the hallmark of J. Lelewel's early nineteenth century scholarship, but while he captures the ethos of primitive Slav society he fails to acknowledge the essential role of the aristocracy in medieval nation-building and by seeing the alliance of Catholic Church and Holy Roman Empire as the basis for feudal subjection tends to erect one of the unfortunate barriers which have cumulatively driven a wedge between the Germans and Slavs.[25] He was forced to emphasise the opposition of Poles to Christianity and feudalism but without acknowledging the contradiction between rejection of the prevailing ideology and formation of a viable state.

Hungary

Looking at a topographical map of Eastern Europe the great plain of Pannonia (Alföld) stands out as an extensive lowland and an obvious base for a powerful nation state. The logic is sustained by imperial Hungary when the integration of the plain with the surrounding mountain country provided one of the most impressive examples in Europe of political boundaries harmonising with a natural region. The capital has however at best stood on the edge of the plain, indicating not only the importance of defence but also the limited agricultural potential of much of the lowland in former times. For while the areas with well-drained loess soils sustained high yields of cereals the extensive areas of marsh, salt and sand were not historically capable of intensive use and this is reflected in the pastoral ethos of the puszta as salt-encrusted areas like the Hortobagy near Debrecen were used extensively as cattle and sheep grazing. The first core area lay just west of the Danube in the hill country between the great plain and the little plain (Kisalföld) with a royal residence at Székesfehérvar and a religious capital at Esztergom. But after some three centuries the capital was moved to Buda on the Danube, at the southern end of a scenically attractive section of the valley where the river cuts through the northeast-southwest trending hill zone. An elevated site, offering abundant scope for fortification, was combined with islands in the river which simplified the crossing and provided opportunity for further defences as well. Eventually a large settlement grew up on the eastern side of the river opposite Buda and this commercial and industrial city, known as Pest, amalgamated with Buda in the late nineteenth century. Buda (today Budapest) has been capital of Hungary continuously through to the present apart from the Turkish period when there was a retreat to Pozsony (Bratislava).

The Magyars who built the Medieval state in Pannonia were nomadic horsemen allegedly forced away from their homeland on the steppes due to the pressure of the Petchenegs in c.889. They arrived in Pannonia under the leadership of Arpad and encountered so little opposition that the whole nation settled by 896. Arpad's own horde settled in Transdanubia (Dunantul) between Székesfehérvar and Buda while other groups set down their roots further west or else along the Tisza valley. They were a serious challenge to the established order in Europe and not until their defeat in

955 did they settle down in Pannonia to rule over the indigenous population of Avar and Slav extraction. Prior to this they had launched more than thirty expeditions all over Europe, 'striking terror into the hearts of their victims with the suddenness of their descents (for their little horses outdistanced any news of their coming), the ferocity of their attacks, their outlandish and to western eyes hideous appearance and their blood-curdling battle-yells'.[26] The Franks were repulsed by 900 and Moravian control was removed from the northwestern part of Pannonia in 906. A Bavarian army was defeated the following year and Magyar rule then extended to the old Avar frontier at the confluence of the Danube and Enns. However the instinct for battle seems to have gradually been lost and while more civilised behaviour may have emerged out of war losses and intermarriage with the native population there can be little doubt that it was also inspired by Christianity.

Both churches were interested in extending influence to Hungary but the Catholic Church enjoyed some advantage through the earlier conversion of Moravians and Slovenes (many of whom were now subjects of the Magyars) and through the missionary activity of the Bavarians with whom Hungary had developed quite cordial relations. This followed from the momentous decision of the new king Géza to abandon raids in c.970 and send ambassadors to Otto's court. Géza surrounded himself with Bavarian knights and baptised his son under the name of Istvan (Stephen). Although the succession was disputed Stephen was able to maintain his position thanks to the support of Bavarian cavalry, assured through his marriage to the sister of Emperor Henry III, and was fortunate in receiving papal recognition as king of Hungary in the year 1000. Stephen's position was now secure and he could claim all the recognised prerogatives of Medieval kingship while his people were admitted to the Christian family of nations and thereby became largely immune from the attacks by Christian princes to which their earlier status as outlaws had rendered them vulnerable. The conversion of the entire population was now undertaken and a complete ecclesiastical organisation was achieved during Stephen's lifetime, with two archbishoprics and eight bishoprics as well as a parish church for every ten villages. Stephen died in 1038 but was declared a saint in 1083: hence the reference made thereafter to the crown of St. Stephen.

The development of Hungary in the eleventh and twelfth centuries was almost inevitably constrained by dynastic warfare, especially since many claimants to the throne summoned assistance from abroad, leading to foreign interference and sometimes to a loss of territory.[27] But leadership was generally competent and Hungary was able to benefit from the fairly peaceful conditions on the steppes. She was also able to live peacefully with neighbouring Christian states for there were no great inequalities in strength and a network of dynastic marriages contributed to stability. But while the prevailing outlook rendered inconceivable any thought of Hungarian rule over Bohemia it is perhaps too sweeping to assert that all tendencies to imperialism were resisted. Croatia was a dynastic acquisition and the country was never treated as an integral part of Hungary, being administered by a viceroy (ban) on the basis of its own institutions.[28] The Croats incidentally had flourished south of the Drava in the interlude between the Avar and Magyar incursions and despite some Byzantine/ Orthodox influence it was the Latin church which made progress. A core area was initially based on Nin near Zadar. But it was at Zagreb where the bishopric was established when the Hungarians took control in 1091. There was less sensitivity shown towards the Romanians, Slovaks and other groups encountered by the Magyars on their eastern frontier, although here the apologist would emphasise the importance of defending the Carpathian passes and of encouraging settlement for this purpose. The frightful destruction wrought by the Tartars in 1241-2 provides dramatic proof of the danger: many towns were reduced to rubble although Székesfehérvar was protected by the marshes and the citadel at Esztergom also held out. King Béla became virtually the country's second founder, such was the scale of the rebuilding and resettlement, and it is noticeable that Hungarian administrative and military efficiency was sufficient to generate a constellation of 'Banats' or client states including Bosnia, Cumania (Wallachia), Galicia and Severin. Relationships cannot easily be clarified, especially in view of the subsequent disruption by the Turks.

Transylvania was of immense strategic significance to Hungary. The province had a distinct administrative status under a vajda (voivod) with practically independent viceregal powers dating from the late thirteenth century, which included the right to appoint administrators for the various counties. Only the Croatian ban enjoyed similar autonomy. Transylvania achieved further distinction in ethnic terms for in addition to Hungarians and Romanians there were many Germans and Székely (closely linked ethnically and linguistically with the Hungarians). The Romanians claim to be the original settlers with continuity stretching back into prehistory yet in Medieval times they were the only one of the four major ethnic groups not formally recognised as a 'nation': they remained essentially a servile peasant community although social mobility was such that Romanian families could join the Hungarian nation, like the Hunyadis who later ruled the province. The most recent arrivals were the Germans invited to settle in strategically-important mountain country along the Carpathian frontier by King Géza II in the mid-eleventh century.[29] Their privileges were extended by King Andrew II early in the thirteenth century when their 'nation' was recognised territorially as extending along the northern flanks of the Transylvanian Alps. The towns of this area, notably Hermannstadt (Sibiu) and Kronstadt (Brasov) has displayed a strong German character ever since.

The powerful drive to expand beyond the confines of the Great Plain into alien territory may be linked forwards in time with aggressive nineteenth century Magyarisation, following the famous compromise of 1867, and the implacable resistance to the Trianon settlement of 1920 which allowed self-determination for the minorities. Yet notions of insatiable territorial ambition should be tempered by the trauma of the Turkish occupation which altered the ethnic character of the plain, a process continued by the flight of Bosnians and Serbs from the south and the systematic Impopulatio carried out by the Habsburg authorities in Banat using Germans, Romanians and Slavs.[30] By the time this programme had run its course Magyars comprised little more than a third of the total population. Hungarian policy in the nineteenth and twentieth centuries should also be seen in the context of the previous Habsburg subjection of the country with German the language of administration (and for a time even the sole language of instruction in the schools) as well as the language of commerce. The recent excesses may be more a reaction to the degradation of the immediate past rather than an arrogant extension of Medieval triumphs.

The Balkan States: Bulgaria

The names of many topographical features indicate heavy

Slav penetration of lands south of the Lower Danube through both the well-wooded Dobrogea and the mountainous Stara Planina which the Byzantines would have found difficult to defend. But the origin of the state lies in the conquest of Slavs by Bulgarians in 679 and the merging of cultures. Under a treaty of 681 signed with the Emperor Constantine IV the independence of the state within the Byzantine Empire was recognised.[31] There was rapid expansion through conquest northwards across the Danube as far as Pannonia and westwards through Macedonia to Lake Ohrid. The full statehood of Bulgaria may be dated from 716 when a political and commercial treaty was signed with the empire. Inland towns like Niassa (Nis) and Singidunum (Belgrade), perhaps with some lingering commercial importance, could now develop contacts with Constantinople and Thessalonica. The frontier to the south was demarcated by the Erkesiya (Great Fence) running from Develtus on the southern edge of the Bay Burgas to Microlivada (Uzundzhova) at the Azmak-Maritsa confluence. But the state soon expanded beyond this limit with Adrianople (Edirne) and Ohrid both incorporated into what became known as the First Bulgarian Empire. It seems that although individual rulers had been converted to Christianity since the early seventh century the predominantly pagan outlook of the military aristocracy prevented widespread conversion until the more amenable Slavs (who looked to the Bulgarians for military protection) had begun to inflitrate the higher levels of society to the point where they were assimilated by the Slav culture and language. This occurred early in the ninth century by which time a line of particularly able rulers was achieving fresh military success and bringing a considerable Christian population under its rule including high-ranking Byzantine officials and army officers. The new era in Bulgarian history began in 852 with the accession of Boris (who changed his name to Michael when converted to Christianity). Paganism seemed inferior both spiritually and politically to Catholic and Orthodox Christianity as well as the Islamic faith of the Arab caliphs. To Boris paganism was associated with social illiteracy as well as potential feudal resistance to royal power whereas Christianity offered not only cultural progress but a framework for the strengthening of the monarchy. 'In Byzantine Christianity especially the sovereign was conceived of as a divinely anointed autocrat and a lay pontiff with supreme authority not only over the state and people but over the holy church itself'.[32] Boris saw good prospects to secure both the acquiescence of the remaining recalcitrant members of the elite and a degree of independence for the Bulgarian church (vis-à-vis the emperor and patriarch in Constantinople) appropriate for national dignity.

With Byzantium to the south and contacts with the Franks through Moravia to the northwest it was perhaps inevitable that Bulgaria would seek to manipulate these rival influences to gain bargaining power. While Greek bishops held sway in Bulgaria immediately after Boris' baptism by the Patriarch of Constantinople in 864 or 865 the impact of Cyril and Methodius in Moravia was sufficient to allow the concession that the Bulgarian church should be bilingual. On this basis Boris went ahead with an ambitious building programme which focussed on his capital of Pliska, a former Roman military camp whose basilica may have been restored, but included churches at Ohrid and Vodocha (near Strumitsa) and the monastery of St. Panteleimon opposite the royal residence of Preslav to which he retired in 889. He lived long enough to see his son Symeon appoint Clement (a follower of Cyril and Methodius) as Bulgaria's first Slav bishop, with a base probably at Veles (Titov Veles) on the Vardar which would have been an appropriate centre for Clement in fending off Greek encroachments from Thessalonica. Clement was responsible for the building of churches and monasteries in the strategically-important Ohrid region and the cultural emphasis on Macedonia provided something of a counterweight to the state capital which was transferred in c.893 from Pliska to Preslav, an entirely new walled city, founded in 821 by Omourtag.

Standing on the Great Kamtchik river near the modern Pravadi, Preslav controlled the Kazan Pass through the Balkans and also the route to the Danube crossings at Ruse and Silistra. Although Byzantine culture was now fully reflected in court life the Slavonic influence in the church was strongly projected. The new churches and monasteries at Preslav did not copy contemporary structures in Constantinople and a council held in 893 decreed the general use of the Slav language and approved a perfected Cyrillic alphabet. This spelt the end of Hellenisation, at least until the collapse of Bulgarian independence at the end of the tenth century. Finally Symeon unilaterally elevated the head of the Bulgarian church to the rank of patriarch (c. 918), recognised by Constantinople in 927. At the height of his power the patriarch controlled some two dozen bishoprics embracing territory more extensive than the Bulgarian state. In view of these extensive domains in the western Balkans the Bulgarian capital shifted in the tenth century to the Via Egnatia, using three former Roman centres: Ohrid, Prespa and Vodena. However, the economic focus remained in the northeast where contact with long-distance traders was made through the port of Little Preslav (near the modern Tulcea): honey, skins and wax came from Kiev, complemented by shipping from Greece bringing textiles and wine. But there was also some overland trade in precious metals with Bohemia.

Conflict between Bulgaria and Byzantium flared up again during the reign of the Tsar Peter (927-969) when a demand for tribute from the Emperor Nicephorus was not only rebuffed but followed up by inducements to the Varangian Prince Svyatoslav to suppress the Bulgarians. Svyatoslav overran the important Danubian trading emporium of Little Preslav in 967 and proceeded to Great Preslav and Philippopolis two years later. The tactics now rebounded on the Byzantines who had to make herculean military efforts to hold the Varangians. Great Preslav was regained in 971 and Svyatoslav was forced to capitulate after a long seige of Silistra. The amazing see-sawing of events was to continue however, for the suppression of the Bulgarian monarchy and the independent church hierarchy lasted only until the death of Emperor Tzimiskes in 976. Samuel now built another Bulgarian Empire in Macedonia, first based on Prespa but later Ohrid, where the Bulgarian patriarchate was re-established 'after its various peregrinations to Sofia, Vodena, Moglena and Prespa'.[33] But after gains in Epirus and Serbia there was only a temporary re-occupation of the Bulgarian heartland (the region of Pliska and Great Preslav) between 997 and 1001. Byzantine Emperor Boris II then regained this northeastern most part of Bulgaria, as the patriarch retreated from the Danube to Ohrid and Preslav and Pliska fell in 1002. He also conducted a war of attrition culminating in the rout of Samuel's army in 1014. Bulgaria's struggle for independence lasted only another four years and in 1018 Basil II, now known as Bulgaroktonos (the Bulgarian slayer) made a ceremonial entry into Ohrid. The patriarch still controlled about two dozen sees embracing territory (as far afield as Albania, Bosnia and Epirus) beyond the limits of the Bulgarian state at its height of power. But Ohrid was demoted to the status of archbishopric in 1019 and its territory drastically restricted, ultimately to Macedonia. There was much informal Hellenisation and the Greek monasteries of Mount Athos became prominent landowners in Macedonia. Nevertheless the First Bulgarian Empire had played a role of historic importance in forging the Slavs of the area into a nation and in resisting the Byzantine assimilation that was the fate of Slavs who settled in the coastal areas to the south.

The tide again turned with the economic and military weakness of Byzantium apparent in the late twelfth century. By 1186 the Second Bulgarian Empire could be proclaimed, this time with its ecclesiastical and political base at Turnovo. However, the re-establishment of a patriarchate was not a straightforward issue given the nature of Byzantine intrigue over aspirants to the Bulgarian throne. The best hope seemed to lie with Rome, especially in view of the diversion of the Fourth Crusade to Constantinople and the capture of the city in 1204. But the Latins would recognise only a primate and subsequently Bulgarian arms made common cause with the Greeks, on which basis the imperial city was recaptured and the Bulgarian national patriarchate ultimately recognised in 1234. The patriarchal church was built beside the imperial palace on Tsarevets Hill in Turnovo with the precipitous slopes of the river on three sides and a strong wall on the fourth.[34] Town development was also evident in the new towns of Cherven and Lovech and in rebuilding of citadels in old towns, like Ohrid, Plovdiv, Sofia and Vidin. These symbols of independence were then destroyed by the Turks in 1393-6 and the Bulgarian church once more subordinated to the Patriarch of Constantinople who now held unprecedented authority. It is evident, however, that whereas the medieval capitals of Bulgaria were situated on the loessic platform between the Danube and the Balkan Mountains modern Bulgaria has settled for a capital at Sofia, the old Turkish administrative centre, which offers easy access to the provinces via the Iskar, Maritsa and Struma valleys and has some claims as a historic cultural centre through the nearby Rila monastery.

Serbia

Settling in remote and rugged upland country far inland from the Adriatic coast and away from the main land routes across the Balkans, the Serbs remained quite untroubled by the outside world for some considerable time. But they were hardly passive members of the imperial community in view of their original role in establishing a frontier zone against the Avars and subsequently the Magyars. The effective organisation was the clan but a particularly assertive and talented leader (zupan) might construct a larger political organisation, embracing such territories as Raska and Zeta. The physical potential for nation-building was not compelling: not only was the terrain quite elevated but there was a lack of unity arising from the dispersal of drainage in three separate directions, towards the Black Sea (via the Morava and Danube), Adriatic (Drin) and Aegean (Vardar). However, there was ample pasture and cultivation was possible in the polja, tectonic basins formerly occupied by lakes. Four depressions stand out: Kosovo (drained by the upper Ibar), Metohija (upper Drin), Tetova (upper Vardar) and Skopje/Kumanovo (between the Morava and Vardar). The main axis developed between the Ibar and Vardar valleys extending from the first capital of Ras on the Ibar south to Pristina (Kosovo) and Skopje. It was always desirable to link such lands with the Adriatic coastal strip because of the trading opportunities and also the scope for transhumance between summer pastures in the mountains and the wintering grounds around Kotor and Ragusa (Dubrovnik).

An embryonic Serb state first appeared in history in c.850 under Vlastimir in the context of territorial aspirations by both Bulgaria and Byzantium. A Byzantine occupation led to the imposition of suzerainty in the later decades of the century but after 897 Serbia was a Bulgarian dependency and cultural influence from that quarter then prevailed. This is reflected in the organisation of the church because the conversion of the Serbs by Byzantine missionaries led in the 870s to the foundation of a bishopric at Raska (in the Ibar Valley near Novipazar and the political centre at the time) subordinate to either Durrës or Split. But as a Bulgarian province ecclesiastical authority passed to the Patriarch of Ohrid. Further changes then followed for the collapse of Bulgaria resulted in Ohrid's demotion to archbishopric and one in which Greek influences were felt. But only for Latin influences to spread from the Adriatic during the eleventh century as a Slav ruler in Zeta extended his power inland into Hercegovina and Serbia and received ecclesiastical underpinning through the creation of the Latin metropolitan diocese (Dioclea) with its centre at Bar. This development went hand in hand with the decline of Byzantine influence on the Adriatic coast north of Durrës first through the temporary Bulgarian seizure of Durrës, terminal of the Via Egnatia and second through the rise of Venice. However, Latin influence in Bar (once a Byzantine dependency of Durrës) was not overwhelming and it is doubtful if the archbishop was ever able to draw the Serbs away from the authority of Ohrid.

The impluses from the coast faded in any case in the twelfth century with the collapse of Zeta and subsequently the demotion of the archbishopric of Bar in favour of Ragusa. Opportunity for the Serbs now arose through renewed Byzantine weakness which ushered in a Serb state contemporaneous with the Second Bulgarian Empire. Once again the interior was linked with the ports (Bar, Budva and Kotor), but the Orthodox influence was predominant although the power of Ragusa had to be accepted as a reality and a commercial treaty was signed in 1186. The desire on the part of both Bulgaria and Serbia for political independence was not linked with any readiness to accept papal authority. The Serbs won their own patriarch and although Latin influence continued at Bar, the Slav language was permitted and the authority of Rome overthrown. As A.P. Vlasto comments: 'in the long run the centuries-old Byzantine culture of both Serbia and Bulgaria and their possession of the Slav ecclesiastical language made them consciously or unconsciously strive for national churches in the Eastern manner and reject the universalism of the papacy which had more than once come close to catching the Balkans in its net. Whereas to be politically independent of Byzantium was their constant ambition alienation from her communion was not'.[35]

Serbia entered her most successful period as a Medieval nation in 1169 when Stephen Nemanja became zupan of Raska and founded a dynasty that was to last for two centuries. He shook off Byzantine suzerainty, incorporated the adjacent Slav territory of Zeta and laid the foundation for an independent Serb church: his youngest son became a monk on Mount Athos and returned under the name of Sava to become the first archbishop of an autocephalous Serbian Orthodox Church in 1219. Péc became the centre of the Serbian church, now freed from the jurisdiction of the Archbishop of Ohrid. The family ties between church and state under the Nemanjid dynasty (with both Sava and Symeon recognised as national saints) provided an excellent basis for applying the Byzantine principle that spiritual authority and temporal power should work hand in hand to guide the state. Since the Magyars posed a formidable barrier to progress in the north the Serb state sought expansion in the south and at the turn of the twelfth century made progress against both the Byzantine and Second Bulgarian empires. But it was Stephen Dusan (1331-55) who for a time achieved incredible success. Dusan's rule was an enlightened one with the elevation of the Archbishop of Péc to patriarch and the publication of the famous Zakonik legal code which combined Byzantine law with Serb custom. He was confident enough to take the fatal step of advancing his capital from the Pristina/Prizren area, in the very heart of Serbia, forwards to Skopje and set his sights firmly on Constantinople, possibly with the idea of blocking any threat of a Turkish invasion of Europe.[36] His untimely death at the start of the crucial campaign had most serious consequences for not only did Serbia lose its coherence but the way was now open for an advance by the Turks who had been recruited by the Byzantine Empire as mercenaries to oppose Dusan's campaign. The Serbs retreated from Skopje, a dangerously exposed capital well outside the ecumene of the state in Raska, to the seclusion of Krusevac on the Ibar in 1371. They also accepted Constantinople's supremacy over their church. The Turkish onslaught completely overwhelmed the state and the abolition of the patriarchate in 1453 was followed ten years later by the elimination even of the bishopric of Péc. However, Péc was to emerge again as the centre of an archdiocese in 1557 and in the meantime the monasteries stood as the main foci of Serb culture. A small fragment of Zeta was left virtually undisturbed by the Turks on account of its remoteness and this was to become the core of the future state of Montenegro.

Bosnia

Bosnia's history is largely obscure but what little is available is certainly intriguing, for the small state experienced fluctuating fortunes in sympathy with events in neighbouring countries. The Bosnian tribes are thought to have entered the region in the seventh century. The original core area seems to have been in the Bosna Valley with a commercial centre at Visoko between Sarajevo and Zenica and a royal residence at Sutjeska to the northeast close to the castle of Bobovac. But the capital was finally established further to the northwest at Jajce, close to a pass which offered easy communication with the fortress city of Travnik. Bosnia was certainly most powerful under Stephen Tvrtko who took the title of 'King of Bosnia and Serbia' in 1377, but by this time a Bosnian bishopric, which may date to the eleventh century, had already been subordinated successively to Split, Ragusa and Kalocsa. However, while an independent ecclesiastical hierarchy was not attainable the Bosnians consciously or unconsciously sought distinction through the Bogomil heresy, recognising Satan (as God's rebel elder son) to be creator of the universe: 'all matter therefore derives from an autonomous evil principle at war with God'.[37] Bogomil's teaching in Bulgaria in the tenth century was evidently dispersed through the Byzantine reconquest and Bosnia then became the most infected area. This may have arisen initially because Bosnia was not firmly associated with any Balkan archbishopric, but the cult took firmer root as heretics from Croatia and Dalmatia sought sanctuary from persecution while the rulers of Bosnia in the late twelfth and early thirteenth centuries tolerated the movement for political reasons. So national sentiment may well have focussed on Bogomilism and helped Bosnians to continue a balancing act between Catholicism and Orthodoxy right up to the Turkish conquest, when in contrast to other South Slav peoples they willingly embraced Islam and so continued to project their homeland as a culturally distinct province which it remains at the present day.

The Romanian Principalities of Moldavia and Wallachia

A Romanised Thracian population was able to defend its cultural heritage through the Dark Ages despite considerable pressure from the Slavs, pressure which in most other parts of the Balkans led to an almost complete cultural replacement. Slav influence was followed by Magyar pressure as the Hungarians advanced eastwards from the Pannonian Plain to reach the Somes river by 900 and the Eastern Carpathians by 1200. Like the Norman Conquest in England, this penetration had the effect of planting a new aristocracy and introducinng a feudal system through the arrival of clerics and soldiers. There was, however, a substantial flow of Magyar peasants into eastern Transylvania while the German Drang nach Osten had implications for the province through the arrival of German farmers and miners in strategically sensitive areas where the Hungarian kings invited them to settle. Yet while there is no doubt that the Romanians comprised the bulk of the peasantry in

Transylvania there has always been a strong difference of opinion between Romanian and Hungarian historians over the origin of the Romanian community: Romanian historians insist that their ancestors have lived in Transylvania continously since prehistoric times while their Hungarian colleagues argue that the Romanians arrived from south of the Danube only in Medieval times after the arrival of the first Hungarian settlers. This notion was propounded by R. Rössler in his book on Romänische Studien, published in Leipzig in 1871. These rival theories have, of course, been presented and articulated over quite a long period of time in connection with rival territorial claims to Transylvania by the Hungarian and Romanian states. Neither argument can be proved conclusively although the Romanian interpretation of the settlement history seems the more plausible of the two.

There is a wealth of archaeological evidence showing continuity of settlement by the Thracians in Iron Age and Roman times, and there is also a significant fund of archaeological evidence showing traces of Daco-Romanian occupation in Transylvania during the critical Dark Ages. Furthermore, anthropological evidence can link modern Romanians with their Thracian ancestors. In one mountain district it is claimed that Geto-Dacian roots do not have to be revealed by digging: the evidence lies on the surface in the physique of the people, their buildings, language and life style including 'the way in which the present day people understand their history'.[38] While it is possible that the Romanised Dacians could have left Transylvania with the Roman forces when the province was abandoned and centuries later moved back there from Bulgaria, there is no logical reason why either event should have occurred and no evidence to suggest that such movements did take place. Certainly Orthodox Church ritual does not show the links with Bulgaria that would be expected: if the Romanians had migrated from south of the Danube they would have recognised the Orthodox patriarch at Turnovo, installed under the Second Bulgarian Empire, yet in fact it was the authority of Ohrid that was recognised, until Stephen the Great's time. On the other hand, the Hungarian claim that Transylvania was deserted when they arrived rests on a very casual documentary reference which is too insignificant to bear the heavy weight of hypothesis which has been placed on it. When the Hungarians entered Transylvania it may be assumed that they were confronted by Romanians organised in large tribal groups in Crisana (under Menumorut), the lower Mures valley (Glad) and the Cris/Somes valleys (Gelu). It is however quite possible that the Dacians were forced to retreat to the mountains because of pressure from the Slavs and then reoccupied the low ground by a process of descent (descalecare) that could conceivably have been more or less contemporaneous with the arrival of the Hungarians. The Slavs in Bulgaria could have displaced some of the natives northwards across the Danube but that does not mean that the entire Romanian population originated in this way.

If continuity in quasi-refuge situations is accepted as mostly likely it would tend to emphasise the Carpathian depressions, especially the marginal ones which provide a combination of land resources and a measure of security against invading forces on the plains. Such a view would draw support from the tradition of the depressions as 'lands' such as Tara Maramuresului and Tara Oasului. Medieval political development certainly seems to focus on these sheltered districts for there is some evidence that powerful Romanian rulers such as Gelu in Crisana opposed the Hungarian advance and after alien authority had been imposed in the more accessible areas of Transylvania Romanian power persisted in Maramures and in the Olt Valley district of Fagaras. Moreover, when the Angevin kings of Hungary pressed for more direct control in the fourteenth century, for economic reasons (to win the same valuable resources which the Romans had previously coveted) and for strategic gain (to extend the frontier to the crests of the Carpathians), there was settlement by both Germans and Magyars and also recognition of Romanians as feudal authorities in areas (like Crisana and Maramures) where they enjoyed numerical strength or effective political organisation. Again, while the mountain crests separating Transylvania from the Danube plains constituted a clearly defined and defensible frontier line, there were economic interests for the Hungarians in the lands to the east by virtue of the trade routes from the Danube delta leading through Transylvania into Pannonia, while Poland had interests in the steppes through the Amber Route connecting the Baltic coast through Lwow (Lvov) with Cetatea Alba (Belgorod) at the mouth of the Dniester: the possibility therefore arises that the Principalities of Moldavia and Wallachia were based on close political links with Poland and Hungary respectively as economic and strategic interests justified protection of Romanian princes who were prepared to extend feudal control across the mountains.

It would appear that political development on the outer side of the Carpathians did not go beyond the level of the judet until fourteenth century migrations took place from Fagaras and Maramures over the Carpathians to Cîmpulung and Baia, the first capitals of the principalities of the Wallachia and Moldavia respectively. The crucial question, of course, is the motive for these migrations and subsequent efforts by the leaders to create new territorial units. The events may have occurred spontaneously as a result of growing pressure of population, for it is widely believed that the fourteenth and fifteenth centuries witnessed a significant growth of population expressed in a wave of secondary settlement indicated by place name elements referring to duals like 'great' (mare) and 'little' (mica) or 'upper' (de sus) and 'lower' (de jos). And more generally there is a long-standing tradition of settlers from Transylvania crossing the mountains, a movement that may most logically be interpreted as a balancing process to match people with resources. For the agricultural potential of the outer slopes (with their extensive foothills and depressions) is far greater for climatic and topographical reasons than the corresponding flanks in Transylvania. Once again the place name dual Ungureni (i.e. from territory under Hungarian administration) and Pamînteni (referring to a community of people native to the locality) indicates the process. However, particular circumstances could have the effect of triggering migration at particular times and it may be asked therefore if the movements from Fagaras and Maramures were sparked off by excessive Hungarian pressure on the autonomy of capable Romanian leaders who crossed the mountains and introduced the new political-territorial model without interference (just as, in later times, Romanians in Transylvania were to settle on the other side of the mountains in order to escape religious persecution). Yet there is an equal possibility that the Romanian leaders were acting in concert with the kings of Hungary and Poland.

The Wallachian state, with its twin capitals at Cîmpulung and Curtea de Arges, was founded by Basarab (1324-1351) who extended his realm across the steppes to Dobrogea and lands east of the Prut. Bessarabia, the name of the latter territory (eventually ceded to Russia in 1812), is in fact derived from Basarabia, although it is doubtful if it was held by Romanians until the turn of the fourteenth century when Prince Mircea the Old was able to make further gains in the east. Moldavia was developed some years after Wallachia and eventually took over some of the latter's territory in the early fifteenth century: this would justify the Romanian name for Wallachia (derived from <u>vlach</u>) being Tara Romȃneasca (<u>the</u> Romanian land). It was about 1350 that Bogdan, the ruler of Maramures, moved across the mountains to the Moldava Valley to found the <u>Tara de Sus</u> (Upper Country), initially a military borderland facing the Tartars. This territory was consolidated by Petru Musat (1374-1392) with a chain of strongholds including Tîrgu Neamt and Suceava and an agreed frontier with the Hungarian territory to the west. Relations with Wallachia constitute a largely unexplored topic yet it must surely be an intriguing one in view of the territorial expansion of Moldavia to embrace some of the Wallachian lands. This applies not only in areas like Covurlui (Galati) and Vrancea which became the southernmost districts of Moldavia but also Bessarabia. With a chain of strongholds along the Dniester including Hotin, Tighina and Cetatea Alba Moldavia clearly took over Wallachia's function of guarding the settled agricultural lands from nomadic invasion. It is not at all clear either how closely the Moldavian prince aligned himself with Hungary when he departed across the mountains, but there was some rural colonisation by Magyar groups and a close trading contact with Transylvania (notably with Bistrita and Rodna). The Germans organised some of the trade from Bistrita into Moldavia and the place-name element <u>Neamt</u> as in Piatra Neamt and Tîrgu Neamt could relate to a German community (German in Romanian being <u>nemtesc</u>). But there were economic links with Poland too and the Moldavian capital gradually inched its way from the seclusion of Baia, first to Suceava and later to Iasi to be well-placed on the trade routes from the Baltic to the Black Sea, just as the Wallachian capital was transferred first to Tîrgoviste and then to Bucharest.

Romanian historians have, therefore, recognised the primacy of Polish influence in Moldavia. But of course the princes in both principalities took advantage of any opportunity to increase their independence and the end of the Arpad dynasty in Hungary provided one such opening for Wallachia: a newly-won autonomy was then maintained with Bulgarian help against Hungarian attempts to regain authority at the battle at Posada in the Olt valley. For some time after the Wallachian prince maintained feudal interests in Fagaras, while nevertheless supplementing the trappings of independence by the appointment of an Orthodox metropolitan (1359) and the licensing of traders to cross Wallachian territory as far as the Danube port of Braila. The long-distance trade routes across the Carpathians were certainly maintained (to say nothing of the 'salt roads' which converged on the mines of Ocnele Mari and Tîrgu Ocna) and this acted as a precedent for long-wave transhumance between the mountains and the steppes. For it is curious that many of the villages most involved are concentrated in clusters on the inner side of the mountains: it is possible that initiative was stimulated through contact with German and Hungarian settlers and their relatively advanced techniques in agriculture and rural industry. Documents refer to transhumance in the fifteenth and sixteenth centuries with some of the earliest references to the Brasov area, specifically the suburb of Schei and a cluster of neighbouring villages known collectively as Sacele. Development may have occurred in parallel with a growth of trade with Wallachia, benefitting from the privileges awarded to Brasov merchants and from the expertise of that area in dealing with Romanians on the southern side of the mountains. It is equally interesting to note that the second important area to emerge in the documentary record is Marginimea Sibiului and other villages in the vicinity of the trading city of Sibiu.

The autonomy enjoyed by Moldavia and Wallachia must be related in part to the wider political context in which the Habsburg Empire and Poland were important powers in containing Ottoman expansion. These two Catholic states were both receptive to the culture of the Italian Renaissance but they maintained separate foreign policies and Poland generally stood aloof from Habsburg attempts to incite opposition to the Turks, preferring a strategy of peaceful coexistence which would allow trade to flourish. In a sense, therefore, the autonomy of the Danubian Principalities as buffer states may be related to the delicate relations between powerful neighbours. At times the pressures became too great and right at the turn of the sixteenth century Transylvania became a battle ground for the three powers, with Wallachia's Michael the Brave able to take advantage of the chaos to effect a short-lived union of the three Romanian provinces (1600-1). But on the whole Romanians benefitted from their semi-independence and were certainly exposed to more western influence than would have been tolerated had they been subject to outright Ottoman occupation.

The whole issue is made all the more enigmatic by the gloss which has been added by Romanian historians since the First World War. It is entirely appropriate that Romanian history should be presented in such a way as to fully rationalise the changes made to the frontiers by the union of the late nineteenth century kingdom (regat) with Transylvania and some smaller neighbouring territories. In the same way Romanians vigorously deny Soviet claims that the Carpians (ancestors of the native inhabitants of Bessarabia) are not part of the Geto-Dacian community so that no fundamental ethnic distinction can be drawn between Romania and the adjacent Moldavian Republic of the USSR which embraces the 'lost province' of Bessarabia.[39] But this has tended to portray Transylvania and the Carpathian girdle as the historic fortress of the nation (cetatea pamîntului românesc). The evidence from the earliest times does not fully support this view and in the Medieval period it is evident that the mountains hardly comprised a watertight barrier, for the passes have a historic role as communication routes and town development emphasises the contact point on either side. The supposed core of the Romanian state has in fact seen considerable ethnic intermixing with the Germans and Hungarians following the Bulgarians and Slavs. And it has not acted as an ecumene for any empire or nation state: rather the impulses have come externally, either from Pannonia or from the lower Danube. This does not diminish in any way the achievement of the Romanians in maintaining the culture of the Romanised Dacians into modern times on the Carpathian-Danubian territory but merely suggests that crude topographical determinism is unhelpful and that an understanding of the political development of the Romanian people is enhanced by treating relations with Germans and Hungarians as sympathetically as earlier relations between Dacians and Romans.

Albania

Observers of the Medieval scene in the Balkans must also come to terms with the anomaly of the Albanians. How did this ethnically distinct group survive in an area of contact between Byzantines and Slavs? The conventional explanation would relate the Albanians to the Illyrians and postulate a continuity of settlement largely undisturbed by the Slav migrations. However, the argument is weakened by lack of evidence of any Albanian names before the twelfth century, and by the absence of that Greek influence in the placenames that would surely be evident if the Albanians had inhabited their present homeland continuously. An intriguing thesis by A. Dabinovic takes remarks by Ptolemy to suggest that there may have been a migration of Albanians either from the Baranya, the southern part of the Pannonian plain, or from the Nis area of the Vardar valley.[40] The migration from the former location might have been triggered by Magyar pressure against Vlach shepherds, while movement from the latter might reflect displacement of Albanian frontiersmen (a people of Caucasian origin settled on the Bulgarian frontiers by the Byzantines) during the fourth crusade at the very beginning of the thirteenth century. In either case the Albanians headed westwards into the lands around Durrës and Vlorë between the Dinarics and the Pindhus, whereupon the Slav population in the countryside was assimilated and the ancient prosperity of the towns (with their mixed Latin/Greek population) undermined. Dabinovic also suggests that a second wave of Albanian settlement, involving people now converted to Islam, followed the Ottoman conquest and took over the towns. Although speculative this interpretation does help to account for the readiness of the Albanians to project their national interests within the fabric of the empire and to contemplate complete independence only when the Turkish position in the Balkans became quite hopeless at the turn of the nineteenth century. Otherwise determined resistance was restricted to Gjergj Kastrioti and his fellow tribesmen in the middle of the fifteenth century. As a child he was placed in the service of the Turks who renamed him Skenderbeg. But he deserted at Nis in 1442 and with the support of Naples was able to establish the independence of his Kastrioti homeland, based on the town of Krujë, and maintain it up to his death in 1468. The Turks did not regain control of Albania until 1501.

OTTOMAN POWER IN THE BALKANS

The political structure of Eastern Europe was a highly unstable one and only a few of the Medieval vicissitudes have been outlined. The most traumatic changes arose through the Ottoman conquest of the Balkans in the fourteenth and fifteenth centuries. In fact their presence in the Balkans dates right back to the ninth century for mercenaries were recruited by Byzantium and Emperor Theophilus settled Turks in the Vardar area of Macedonia. But an increasingly well-organised force built up in Asia: a remarkable piece of concerted political action contrasting with the 'feudal particularism' of the regimes which were placed in mortal danger as the Turkish invasions of Europe began in 1345. The assault on the Balkans seems to have arisen out of a desire to control the Dardanelles and the trade that passed through. The commercial activities of the Genoese were to be eliminated and cereal surpluses diverted to Istanbul. A frontier in Europe was first established through the movement of soldiers into Thrace and the displacement of Christians. But while the Turks could profit from the weakness of the Byzantine Empire and the Balkan states (for even Serbia lost its cohesion after the death of Dusan) they lacked a navy and heavy artillery. Hence their conquest was by no means assured. The Turkish crossing of the Bulgarian frontier in 1366 led to defeat at Vidin and shortly after this a crusade launched by the pope was able to restore Gallipoli to Byzantine control. But this was held only until a Turkish assault on Bulgaria and Macedonia in 1576 reduced all these lands to vassaldom. Serbia was defeated in 1389 and Wallachia was forced to capitulate despite a stubborn resistance which included one notable victory by Mircea the Old in 1395. By 1400 much of the Balkans lay under Ottoman control and the Byzantine Empire was reduced to the imperial city alone. Mehmet I thus achieved a frontier along the Danube from the Iron Gates to the sea, defended by garrisons at important crossing places like Isakci (Isaccea), Tutrakan and Vidin. After the diversion of a Mongol attack on Anatolia the pressure was resumed, leading not only to the fall of Constantinople (with its great arsenal and dockyard) but also to the elimination of Hungarian and Venetian influence through victories at Varna (1444) and Kosovo (1448).[41]

Further adventures may have been precipitated by the attitude of the military class, for there may even have been an imperialist mentality of conquest for its own sake which made it impossible for the empire to live at peace. C.M. Kortpeter considers that 'the Ottoman elite, acting upon expediency, found it easier to employ its armies to make war upon a neighbouring state, in the hope of seizing that country's movable wealth and population, than to create a healthy social environment and to use wisely its own vast physical and human resources'.[42] However, the advances of Mehmet II may also be interpreted as attempts to gain security against further crusades and prevent the Habsburgs from profiting from the weakness of Hungary during the minority of Laszlo V (who succeeded on John Hunyadi's death in 1458). The situation north of the Danube was certainly chaotic in the late fifteenth century with both Hungary and Moldavia seeking to place their own nominees on the Wallachian throne and reject Turkish suzerainty. Vlad the Impaler was installed in 1456 by John Hunyadi and embarked on a notorious six year reign marked by a solid defiance of the Turks, including raids south of the Danube and wholesale executions of Turks by impalement. Ottoman suzerainty was reimposed in 1462 but in Moldavia stout resistance was maintained by Stephen the Great (including capture of the trading settlement of Chilia at the mouth of the Danube) until his submission in 1492. But Hungary still remained a threat to the Turkish position in Wallachia and some irritation may have arisen from the status of the Banat of Severin which fluctuated in its subordination between direct Hungarian authority and overlordship as part of the Wallachian principality. It seems to have been in dispute again between Hungary and Wallachia when the latter was an Ottoman dependency although precise details are lacking. The decisive move against Hungary was, however, delayed until 1526 when a disunited country (weakened by the peasant revolt of 1514) was again ruled by a young king. Once again Pannonia became an important frontier province, so much so that parallels might be drawn between Ottoman palanka and Roman limes. Certainly Buda was one of the most important places in the empire and the link with Istanbul (by way of Belgrade, Nis, Filibe (Plovdiv) and Edirne, was the principal road in the Balkans, flanked by the eastern route to the lower Danube and Moldavia and the western route from Selanik (Thessaloniki) to Monastir (Bitola), Ohrid and Durrës.

Hungary marked the northern limit of Ottoman advance and although Vienna was threatened in both 1529 and 1683 the city was able to hold out, supported on the latter occasion by Poles who had previously encountered Turks on the steppes of Ukraine. The capacity and motivation of the Turks for control of significant additional territories may certainly be doubted but nevertheless there is credibility in the view that stubborn resistance to the Ottoman advance by the Christian states of the Balkans protected Western

Europe at a critical time when political divisions might have inhibited effective opposition. The respite also coincided with the overseas discoveries which were to 'endow Western Europe with a technical superiority over the rest of the world and thus the possibility to defy even the Ottoman Empire which adapted to new inventions with great difficulty'.[43] The Turks plainly did not have the resources to settle all the newly-conquered lands and hence their readiness to enter into vassalage agreements which gave them strategic advantages and supplies of soldiers in return for local autonomy. So long as the Ottomans did not face treachery or attempts to regain full independence on the part of their clients they stuck to these covenants. Much of the empire was administered by Turkish governors through a system of civil and military regions (sancaks), subsequently subdivided into eyalets; there were also autonomous regions of hükümet sancaks embracing Ragusa (Dubrovnik) and the Romanian provinces of Moldavia, Transylvania and Wallachia.[44] For the peasant population of these areas the arrangement was not necessarily a blessing since rulers might be too weak to prevent oppression by feudal authorities (both lay lords and monasteries) while the payment of tribute would impose further hardships.

Here the position of the Romanian Principalities is instructive. Both Wallachia and Moldavia submitted to the Turks because on the one hand support from Christian states like Hungary and Poland was inspired only by desires to press claims for overlordship while on the other the Turks were prepared to offer reasonable terms. Hence Stephen the Great of Moldavia maintained a stout defence against the Turks during most of his lifetime with the support of a badly-equipped peasant army but disillusionment with his Christian neighbours led him to settle with Istanbul on the best terms available. Only a moderate tribute (4000 ducats in 1503 compared with 8000 for Wallachia) was levied initially and with Ottoman backing Stephen was able to wrest control of Pocutia (Bucovina) from his previous overlord, Poland. Under Ottoman suzerainty the prince was elected by the nobles: supporters of the winning candidate would expect substantial patronage and hope for a reign long enough to make considerable profit. The election of Orthodox princes had to be confirmed by the Porte and payments made: both an accession gift and tribute. There were no Muslim settlements or military fiefs although bridgeheads like Giurgiu, Ibrail (Braila) and Turnu Magurele gave the Turks garrisons on the northern side of the Danube and additional forces could be maintained in Dobrogea. The princes had only limited power to deal with the nobility and attempts to gain support by bestowing land or by tolerating greater pressure on the peasantry could only make the situation worse in the long run. Even the most able rulers like M. Basarab (1632-58) in Wallachia and V. Lupu (1634-53) in Moldavia could not hope to reverse the trend and any scope for greater bargaining power with the Turks was undermined by their wars with each other, on three occasions during the mid-seventeenth century. Indeed Greek Phanariot families gained an important springboard in the principalities at this time.

Transylvania was most favourably placed, however, for the terms of Ottoman overlordship were relatively light (with no Turkish insistence on garrison rights) and the level of development was higher, thanks to superior natural resources and a fairly comprehensive urban system which owed much to German efficiency. However, it is evident that Romanian nationalism was not the potent force it became in the late nineteenth century when the fusion of Moldavia and Wallachia gave rise to speculation about a 'Greater Romania' that was eventually achieved in 1918. There was a curious lack of cooperation between Transylvania and the two Danubian principalities and only for a very short time, under the charismatic leadership of Michael the Brave in 1600 was there any kind of union. Of course the rulers of Transylvania did not have any territorial conception of 'Romania' and naturally despised the Romanian peasantry, while the Danubian principalities maintained their own separate establishments. Yet there was no explicit national hatred and P.F. Sugar has suggested that Transylvania had the greater potential as the nucleus of a strong non-Habsburg Christian state.[45] But he also argues that the possibility of limited progress in the Danubian sphere in the sixteenth and seventeenth centuries was obscured by an imperialistic policy to combine the three principalities with Hungary and Poland, so 'going beyond the objectively achievable or the religiously and even politically desirable'.[46]

LANDHOLDING AND SETTLEMENT

'The whole land belongs to the Caliph' was the fundamental principle of Turkish rule in the countryside. Land was allocated to true believers and so only those members of the native aristocracy who would accept Islam were able to keep their land. Those dispossessed were reduced to the class of subject people (raya) with restricted economic and cultural opportunities, although they could always win some favours (as voinitsi, holding land free of tax) by making themselves useful as builders, estate managers, foresters or guards. And they might also retain some status in mountain areas where Turkish control was tenuous and where privileged villages sheltered a chorbadzhii class of Christian landowners and merchants. For non-Muslim boys seized as slaves through the devshirme system there was the prospect of a distinguished career in the Ottoman army (often in the famous infantry group known as the Janissaries) or in the sultan's household. However, all Christians and Jews were tolerated, thanks to the recognition of a common bond of monotheism between Islam, Christianity and Judaism: 'any monotheist who accepted the political supremacy of Islam and was willing to live in a Muslim state under stipulated conditions became a zimmi, a protected person'.[47] Such status involved a type of self-government under the millet system, a sort of minority home-rule policy based on religion. There was four millets, covering Armenians, Jews and Orthodox Christians as well as Muslims. The Christians were all theoretically subject to the patriarch at Istanbul but there were two autocephalous churches (the Greek and Serbian) with jurisdiction over different combinations of ethnic groups. The Orthodox Church certainly continued to flourish, with increased power for the patriarch in Istanbul arising from the suppression of the Bulgarian and Serb patriarchates.

The peasantry paid tithes of different kinds as well as taxes to the state. As long as administration remained efficient the latter were reasonable and equitable which 'explains why so many Southeastern Europeans helped the Ottomans during their conquests and why living under direct Ottoman rule was preferable to living under a local lord'.[48] Peasant rights were safeguarded and their tenure was more secure than in most other parts of Europe, although people could not leave their land unless their property rights (tasarruf) were taken over in a manner acceptable to their superiors and fellow villagers. The basic unit of land ownership was the timar: in effect a military fief since the bulk of the regular army was made up from timar holders who had to provide a number of horsemen commensurate with the size of the property and serve as cavalry themselves. Ottoman agents (mevkufchus) kept a check on the system to deal with defaulters. Estates were periodically redistributed, usually at the accession of a new sultan (who could claim penultimate ownership of all land) having regard to the military services rendered. Thus the timar holders tended to have a vested interest in further conquest in order to provide more land for distribution. All in all the system of Ottoman land tenure was very different from the regime of peasant serfdom which is usually associated with the feudal state in economic development. However the high level of conformity with the obligations of timar holding suggest that the system was quite old and was perhaps borrowed from the Byzantines and their Muslim contemporaries.

Important migration currents were associated with the Ottoman advance. There was some settlement of Turks on the land and considerable recruitment of Christian children for the Janissaries. In the towns a 'Greek' business community became a commonplace. But there were also important shifts among the indigenous rural population. Some Serbs went north with the Turks into Bosnia in a military capacity and these soldiers, the so-called Martolozi, settled with their families in the border regions, particularly in northwestern parts abandoned by the Croats. The movement of Serbs in various contexts was great enough to depopulate Kosovo in large measure. Some Anatolian peasants were settled on the land but the most prominent compensatory movement was by Albanians who embraced Islam and (by the late seventeenth century) moved down from the mountains to the west, almost an instinctive response by this pastoral people. Radical change occurred in Hungary which best exemplifies the frontier (palanka) in the Ottoman Empire. Although many settlements, including Buda and Pécs, fell undamaged into Turkish hands the hostility shown to the natives made certain that the initial flight by the nobility would be followed, gradually, by almost the whole Magyar population. Empty buildings were occupied by Turks and by a stream of Balkan artisans (many Bosnians and Serbs) who came to provide services for the sancak governors and military commanders. Substantial fortifications were erected but very little was done to raise new buildings or repair old ones, so that travellers reported many ruined buildings and whole districts with the appearance of shanty towns. Some Hungarian craftsmen supplied the Turkish garrison but generally speaking the towns became alien military colonies without any significant contacts with the surrounding rural area.

In the Pannonian countryside a small population remained to seek a meagre living in a badly-devastated area, perhaps raiding across the frontier and so demonstrating sufficient military prowess to be recruited as regular soldiers. The depopulation was quite remarkable considering that there may have been three to five million people present before the Ottomans arrived. But the area seems to have been approaching an ecological crisis in any case, for steady deforestation was reaching the point where it threatened the water supply for crop production. The arable farmers could just cope under these difficult circumstances but the land rapidly deteriorated when they were disturbed by the Turks and replaced by Serb and Romanian immigrants. There was also a great loss of life through disease, for the newly-created marshes and semi-deserts 'produced a great variety of disease-carrying insects which made the land between the Danube and Tisza probably the least sanitary region of Europe at the time'.[49] This in turn had a depressing effect on town life so that the major Ottoman administrative centres (Pécs and Szeged along with Buda) became true Muslim towns with virtually no indigenous population. However, another distinctive feature of the settlement pattern was the pattern of prairie towns (mesövarosok) on to which the remaining rural population fell back. Deserted village lands were therefore functionally related to these towns which now became the centres of extensive pastoral farming systems seeking to make the best use of the degraded land. And in contrast to the major centres already mentioned prairie towns like Cegléd, Kecskemét and Nagykörös had no Muslim settlers: Ottoman representatives would appear only from time to time to collect taxes. A distinctive frontier ethos also obtained on the Habsburg side through the establishment of the military frontier in Croatia.[50] This was done basically to oppose further Turkish advance but it had an important side effect through control of the Hungarian nobility. The frontier concept developed through arrangements to defend Austrian duchies, followed by agreements with the Croatian estates in 1523 and 1527 which placed Croatia under Habsburg protection and paved the way for a Habsburg claim to the Croatian crown. Policies for the settlement of the area are discussed in Chapter 7.

Economy

In both cultural and material terms the Ottoman impact on the Balkans has often been considered a strongly negative phenomenon. One sweeping judgement by S. Vryonis involves an analogy with the Mongols in Russia, interrupting the natural pattern of development and modernisation. Contact with the west was broken off until the nineteenth century 'at which time the Balkan peoples were faced with the impossible task of bridging the gap between the Renaissance and the Industrial Revolution in a very brief space of time'.[51] On the whole however it seems more reasonable to follow Carter's proposition that derogatory ideas about Ottoman civilisation relate most appropriately to the later stages of Turkish rule, a time of persistent decline. 'It is possible that in the earlier centuries the various Ottoman institutions offered the Balkan population a situation which was an improvement on the one previously tolerated under native feudal governments'.[52] It would certainly be a gross oversimplification to suppose that the government was opposed to commerce and industry. P.F. Sugar states categorically that 'the Ottomans regarded economic pursuits, including manufacture and trade, as essential to the well-being and financial stability of the state'.[53] Patents for traders organised into various branches of commerce were quite readily forthcoming, for merchants were extremely valuable as an entrepreneurial class well able to make loans to the government and act as intermediaries with the people over taxation. They also acted as agents and ambassadors, over and above their basic commercial functions of supplying food to the townspeople and luxury goods to the elite. Naturally the state's attitude showed a streak of ambivalence because excessive speculation by the merchant (<u>tüccar</u>) could result in unacceptably high food and raw material prices: some confiscation of merchant wealth could then appease the guilds and the consumers in general. Nevertheless the prevailing view favoured the migration of wealthy merchants to Ottoman cities as one of the most effective methods of enriching the country and filling the treasury.

The merchants constituted the elite in the urban settlements and were the counterparts of the rural <u>âyans</u>, chiefs or state officials who often held extensive fiefs.[54] They could be both Muslim or non-Muslim but it was Orthodox subjects of the sultan who were particularly prominent in the growth of trade. It has been said that the Balkan Christian family became larger and stronger in contrast to the Muslim Ottomans (with the possible exception of the Muslim Albanians) because of the growth of abortion which seems to have been a consequence of polygamy: Turkish women were anxious to protect their beauty and their ability to compete for male attention, although it is also possible that birth control was a response to economic pressures. Greeks were especially successful in commerce and controlled much of the Balkan trade by the turn of the sixteenth century. Rival traders were gradually displaced: the Venetians' right to navigate the Black Sea ceased by 1540 and between 1592 and 1783 the Black Sea was in effect mare clausum. The hegemony of Genoa and Venice was broken and instead it was Ottoman merchants: Greeks, but also Armenians, Jews and some Turks, who enjoyed privileges abroad (e.g. at Ancona in 1514). At this time the spice trade was an important preoccupation and Pax Ottomanica made Istanbul a logical centre for this activity. However the most important branch of trade was always concerned with the supply of food to the capital and it was the food dealer (celep) who administered many of the monopolies for the Ottoman government. Food was delivered tax-free to the capital in order to keep down prices to urban consumers. But even so the high prices demanded by cereal farmers meant that the successful dealers were forced to rely on malpractice.

After the expulsion of the Jews from Spain in 1494 thousands of them were welcomed by the Ottoman government and allowed to settle in the port towns where they collected taxes, developed local industries and handled trade with Western Europe. For example Jewish settlement in Selanik resulted in the growth of a woollen industry which supplied the Balkans as well as Istanbul, where the Janissaries maintained a large demand for clothing. This helped to switch the geography of production away from Anatolia. The Balkans served as Selanik's hinterland for this external centre, sending out raw wool (especially in the case of Macedonia) and receiving back the finished cloth. Much of the commerce was based on Edirne: English and Florentine cloth as well as the production from Selanik was marketed through Bulgaria and Serbia. But there was also some overland trade and merchants from Hungary were able to reach Vienna to purchase woollen cloth from Bavaria, Moravia and Silesia (and English goods sent out via Hamburg and Nürnberg) for sale in the empire.[55] However, the Jews did not retain their prominent position in Balkan towns and there appears to have been a significant westward movement in the seventeenth and eighteenth centuries which reduced the Jewish population in both the Ottoman Empire and Poland. Growing intolerance seems to have been an important factor, though evacuation through war may have been a more immediate cause in some cases. Selanik's Jewish population amounted to some 40,000 in the 1660s but was down to around 12,000 by the end of the eighteenth century: at the same time there was an increase in the population of Greeks as well as Albanians and Slavs.

CONCLUSION

The construction of a new political geography in Eastern Europe was a great achievement of the period. Although the balance between local and imperial power was not a particularly stable one, as events in the Balkans amply demonstrate, important progress was made towards the crystallisation of national consciousness which provided inspiration in later times. Arguably the church acted as a catalyst in the development of states and in the creation of some sense of community in the region as a whole, providing a set of standards conducive to civilised behaviour within and between nations. The churches were able to bolster national consciousness while maintaining considerable independence of action. There was certainly no blind submission to the power of the state. Although for a time the kings did control their churches the early thirteenth century brought an important breakthrough. By 1217 in Poland, 1222 in Bohemia and 1231 in Hungary the church was generally speaking administering its property and cathedral chapters were electing bishops. 'The bishops and abbots thus acquired political rights in church affairs equivalent to those of the lay nobility in secular matters'.[56] Ecclesiastical territories in Eastern Europe did not develop into principalities but the scale of property ownership was sufficient for the church to continue its role in agricultural development and rural colonisation which had started with the foundation of Cistercian and Premonstratensian monasteries (like Osek in Bohemia and Zsambek in Hungary). In the late thirteenth century the Bishop of Olomouc colonised his diocese in Moravia on progressive lines and the same development can be seen a little later in the case of Krakow and Wrocław. So despite imperialistic overtones at the missionary stage the Catholic Church became an important force in the prosperity and stability of the state, identifying with national interests without necessarily endorsing the policies of secular government. This has arguably provided mechanisms for social change as in the case of the Hussites in Bohemia with resistance to authority justified on the grounds of faith, so allowing the church to become a force for disciplined revolution.

But the role of the church was arguably less constructive in the Balkans because of the fundamental divide across this region, reflecting the Roman legacy of division between Rome and Istanbul in religious practice as well as administration and language. Ecclesiastical organisation by the two churches (Catholic and Orthodox) certainly developed the existing clan and tribal relationships thereby paving the way for the creation of broader national groups and firm state organisation. And the Balkan peoples were able to exploit this once alien ideology and saw a national ecclesiastical establishment as an important factor in political development. However, the boundary line between Orthodox and Catholic churches cut across the Southern Slav lands: Croat independence was furthered by the crown received by King Zvonimir from the hands of the papal nuncio while the Serbs looked to an autonomous Orthodox Church as a means of reducing dependence on Istanbul. But different churches meant different alphabets and different cultural influences separating Croats and Slovenes from Macedonians, Montenegrans and Serbs as regards mentality and national consciousness. The Christian-Moslem divide also lay on South Slav territory with Moslem Slavs in Bosnia, descendants of feudal landowners who embraced Islam at the time of the Turkish onslaught in order to retain their property and social position: their particularly close links with the ruling classes of the Ottoman Empire gave the Arabic/Turkish oriental culture a formidable impact and in effect made the Bosnians a distinct ethnic community. Meanwhile the Orthodox Christians attached increased importance to their church (with its cultural-educational function as well as a spiritual role) as a proxy for the less of independent government and campaigned strongly for the restoration of the Patriarchate of Péc (and with it the independence of the Serbian Orthodox Church). On the other hand the Croats and Slovenes fitted less uneasily into the multilingual Habsburg

Empire with its Catholic ideology, especially when this affiliation brought considerable material advancement. Although the supra-territorial ideal seemed increasingly anachronistic in the late nineteenth century (witness the Grossdeutsche/Kleindeutsche struggle which was resolved in favour of Protestant Prussia acquiring control over one linguistic community) a South Slav state was by no means a foregone conclusion and since its establishment Yugoslavia has been embarrassed by conflict between Croats and Serbs with their rival industrial and political establishments. And this is to say nothing of the problems of boundary delimitation vis-à-vis Albanians, Hungarians and Italians, the former problem arising from Serb migration away from their historic core area and the enigma of Macedonia.

It may also be observed that in most parts of Eastern Europe the Reformation was not a powerful force, being either non-existent or subject to determined Counter-Reformation. The region did not therefore experience the impact of Protestant churches as central agencies in nation building and instead the church remained supra-territorial in outlook. This helps to explain the irreconciliable conflict in Eastern Europe between the multilingual empire and the ethnically-unified nation state. However it would be wrong to regard the church as the overriding force in moulding political structures and ecclesiastical organisation had inevitably to take into account the realities of empire-state relationships. Furthermore the political developments discussed in this chapter were undoubtedly conditioned by economic considerations and it is to the study of settlement and trade patterns that discussion must now turn.

NOTES

1. D.S. Rugg 1978, 'The geography of Eastern Europe' (Lincoln, Nebraska: Cliffs Notes) 32.

2. N.J.G. Pounds and S.S. Ball 1964, 'Core areas and the development of the European states system' Annals Association of American Geographers 54, 24-40. See also J. Breu 1971, 'Emergence of empires in the Danube area' Geoforum 2 (6), 7-19; J.H. Shennan 1974, 'The origins of the modern European state 1450-1725' (London: Hutchinson).

3. R. Bean 1973, 'War and the birth of the nation state' Journal of Economic History 33, 202-221.

4. Ibid. 220.

5. A. Kahan 1973, 'Notes on serfdom in Western and

Eastern Europe' Journal of Economic History 33, 86-99 (quote pp. 91-2). See also D.C. North and R.P. Thomas 1971, 'Rise and fall of the manorial system: a theoretical model' Journal of Economic History 31, 777-803.

6. W. Conze 1979, 'The shaping of the German nation: an historical analysis' vols. 3 and 4, (London: George Prior). See also G. Barraclough ed. 1938, 'Medieval Germany 911-1250: essays by German historians' (Oxford: Blackwell); G. Barraclough 1946, 'Factors in German history' (Oxford: Blackwell); G. Barraclough 1950, 'The medieval empire: idea and reality' (London: Historical Assoc.) F. Bäuml 1969, 'Medieval civilisation in Germany' (London: Thames & Hudson); H. Böhme 1978, 'Introduction to the social-economic history of Germany' (Oxford: Blackwell); C.N.L. Brooke 1964; H. Fichtenau 1957, 'The Carolingian Empire' (Oxford: Blackwell); V. Press 1987, 'The Holy Roman Empire in German history,' E.I. Knouri and T. Scott, eds. 'Politics and society in Reformation Europe' (London: Macmillan) 51-77.

7. S.H. Steinberg 1966, 'The Thirty Years War' and the conflict for European hegemony 1600-1660' (London: Arnold) 2. See also G. Benecke 1978, 'Germany and the Thirty Years War' (London: Arnold); J.V. Pelisvensky 1971, 'The Thirty Year War' (London: Batsford).

8. J.G. Gaghardo 1980, 'Reich and nation: the Holy Roman Empire as idea and reality 1763-1806' (Bloomington: Indiana University Press) viii.

9. S. Vryonis 1967, 'Byzantium and Europe' (London: Thames & Hudson) 424. See also P. Charanis 1953, 'Economic factors in the decline of the Byzantine Empire' Journal of Economic History 13, 412-24; D.M. Nicol 1979, 'The end of the Byzantine Empire' (London: Arnold).

10. S. Vryonis 1967, op.cit. 171.

11. A.H.M. Jones 1971, 27.

12. D.S. Chambers 1970, 'The imperial age of Venice 1380-1580' (London: Thames & Hudson); F.C. Lane 1966, 'Venice and history: collected papers of F.C. Lane' (Baltimore: Johns Hopkins Press); C.T. Smith 1967, 343-69.

13. B. Pullan 1968, 'Crisis and change in the Venetian economy in the sixteenth and seventeenth centuries' (London: Methuen); A. Tenenti 1966, 'Piracy and the decline of Venice 1585-1615' (London: Longman).

14. G. Ostrogorsky 1963-4, 'Byzantium and the South Slavs' Slavonic & East European Review 42, 1-14 (quote p.14).

15. F. Seibt 1970, 'The religious problems', G. Barraclough ed. 83-124 (quote p.86).

16. K. Bosl 1970, 'Political relations between east and west', G. Barraclough ed. 43-82 (quote p.57).

17. Ibid. 61.

18. A.P. Vlasto 1970, 142.

19. K. Bosl 1970, op.cit. (note 16) 71.

20. M. Biskup 1966, 'The role of the order and state of the Teutonic Knights in Prussia and the history of Poland' Polish Western Affairs 7, 337-65.

21. S.H. Thomson 1965, 'Czechoslovakia in European history' (Hamden, Conn.: Archon Books).

22. A.P. Vlasto 1970, 107.

23. R.R. Betts 1946-7, 'The place of the Czech reform movement in the history of Europe' Slavonic & East European Review 25, 373-90; J. M. Klassen 1978, The nobility and the making of the Hussite revolution (Boulder, Col.: East European Monographs); O. Odlozilik 1965, 'The Hussite king: Bohemia in European affairs 1440-1471' (New Brunswick N.J.: Rutgers University Press).

24. A.P. Vlasto 1970, 126.

25. J.S. Skurnowicz 1981, 'Romantic nationalism and liberalism: Joachim Lelewel and the Polish national idea' (Boulder, Col.: East European Monographs). See also M.K. Dziewanowski 1962-3, 'Dualism or trialism: Polish federal traditions' Slavonic & East European Review 41, 442-66; B. Zientara 1970, 'Nationality conflicts in the German-Slavic borderland in the thirteenth-fourteenth centuries and their social scope' Acta Poloniae Historica 22, 207-25.

26. C.A. Macartney 1962, 'Hungary: a short history' (Edinburgh: Edinburgh University Press) 10.

27. Z.L. Kosztolnyik 1981, 'Five eleventh century Hungarian kings: their policies and their relations with Rome' (Boulder, Col.: East European Monographs).

28. P. Teleki 1923, 'The evolution of Hungary and her place in European history' (New York: Macmillan).

29. H. Lenz 1967, 'The German cultural influence in Hungary before the eighteenth century' (Ohio State University: Ph.D. thesis).

30. J.M. Bak and B.K. Kiraly 1982, 'From Hunyadi to Rakoczi: war and society in late Medieval and early Modern Hungary' (New York: Columbia University Press); S. Guldescu 1970, 'The Croatian-Slavonian kingdom 1526-1792' (The Hague: Mouton).

31. R. Browning 1975, 'Byzantium and Bulgaria'

(Berkeley: University of California Press); S.G. Evans 1960, 'A short history of Bulgaria' (London: Lawrence & Wishart); V. Georgiev 1966, 'The genesis of the Balkan peoples' Slavonic & East European Review 44, 285-97; R.F. Hoddinott 1975, 'Bulgaria in antiquity' (London: Benn).

32. D.M. Lang 1976, 'The Bulgarians from pagan times to the Ottoman conquest' (London: Thames & Hudson) 56.

33. Ibid. 69. See also P. Charanis 1976, 'The Slavs Byzantium and the historic significance of the first Bulgarian kingdom' Balkan Studies 17, 5-24; S. Runciman 1930, 'A history of the First Bulgarian Empire' (London: G. Bell).

34. G.D. Hubbard 1946, 'Turning of Turnovo' Economic Geography 22, 109-15.

35. A.P. Vlasto 1970, 221.

36. M. Burr 1949-50, 'The code of Stephen Dusan' Slavonic & East European Review 28, 198-217; F.W. Carter 1969, 'An analysis of the Medieval Serbian oecumene: a theoretical approach' Geografiska Annaler 51B, 39-56.

37. A.P. Vlasto 1970, 227. See also V. Cornish 1935, 'Bosnia: the borderland of Serb and Croat' Geography 20, 260-70; D.A. Dyker 1972, 'The ethnic Muslims of Bosnia: some basic socio-economic data' Slavonic & East European Review 50, 238-56; N. Nikoloff 1956, 'The Bogomil movement: an investigation of the essential characteristics of the 'Bulgarian Heresy' (New York University: Ph.D. thesis); W.S. Vucinich 1949, 'Yugoslavs of the Moslem faith', R.J. Kerner ed. 'Yugoslavia' (Berkeley: University of California Press) 262-3.

38. Quoted by D. Turnock 1980, 'The human geography of the Romanian Carpathians' (Nottingham: Geographical Field Group) 15. See also D.C. Giurescu 1981.

39. G. Cioranescu 1976, 'The political significance of the Thracians' Radio Free Europe Background Report 218.

40. A. Dabinovic 1937-8, 'Early Balkan migrations' Slavonic & East European Review 16, 393-411. See also V. Georgiev 1966, 'The genesis of the Balkan peoples' Ibid 44, 285-97; W.S. Vucinich 1962, 'The nature of Balkan society under Ottoman rule' Slavic Review 4, 597-616.

41. F.W. Hasluck 1929, 'Christianity and Islam under the sultans' (Oxford: Clarendon Press); H. Inalcik 1973, 'The Ottoman Empire: the classical age 1300-1600' (New York: Praeger); V.J. Parry et al. 1976, 'A history of the Ottoman Empire' (Cambridge: Cambridge University Press); D.E. Pitcher 1972, 'An historical geography of the Ottoman

Empire from the earliest times to the end of the sixteenth century' (Leiden: E.J. Brill); S. Shaw 1976, 'History of the Ottoman Empire and modern Turkey' (Cambridge: Cambridge University Press).

42. C.M. Kortpeter 1972, 'Ottoman imperialism during the Reformation: Europe and the Caucasus' (New York: New York University Press) 244.

43. J.C. Dragan 1976, 'We the Thracians and our multimillenary history' (Milan: Nagard) II 137-8.

44. I.M. Kunt 1983, 'The Sultan's servants: the transformation of Ottoman provincial government 1550-1650' (New York: Columbia University Press).

45. P.F. Sugar 1977.

46. Ibid. 166.

47. Ibid. 5. See also A.H. Lybyer 1913, 'The government of the Ottoman Empire in the time of Suleiman the Magnificent' (Cambridge, Mass.: Harvard University Press); N.J. Pantazopoulos 1967, 'Church and law in the Balkan peninsula during Ottoman rule' (Thessaloniki: Institute for Balkan Studies); T. Stoianovich 1953, 'Land tenure and related sectors of the Ottoman economy' Journal of Economic History 13, 398-411.

48. P.F. Sugar 1977, 96.

49. Ibid. 108.

50. G.E. Rothenburg 1959-60, 'The origins of the Austrian military frontier in Croatia' Slavonic & East European Review 38, 493-8.

51. S. Vryonis 1967, 'Byzantium and Europe' (London: Thames & Hudson) 194.

52. F.W. Carter 1977, 'Introduction to the Balkan scene', F.W. Carter ed. 1-24 (quote p. 3-4).

53. P.F. Sugar 1977, 72. See also H. Inalcik 1969, 'Capital formation in the Ottoman Empire' Journal of Economic History 29, 97-140; B. McGowan 1981, 'Economic life in the Ottoman Empire: taxation trade and the struggle for land 1600-1800' (Cambridge: Cambridge University Press).

54. T. Stoianovich 1960.

55. W.G. Endrei 1974, 'English kersey in Eastern Europe with special reference to Hungary' Textile History 5, 90-9.

56. F. Seibt 1970, op.cit. (note 15) 106.

5

Economic Development

The expansive economy of the Middle Ages was evident everywhere in Europe by the year 1000, although the upward trend was probably longest delayed in the east. N.J.G. Pounds considers that the expansion, persistent apart from the recession in the fourteenth century, can be traced through five different indicators.[1] Of prime importance was the system of European states, emerging in the tenth century when Saxony (previously conquered by Charlemagne) supported the first German imperial dynasty. The Czech (Bohemian) and Polish states also made their appearance while the Magyars consolidated their hold on the Pannonian Plain and stirrings of statehood became apparent in the Balkans too. M. Malowist then refers to a politically-explosive eleventh century, with frequent war between emerging states geared to both territorial acquisition and capture of slaves, leading to more stable and enlightened times by the thirteenth century. Bohemia, Hungary and Poland were equally matched with feudal systems already switching from labour services and commodity deliveries (often highly specific in 'service villages' required to meet princely needs for particular agricultural and industrial products) to cash payments.[2] Given a basic security system there emerged a stimulus to clear more land and support a growth of population which was fundamental to Medieval economic growth. If anything, population in Europe grew too quickly and the set-backs of the fourteenth century may be interpreted as a classic Malthusian check. The impact of epidemic disease, along with war and crop failure, seems to have been much greater in the fourteenth and fifteenth centuries than in the three preceding centuries. However, information is particularly sparse for Eastern Europe in view of the limited number of areas which have documentary evidence of any kind relevant to demography, and the implication of this may be that Eastern Europe did not experience any Malthusian check to population in the fourteenth century. The population of Poland is thought to have grown quite steadily at a rate of 0.35 percent per annum from some two million in c. 1250 to reach 7.5 million in the sixteenth century, which would give a density of just twenty-one per square kilometre. Even so this figure is probably quite high in comparison with other parts of Eastern Europe since the estimate of 3.6 million for Hungary at the turn of the fifteenth century means less than twenty people per square kilometre and the five million derived as an estimate from the Ottoman hearth tax of 1520-35 gives less than ten, although account must be taken of the war losses associated with the Ottoman conquest, losses from which Eastern Europe had previously been immune.

The growth of population called for an increased food output and trade in agricultural commodities underpinned a growing urban network, with a large number of new towns established through the twelfth and thirteenth centuries (Figure 5.1). Yet economic growth could not take place at an even rate through Europe. Italy may be considered the key by virtue of the trading links with the Levant which developed under the umbrella of the Byzantine Empire while the Low Countries, fringing the Carolingian Empire, commanded the trade routes extending into the pioneer regions of the British Isles and Scandinavia. There was a close association between the two centres, a commercial axis between southern and northwest Europe: 'from the eleventh century until the commercial revolution of the sixteenth it continued to dominate the trading pattern of Europe and to stimulate business along the routes which diverged from it'.[3] Away from this axis growth was relatively slight with isolation and self-sufficiency more pronounced. Population was relatively low in relation to the agricultural potential and there does not appear to have been sufficient demographic pressure to introduce all the available technology, such as the heavy plough which could have been effective on the heavy clays of Poland. The valuation of dioceses in c. 1300 shows levels of wealth (per unit of area) in part of Italy and the Low Countries at least ten times greater than those prevailing in Eastern Europe. The only exceptions apply in the Czech Lands and in the regions of Pomerania and Saxony to the north where German

Figure 5.1: The economy of Medieval Eastern Europe, c.1500

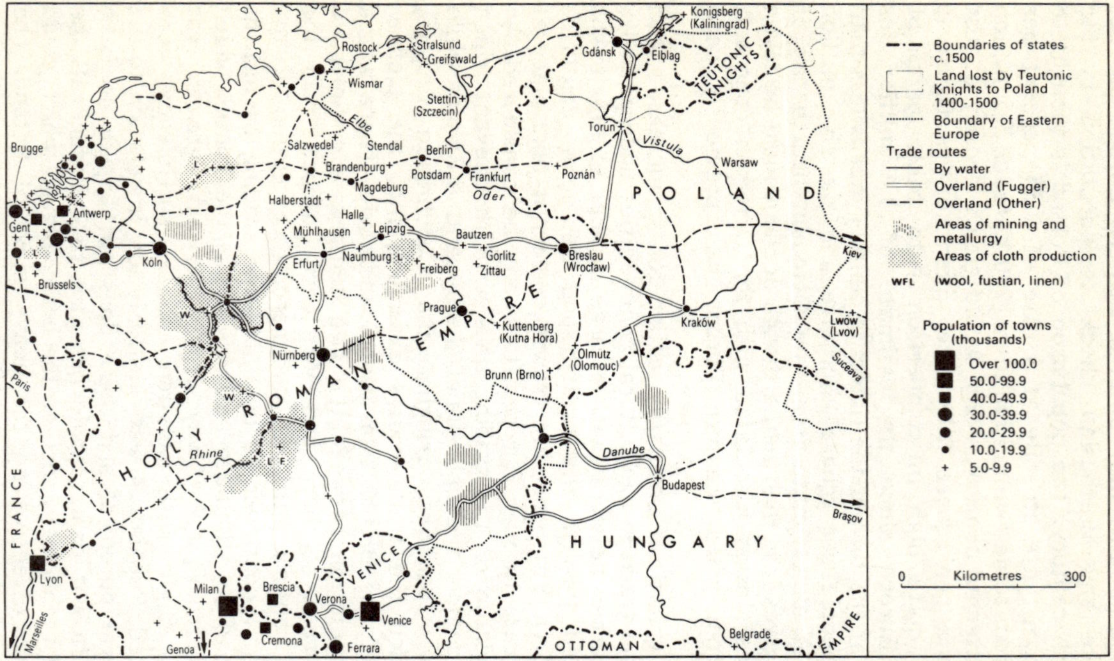

Sources: T. Kraus et al. 1959, Atlas ostliches Mitteleuropa (Bielefeld: Velhangen u. Klasing). Population data from J de Vries 1981, 'Pattern of urbanization in pre-industrial Europe', H. Schmal ed. Patterns of European urbanisation since 1500 (London: Croom Helm) 77-109.

settlement was making a decisive impact.

COLONISATION: NORTH EUROPEAN PLAIN

In Eastern Europe as in the continent as a whole the peasantry comprised the bulk of the population and the most important changes in the human geography arise from a largely unrecorded process of land reclamation which allowed settlements to grow and also permitted the founding of new communities in former virgin territory. The frontiers of settlement were pushed back as people moved from their primary settlements in the valleys to secondary colonies on wooded or moorish interfluves. Of course particularly damp floodplains (as in parts of Poland) on the one hand and poor upland country (like the Harz Mountains) on the other would tend to repel settlement even in the late Medieval period unless there was some particular incentive (like the minerals found in parts of the Harz) to set alongside the decidedly unpromising agricultural potential. Yet while there were local developments occurring in parts of Eastern Europe the core-periphery model, which is frequently applied in the context of modern economic development, may be considered here in the context of settlers from a relatively densely settled 'core' moving into sparsely populated lands to the east. Iberia and Scandinavia may have been affected by long-wave migration but the frontier of Europe *par excellence* certainly lay in the east.

Pounds suggests that the movement to the east, reversing the predominantly westward flow during the Dark Ages, dates from Charlemagne's conquest of Saxony in the late eighth century and the development of trade with the Slavs.[4] But it was between the eleventh and thirteenth centuries that the main colonisation took place: the Elbe was crossed in the twelfth century and the Oder in the thirteenth, with areas like Breslau (Wrocław) and Danzig (Gdansk) colonised by 1300. To some extent the movement was coordinated by landowners who had acquired territory in the east that they wished to exploit: both ecclesiastical and lay lords (like the Archbishop of Bremen and Count Adolf of Holstein respectively) were involved in arranging for colonists to be recruited in the west and then resettled through the agency of middlemen known as *locatores*. C.T. Smith stresses the tremendous amount of organisation required to transfer the peasantry to new settlements and provide equipment to clear forest and build new homes. The size of the movement and high level of planning by the colonising agents differentiates this German settlement from the smaller-scale spontaneous movements of earlier times. 'The locators supplied the floating capital to the migrants while they settled; and it was the locator or his men who recruited settlers and brought them to the site already chosen and prepared. They allocated lands and made themselves responsible for the supply of equipment, seed and even food for the period of the initial settlement. In return they received a holding of land in the village which was often twice the size of the normal peasant allocation and they received it free of tithe or rent'.[5]

Yet the movement has also been seen as an uncoordinated flow by numerous small groups and the instinctive advance of these people into relatively empty lands, where adequate holdings could be taken without burdensome feudal obligations, certainly seems to provide a more realistic perspective than the suggestion of missionary zeal among relatively unsophisticated peoples which flows from the abrasive German slogan of <u>Drang nach Osten</u>. Certainly Slavs would see the migration as one that was as significant for the innovation of new technology (such as the heavy wheeled plough) and the development of trade as it was for the development of peasant colonisation. German political control came a long way behind the initial settlement process and some German settlements in the east never did fall under a German administration, in peacetime at any rate. Initially the Germans settled on empty land, or land reclaimed from forest or marsh. Slavs were not dispossessed but were in many cases integrated into the colonisation process and led by those sections of the native aristocracy amenable to German authority into new lands. The pressure was essentially cultural and economic. Slavs who wished to be assimilated had to accept the German religion (and pay tithe) and also German agricultural methods including the iron plough and three field system. Although the Teutonic Order did not at first allow Germans and Slavs to work side by side, the rule was later relaxed subject to the adoption of progressive farming methods which allowed the natives to be trusted with the heritage of the German peasant.[6] The cultural transformation makes it very difficult to estimate the number of real German settlers. The exercise founders on such imponderables as the ethnic character of villages with German names: many such villages would have contained large numbers of Slavs and would probably have been established as part of a local expansion of settlement by an ethnically mixed community from primary to secondary sites rather than populated from the start by migrants from the west. It may well be that the settlers were less numerous than the natives, as it is estimated by B. Zientara that probably no more than a quarter of a million Germans settled on present Polish territory during the thirteenth and fourteenth centures with some 2,000 people per year leaving the lands west of the Elbe.[7] What is certain is that the colonising movement faltered in the fourteenth century because even if the Black Death did not strike in the east in devastating fashion it certainly reduced population pressure in the west and removed the principal motive for resettlement.

Positive initiative on the Polish side is brought out by the action of the Duke of Wrocław in the early thirteenth century in settling the foothills of the Sudetan Mountains (Sudety). The response came from descendants of Dutch and Flemish settlers on the central reaches of the Elbe and from Franconians in the Ore Mountains (Erzgebirge). Settlement of miners was also sought by Polish nobles and the gold, lead and silver resources of Silesia prompted new settlements at Bytom, Lwowek and Złotoryja while mining of rock salt began at Bochnia and Wieliczka. Privileged groups of settlers were commissioned to search the country for precious metals, usually without success, but at the very least the immigrants (many of them from Goslar and Meissen) brought more advanced technology and the iron industry for example benefitted from the application of water power to bellows and hammers. They also brought with them established principles for negotiating with landowners and these became known collectively in Silesia as 'German law': this does not refer to any general law used in Germany but indicates a code of practice applied to free settlers from the west safeguarding their personal freedom and limiting their obligations to landlords. 'No historian today will necessarily equate settlement according to German law with colonisation by ethnically German immigrants'.[8]

In assessing the relative numerical importance of Germans and Slavs it is important to differentiate between areas lost to German conquest and those lands which remained under Polish administration. In the latter Germans only achieved a majority in parts of Pomerania and Silesia. In rural parts of Great Poland German immigration was hardly noticed and in Masovia even the towns failed to attract significant numbers. The strength of German influence in Pomerania, where the majority was able to push Slavic elements to the very fringes of society, seems to derive from the fact that all social classes were represented in the colonisation process. German clergy and nobility entering Poland (and also Bohemia and Hungary) did not exert any significant cultural influence due to rapid assimilation, but in Pomerania these privileged groups were backed by peasants and townspeople and the assimilation process worked in the opposite direction. Despite the favourable economic trends there must have been antagonism between Poles and Germans, but arguably the sense of unity arising from anti-German sentiment was an important factor in overcoming the fragmentation of the state and thus complementing the ecclesiastical unity of Poland (maintained by the Polish bishops) with a political union of dual territories under the Piasts. 'It may even be that German settlement and the conflicts which emerged from it accelerated the formation of a uniform Polish language and national consciousness'.[9]

FIELD SYSTEMS AND SETTLEMENT PATTERNS

Although considerable variety may be found in areas of Slav settlement the new lands in the east settled by Germans tend to show fairly simple field systems, with large open fields carved up into strips of regular size and shape. On the margins of the Hercynian hill country a common pattern was the *Waldhufen* with each peasant holding consisting of a single long narrow strip which provided crop land and also access to the uncleared forest. The *Hufen* were then taken as basic units for taxation purposes. Similar arrangements applied in areas of heath and marsh. In turn these ideal forms give rise to village types which are easily distinguished with the regular clustered villages in the open field areas taking the form of compact street villages (*Strassendörfer*) with the main street as the focus or *Angerdörfer* where there is grouping around an elongated green. Linear villages with consolidated holdings known variously as *Hagenhufendörfer*, *Marschhufendörfer* or *Waldhufendörfer* may be found in other environments: heath, marsh or forest respectively. Hamlet settlements (*Weiler*) were not common but occurred in certain areas like Mecklenburg through the subdivision of dispersed farms. By contrast in areas of Slav settlement it was suggested by August Meitzen that ethnic differences would give rise to distinctive settlement forms with the Rundling or ring fence village as the characteristic form. This theory seems to draw its inspiration from outdated notions of clear-cut contrasts between German and Slav peoples. J.G. Herder and later G.W.F. Hegel argued that language was a critical factor combining a group of individuals into an organic 'folk' unit. But this view of rival German and Slav civilisations and ideologies has foundered on the more recent revelations of conflict within these groups as much as between them. A democratic Slav society of free men has been compared with a regime of serfdom imposed by German authority but a class system based on an aristocracy (szlachta) has been a fundamental attribute of the Polish state society. Certainly it was a prince and an elite rather than a tribal community of free men that was the crucial factor in the creation of Medieval states and it is evident that the pressures to which minor Slav tribes like the Serbs and Wends were subjected did not arise out of German-Slav antagonism so much as political development by more powerful groups, both German and Slav. 'The conquered Slav inhabitants of these territories were repeatedly sold as slaves to Bohemia and Poland where no more reluctance to purchase and sell Slav prisoners of war was shown than, in an earlier age, was shown by Germans in buying and selling enslaved Scandinavians'.[10] Polish placenames like Pomorzany (Pomeranian) or Prusy (Prussian) suggest settlements founded by the forced planting of groups of war captives, initially distinct but probably quickly assimilated into local society. Thus it may well be unrealistic to anticipate a specifically German or Slav type of house or village: rather than the function of the building or complex, in the context of local resources and available technology should be considered.

Rural settlements in Poland in the twelfth and thirteenth centuries consisted of complexes of individual units known as zrebia, though occasionally the zreb might exist in isolation.[11] Such a unit embraced only arable land and was obtained by each family drawing lots: the meadow and pasture land was held in common. It is generally assumed that the individual fields were square in shape because according to prevailing techniques the field was 'ploughed' twice with an ard, lengthwise and crosswise. The various zrebia in a particular settlement combined together to form a ujazd, a unit of landownership which is encountered initially among church properties in southern Poland during the twelfth century. It was usually within the context of the *ujazd* that agriculture was modernised along the lines of a three field system. Preference for the three field system may be broadly explained in the same way as for Western Europe with rising population requiring the exercise of seigneurial authority to regulate cropping so that maximum production of food could be harmonised carefully with provision of fodder for plough-teams essential for the breakup of the heavy clays.[12] And with the introduction of the heavy plough in place of the *ard* the need for turning space suggested long strips to minimise the amount of land so lost to cultivation. The *lan* therefore replaced the *zreb* as the basic unit of farm land. And growth of population would have required periodic reallocation and a gradual narrowing of the strips even further. The appearance of the three field system was sometimes long delayed and in parts of northern Poland action followed the *włoka* decrees of 1557 (*włoka* relating to a holding in the open fields).[13]

Some open-field villages were established from scratch according to the new pattern at the time of the German colonisation, although the *Waldhufen* villages created in wooded regions with consolidated holdings introduced a distinction that can still be appreciated in certain upland districts of Lublin and Zielona Gora. The open-field system took time to spread across the whole of Poland and did not become a feature of some eastern regions until the sixteenth century: in Lithuania and Podlasie the remeasurement by the *pomiara włoczna* was introduced first on royal property and later on the private estates. Interestingly, however, the introduction of the system did not always produce the irregular nucleated village for cases have been documented to show the persistence of the oval form of the *Rundling* with the small girdle of farmhouses enclosing a common pasture and working arable strips radiating outwards from the settlement. The subsequent emergence of a three field arrangement can then be seen through continuation in the alignment of strips from the original 'central field' into open fields. The traditional form was even perpetuated in some new settlements: notably the regular green villages of Pomerania which in many cases arose through planned settlement under the monasteries. The persistence of the *Rundling* has also been noted along the Elbe valley and interpreted as a response to frontier conditions and consequent insecurity along the old German-Slav ethnic frontier.

Villages seem for the most part to have remained intact right through to the present. A modest reduction of population associated with the Black Death may have led to desertion, perhaps in the Harz Mountains where some abandoned lands have been found with the ridge and furrow pattern generated by the heavy medieval plough plainly in evidence. But most desertions may be best explained through the elimination of small hamlets in a consolidation process that led to the formation of large nucleated settlements with their open fields. However, some attention must be given to the thesis of T. Dunin-Wasowicz that a combination of climatic and economic changes brought about such a change in the drainage system as to promote a substantial shift in settlement from the valleys to the higher ground in the thirteenth century.[14] Some increase in precipitation was involved but the effects were exaggerated by the clearance of woodlands (to provide agricultural land and meet urban demands for timber) which provoked more frequent flooding, and the impact of mineral workings for bog ore and salt. Water-filled depressions form part of the picture of a devastated natural environment and saline waters in Kujawy had a particularly adverse effect on vegetation. New settlements were now founded on higher ground and deforestation pressed ahead in the mountainous areas. Centuries later the rising demand for cereals in the west prompted a land reclamation movement.[15] Dutch settlers advanced up the Elbe, Oder, Notec and Vistula valleys in the sixteenth and seventeenth centuries digging canals and building windmills to help drain marshland and establish model farms.[16] Work seems to have started on the lower Vistula between Gdansk and Torun in the sixteenth century and continued into the eighteenth century on the Oder and Notec.

RURAL SETTLEMENT IN THE BALKANS

Woodland clearance was also taking place on a considerable scale in the Balkans and it is difficult to visualise the open country between Belgrade and Nis as the dense forest that took a week for the Crusaders to cross in the late eleventh century. The need for additional grazing land would have resulted in the clearance of woodland, the Slavs being particularly associated with goat and sheep herding. 'The process of natural seeding was checked continually by the voracity of goats to whose discriminating palates new shoots and young seedlings proved irresistible'.[17] But the timber was also taken for building, smelting and the shipbuilding industry, with the latter's needs responsible for considerable inroads from classical times into the Byzantine, Venetian and Ottoman eras. Forest fires took their toll as did the further destruction carried out for military or security reasons. In many places the loss of the forest cover has been ecologically disastrous with the washing away of much of the soil cover to produce bare rock or at best scrubland and rough pasture. The rural settlement pattern in the Balkans was built around the zadruga: a patriarchal union consisting of several families living in the same house under the authority of a chief (stareisina) and cultivating their land in common. The homestead would be surrounded by its fields, perhaps cleared from the woodland. Perhaps a single zadruga comprised the basic settlement unit, but progressively there seems to have been development to form a cluster of such units, creating first a hamlet and later a larger compact village. The individual homestead might grow in population to over fifty before any resettlement was contemplated. Many of these settlements developed in remote places as a result of insecurity arising from the Bulgarian-Byzantine struggles and later the Turkish advance.

The Romanian Carpathians

Case studies of Medieval rural settlement in the Balkans are not very numerous but the historical geography of agrarian communities in the Romanian Carpathians has been studied closely over the last half century and a fairly clear outline is now available.[18] The village community would appoint a leader (knez) and survey work would be carried out to define its lands in collaboration with representatives of neighbouring groups. Usually the territory would assume an elongated form so as to include all the basic terrain types between valley bottom and mountain top. All this could well have pre-dated the emergence of the Romanian principalities and the necessary authority above the village level would have been provided by the voivode, a ruler of a confederation of village communities. Such local groupings continued to thrive long after the principalities had been formed since the Moldavian prince Dimitrie Cantemir mentions several examples in his Descriptio Moldaviae of 1716. One of them (Vrancea) retained its confederate form until the Second World War, comprising fourteen villages which shared a vast area of mountain grazing administered by a local authority.

An outline of the village economy may begin with emphasis on the importance of the woodland, used as a refuge during times of Tartar or Turkish raiding and cut extensively for fuel and building purposes, thereby giving rise to an entire civilisation du bois. The woodlands also yielded a range of 'secondary products' such as berries (which formed a significant element in the diet) and there was a large wild bee population, enabling the peasants to harvest honey and wax, perhaps from a hive (prisaca) established in a tree trunk. On the other hand there was some fear of the forest (where wild animals were an obvious danger to livestock) expressed in the assumption that without continual cutting the woodlands would overwhelm the community: so right up to modern times the forest has been attacked to frustrate its inexorable advance. It was in the woodlands, in specially-prepared temporary clearings, that animals were grazed: bark would be removed from the base of certain trees and after a drying-out period they would be burnt down to create a small clearing or arsita. But more extensive clearings and corridors would be needed to create permanent arable lands and grazings as population increased. In this case the peasants would instinctively allow the woodland cover to remain on steeply-sloping ground with limited agricultural potential where there was danger of erosion. In their selective approach and in their concern for the quality of the agricultural land created by forest clearance, rather than the commercial value of the timber, the approach of the traditional village community was quite different from the one adopted by the modern timber companies. Trees left standing close to the village would be valued for their leaves and would therefore be pruned in such a way as to maximise the harvest.

Over the years the cleared pasture land (muscel) would occupy a considerable area separating the village from the main stands of woodland. Such land would be put at the disposal of the villagers for grazing but, to allow larger herds to be kept, transhumance techniques were involved to make use of the forests and high mountain pastures in summer and (sometimes) the distant steppes in winter. Traditionally it seems the summer grazing regime stimulated a tremendous sense of liberation, with little attention paid to the boundaries of village lands. Animals were allowed to circulate in the forests and meadows and could only be controlled with difficulty, but growth of population called for more intensive methods and animals were then more carefully controlled. Sheep of course could not be allowed to wander freely at any time in view of the threat from wild animals: they were always shepherded and well-guarded at night in suitable enclosures. The site used for the home enclosure would change, perhaps when the ground became excessively muddy or when temporary homes were needed for seasonal use in the case of grazings that were situated a long way from the village. Various regional names are used for such temporary settlements today, including *odai*, *salas* and *tîrle*. For social reasons outlying huts would be arranged in small groups and their importance tended to increase by the practice of bringing livestock out to the haystores on the hills rather than transporting the fodder down to the village. There was a long-standing convention whereby newly-married couples occupied the temporary farmsteads and gradually by long-term occupance they might convert the settlement into a permanent habitation: a group of *tîrlele* would then become a *catun*, indicating a change in the pattern of occupance rather than in morphology. The hamlet of Lepsa, for instance, is known to have developed from a summer pasture station to Tulnici in Vrancea and other settlements in the district may well have developed in this way. In architectural terms the houses in the areas of dispersed settlement were little different from those in the village cores, but in parts of the Transylvanian Alps isolated farmsteads were built so that a cluster of buildings would almost completely surround a small courtyard, providing both convenience and security in wintertime. Several footnotes must be added to this simple picture however. First, dispersal did not occur everywhere and nucleation, albeit in a linear form, might well persist where the higher ground was unsuitable for cropping, where security or cultural factors were inhibiting or where governments kept the people together for ease of administration and tax collecting. Secondly, the timing of these changes is uncertain and the explosion of permanent settlement, along with subsequent attempts to consolidate for administrative convenience, may have been most prominent in modern times when population evidently increased more rapidly and when government widened its role. Thirdly, a distinction should always be drawn between the occupation of outlying pastures, where villagers established their own cottages and gardens, and the high mountain pastures well above the limits of cultivation where there would be no evolution towards permanent settlement and where the pasture station (stîna) would be worked usually on a community basis.

As regards cropping and haymaking, this has traditionally tended to occupy no more than one third of the land close to the village. The best grass would be reserved for haymaking, protected by simple wooden enclosures that would later be erected around the individual haystacks. Cropping first relied on a very simple wooden plough (working both along and across each surface) or wooden hoe and would follow a shifting pattern with each piece of land being worked for three seasons. The size of these temporary allotments increased with the growth of population leading to some allocation of strips to the various families for their exclusive use while access to the land beyond was secured by corridors that acted as rights of way. The cropping zone would be guarded by fences to prevent incursions by livestock although initially the shifting system continued. But it appears that, as with the infield systems in other parts of Europe, the cropping area became stabilised on what was found by trial and error to be the best land for continuous cultivation. Strips would then be held in perpetuity, to be handed down through the generations, although common grazing rights after the harvest might still be respected. And of course the bulk of the land, apart from the arable strips and small enclosures for vines and fruit trees, remained permanently available for community use. Hence the infield-outfield system: a permanently cultivated infield, with suitable methods evolved to maintain fertility, leaving outfield cultivated on an *ad hoc* basis as need arose and progressively incorporated into the infield as the growth of population required. The pastoral community, organised on egalitarian lines, thus adapted progressively to increasing population pressure on land with substantial variations in quality and accessibility. On these 'outfield' lands, where the resources at first seemed inexhaustible, everyone had the right to use whatever land was genuinely needed. Clearings in the forest would be made on a private basis and although the family concerned would not actually own the land it was accepted that they alone had the use of it: hence the term stapanîre locureasca indicating the status of occupier of a particular parcel of community land. Such land could be transferred from one family to another, but it was the labour in preparing the land for agriculture that was bought and sold (along with the crops and buildings established on it) and not the ownership rights. However, it was understood that each family would take only the land required for its own subsistence and clearings were limited by custom to the distance that an axe could be thrown. If the peasant erected an enclosure or house in a position that the community considered inappropriate there would be pressure brought to bear to bring about relocation and as a last resort buildings and fences could be pulled down. The greatest friction seems to have arisen over mills because of the danger that individual families might try and monopolise certain water courses.

However, this Naturalwirtschaft, evolved by a subsistence community, was transformed by commercial forces expressed through the money economy and a market system. Some peasants then sought to generate surpluses in cereals, charcoal, honey, leather and other commodities by making greater use of the communal lands: carving out more clearings and allotments for the exploitation of which some non-family labour might be used. Land thus came to be regarded increasingly as private property and as the acquisitive peasants began to form a significant group within the village community it became difficult for the assembly to oppose them. Moreover the united stand previously taken against infiltration by strangers broke down in the face of outsiders able to buy their way into an inheritance under the cover of fraternisation. Indeed over a period of years an outsider could establish himself in a powerful position in a former free village community by using various illegal methods, including intimidation and violence, to reduce free peasants to servile status. Once again timing is uncertain but it seems that from the seventeenth century onwards there was a trend towards servility on the part of many formerly free peasants. It is not difficult to imagine such peasants binding themselves to perform certain duties for a wealthy farmer who had made advances to them during a famine or some similar adversity. This would account for the many cases where just a part of the village community was reduced to servile status by 1864, the year of emanicipation in Romania. However, within the ranks of the free peasantry there would be increasing contrasts as more and more of the village lands became allocated to individual families, culminating in a situation where (as in Bucovina) holdings consisted of long strips extending from the river to the mountain top. However, the mountains remained a relatively free area by comparison with the lowlands. This is evident from the 1912 census which enquired into the status of families in 1864 and the extent to which they had received land subsequently. It may seem strange that so many free villages existed in the Carpathian core areas of the Moldavian and Wallachian states. However, it was possible to exploit the free communities by fiscal means and it was in the devastated lowlands, reconquered from the nomads, that feudal dues were levied.

The island of Brac, Dalmatia

In Dalmatia the impact of the Venetians and subsequently the Turks is well brought out by F.W. Carter in the context of Brac.[19] This is an island with a Latin origin, related to the flight of refugees from Salona following the destruction of the city by Slavs in 614. But the Romanised population, formally under Byzantine protection, experienced some immigration by Slavs from the Neretva area of the mainland and it was this community of Neretljani which the Venetians encountered when they first occupied the island in 1000. Although commerce was now encouraged as a supplement to a basically agricultural economy the changing political control of the island made for instability and the problem of piracy increased. The bulk of the population therefore continued to live in the interior: 'constant fear of attack from either the Venetian galleys or from marauding mainland pirates meant that no stable settlements were developed along the coast'.[20] A fifteenth century poet suggests a population of some 6,000 in 1405 concentrated in twelve inland villages. However, a further spell of Venetian rule began in 1420 and that, combined with the defeat of the pirates based at Omis in 1444, stimulated migration to the coastlands of Brac where in addition to commerce and fishing there were opportunities to diversify agriculture by establishing vineyards. This was the time that the basis of the present settlement pattern was created. Evidently Venetian officials encountered some opposition to their plans for more intensive farming and it was necessary to take legal sanctions to restrict the area that could be devoted to the traditional cattle-rearing economy. Vines did particularly well on the south-facing slopes around Bol where land was owned by the Bishop of Hvar and there was a considerable export to Venice. Figs were also in surplus but cereals and olives were generally insufficient to meet the needs of the islanders.

New challenges emerged however through the Turkish expansion to the Dalmatian coast. Further refugees crossed to the islands yet, despite this net in-migration, losses through plague and shipwreck reduced the population in the mid-sixteenth century to little more than half the 1405 level. Further migration was therefore encouraged and the population now recovered quite dramatically to exceed five thousand in 1682 and to reach eleven thousand when Venetian rule ended in 1792. Travellers point to a continuation of established trends in agriculture with the livestock sector declining not only in relation to cereals, figs, olives and vines (the latter enjoying a particularly high reputation) but also in comparison with other parts of Dalmatia. Thus, once security and a commercial infrastructure was provided agriculture could modernise with the appearance of patterns of specialisation which survived right up to the phylloxera epidemic at the beginning of the twentieth century. The Brac population, standing at almost 25,000 in 1900, then suffered further losses as disillusioned farmers began to emigrate to the New World.

MEDIEVAL INDUSTRY

The conventional view of Medieval manufacturing is one of small-scale enterprise, but with considerable growth of production, increasing specialisation and quality control maintained through the urban guilds. Capital was in short supply and few craftsmen made real fortunes. With the growth of towns manufacturing seems to have shifted from a rural to an urban base, in sympathy with a growth of commerce which called for a close association between manufacturing and markets. However, the monopoly of the towns was never complete for some activities such as quarrying would be mainly rural. And even though towns would naturally concentrate on working the stone nearest to hand (or perhaps use locally-produced bricks as at Danzig with its Brick-Gothic architecture) there would still be considerable manufacturing for domestic or local village consumption. Furthermore in the later Medieval years the towns lost much of the pre-eminence they had previously enjoyed. For it is argued that the guilds failed to adjust to the growing demand for medium quality goods (as opposed to luxury goods) while the rural manufacturer was stimulated by the pressure to supplement a meagre income from agriculture, especially in mountainous country like the borderlands of Bohemia and Saxony. Opportunities also arose in the countryside to install the simple water-powered machinery developed for milling corn and various other industrial processes such as blowing air (in iron furnaces), crushing ore, fulling cloth and operating forge hammers. Underlying this trend was a further growth in population after the decline, or at any rate stagnation, of the fourteenth century which pushed colonists into agriculturally marginal environments and gave rise to a disposition to work in ancillary industries for meagre rewards.

In the sixteenth and seventeenth centuries cloth was being sent from Bohemia and Saxony to Hungary and Poland in exchange for foodstuffs, thereby underlining the importance of manufacturing for upland areas with limited agricultural resources, especially when a rapid growth of population was taking place. F.F. Mendels sees the industry as a positive response to population increase and one which may well have been crucial for the emergence of industrial regions over the longer term, with the embarrassment of demographic pressure stimulating effort in job creation right up to the commencement of the factory era.[21] Growth of population in sixteenth century Lusatia therefore induced a linen industry in Zittau, an area physically well suited to the production of flax. The linen hall (Leinwandhaus) erected in the town in 1658 underlines the role of Zittau in organising a rural industry which extended southwards into Bohemia. Cloth was sent to various parts of Germany (Augsburg, Hamburg and Nürnberg) as well as to Hungary and it seems that the recruitment of villagers as purchasers for the Bavarian trading houses introduced an element of competition which led to the village 'interlopers' being regarded somewhat disparagingly in Zittau. In Vogtland on the other hand the stimulus to industry arose earlier for it was in the fourteenth and fifteenth centuries that woollen cloth production started, evidently as a replacement industry when the mines in the Ore Mountains were worked out. The transition may have been eased by the passage of merchants through Plauen, the main oranganising centre, on their journeyings between northern Italy and Leipzig. The industry successfully diversified over the centuries with the first shift (to worsted production) achieved in the seventeenth century in response to English and Flemish competition.

A slightly different perspective is offered by H. Kisch who traces the development of the textile industry in Silesia during the sixteenth and seventeenth centuries when locally-produced linen cloth emerged from obscurity to enjoy an unchallenged position in world markets.[22] The lands north of the Sudeten Mountains were most suitable for flax growing and merchants won the approval of the feudal landowners to transform the rural economy from self-sufficiency to production for the market, organised from Greiffenburg (Gryfow), Jauer (Jawor) and Landeshut (Kamienna Gora). The urban guilds were not responsive to the opportunities, and in any case were constrained by a shortage of timber (needed as a fuel in the bleaching process) and instead there was a sort of colonial penetration with the merchants exploiting the skills of servile labourers and thereby enabling the lords to enlarge their feudal revenues because they could now draw cash payments from the proletarianised peasantry while devoting the demesne land to cash cropping. The industry was depressed by the Thirty Years War and by the Counter-reformation which drove Protestants westwards to Lusatia but the pendulum swung in the opposite direction after Prussia's annexation of Silesia and Protestants began to move back into the province.

Metallurgy and mining

In the iron industry there were relatively heavy capital demands and the relationship with marginal agriculture is not so easy to demonstrate. Production was tied to rural areas through the remoteness of some of the newly-discovered ore bodies. Production of iron seems to have been widespread in the northern half of Eastern Europe where a series of technological innovations may be noted. The water-powered bloomery made its appearance on the northern borders of Slovenia in the thirteenth century (related to the Austrian industry of Carinthia and Styria) and spread northeastwards to Slovakia and Silesia. Some three centuries later the blast furnace was diffused along roughly the same route, although the use of this more sophisticated equipment was extremely limited before the eighteenth century. The innovations relaced the simple wind-furnace which could very easily be built and then abandoned when pockets of ore were exhausted: slag found in the Holy Cross Mountains of Poland bears an ample testimony to these forgiae errantes built, provided there was some wood fuel available, near to small ore bodies that in later times would have been overlooked.

Where more precious metals were involved rulers would normally welcome skilled foreign workers and take some initiatives in developing a legal framework in which the miners would enjoy a suitably privileged status. A distinction between surface rights and mineral rights to land was a useful advance which allowed capitalists like the Fuggers, Paumartners and Welsers of Slovakia to gain control of ore bodies apart from surface land with its superfluous feudal obligations and responsibilities. Where minerals were found close to the surface there would be some inevitable disturbance of agriculture through the churning over of ground and the construction of artificial channels to supply or evacuate water, so clearly progress in ore production would be conditional on privileges which would give priority to the miners over agricultural interests. Privileges were embodied in the 'Laws' of Jihlava (Ger. Iglau) in Bohemia: first codified in 1249 they were subsequently adopted, perhaps with some modifications, throughout Eastern Europe. Most of the miners were German and the growth of mining communities in the Carpathians (such as Banska Bystrica/Neusohl, Banska Stiavnica/Schemnitz and Kremnica/Kremnitz in Slovakia), the Czech-Moravian Hills (Kutna Hora/Kuttenberg and Pribram), the Ore Mountains (Freiberg in Saxony) and even the Balkans (Novo Brdo) may be seen as part of the eastward colonisation of Germans already discussed at the agricultural level. It was incidentally at the silver-mining settlement of Freiberg where the earliest known mining school (Bergakademie) was founded and where the doctor Georgius Agricola studied the mining industry and collected information for his celebrated sixteenth century work De Re Metallica. Mining could be immensely profitable in the late Medieval period. This can be seen through the fortune accumulated by Jan Thurzo at Kutna Hora where silver mining (yielding up to ten tonnes of silver per annum) was controlled by the Bohemian crown and some metal used by the royal mint. In Slovakia too royal interest, this time on the part of the Hungarian kings, was sustained but the scale of production by the sixteenth century was such that considerable supplies of silver and copper could be marketed in the west at places like Antwerp (reached by the Baltic), Nürnberg and Venice. Indeed it could be argued that the upward trend in prices in the sixteenth century was initially related as much to silver from Eastern Europe as to bullion from the New World.

In view of the difficulties in moving bulky minerals overland it was desirable to smelt ore close to the mines and normally this was even more appropriate in view of the forested nature of most upland country which implied a ready supply of fuel. Indeed at the major smelting centres such as Kutna Hora charcoal burning was a major activity in itself. Even so, transport of the refined metal was a lengthy operation particularly in the Balkans where convoys of pack animals negotiated the rugged country of the Dinaric Alps to reach Dubrovnik or Split, the principal shipping points for Italy. It was unfortunate that the Ottoman conquests destabilised the industry (the Fuggers for example withdrew eventually from Slovakia after the Turkish victory at Mohacs in 1526 though their action was partly due to competition from New World silver), but further north mining was more continuous and was constrained only in the modern period through the exhaustion of reserves. Fourteenth century depopulation had a generally depressing effect on European mining for the loss of momentum in forest clearance and the conversion of land to agriculture meant fewer strikes of new mineral resources. However, the setbacks were not so marked in Bohemia and Hungary and these parts of Eastern Europe were well-placed to take advantage of the rising commodity prices of the late fifteenth century. Rising prices allowed mining to become more capital intensive and more sophisticated pumping systems could now extend mining to depths previously considered quite out of the question.[23] Waterwheels or treadmills could work a series of simple lift pumps with subsequent refinements introduced through the modified Arabian chain-bucket pump and by the use of drainage levels too. Ore processing was also improved through larger water-hammers to crush the ore and the employment of pairs of bellows in tandem to allow higher furnace temperatures. The result was a dramatic increase in silver output in Bohemia, Hungary and Saxony at the turn of the fifteenth century. Although silver was a key product it should not be overlooked that considerable amounts of copper and tin were produced. Copper output was about 2500 tonnes of metal in the sixteenth century, coming from Banska

Bystrica in Slovakia and Mansfeld in the Harz Mountains while the smaller tin production came mainly from Bohemia (330t) and Saxony (550t). The towns provided an essential part of the infrastructure for trade but where they were small it was common for periodic fairs to assume particular importance. This can be seen at both Gniezno and Poznan and, most significantly, at Leipzig which was very important in the fifteenth century.

The case of Poland

The main interest has attached to salt production and also to the galena/silver ores found on the borders of Little Poland and Silesia (Olkusz and Sławkow on the Polish side of the border and Beuthen (Bytom) and Tarnowitz (Tarnowskie Gory) on the Silesian side).[24] Salt production seems to have enjoyed a relatively uneventful history. Since the thirteenth century the industry was the monopoly of the king, though workings might be leased from time to time, and output is thought to have increased from some 20,000 tonnes in the sixteenth century to 37,000 in the mid-seventeenth century.[25] The salt mines of Bochnia and Wieliczka near Krakow and the salt springs of Drahobycz and Przemysl) in Ruthenia catered mainly for the domestic market in Poland, though there was some history of trade with Moravia, Silesia and Slovakia and the workings were a significant economic asset for Austria following the partition of Poland. Indeed the rock salt mines have been described as Poland's greatest industrial enterprise prior to the nineteenth century. Originally discovered in the thirteenth century (prior to which a tradition of salt production from springs dates back to the Neolithic) the mines constituted a state enterprise and made an important contribution to the royal treasury. A virtual monopoly was created through control of the Ruthenia salines and of the salt boiling industry around Krakow (using surface waters which had penetrated the mines). Foreign salt, some from other parts of Eastern Europe (Halle in Saxony) and some from further afield including France and Spain, was displaced from Great Poland and Kujawy in the fifteenth century, while market areas were carved out for the two principal domestic suppliers (Bochnia-Wieliczka and Ruthenia). By contrast lead production fluctuated quite considerably, although the general trend was again upwards from 200-500t per annum in the thirteenth century and 2000-3000 in the sixteenth and seventeenth.

Capital investment was particularly important in the lead industry as initial development at low cost by hundreds of small companies gave way to consolidation when drainage works in the mines became crucial. Interest was taken in mining by Polish kings, nobles and clerics, the latter prominent in the thirteenth and fourteenth centuries through the Italian gallici who appeared in Krakow as agents transferring church taxes to Rome. But the Krakow merchants were most active in the thirteenth century because their trade privileges enabled them to export metal by the Vistula waterway: many of them would take up the position of leaseholder (Bergmeister/zupnik) of royal mines, particularly in the Olkusz area where mining was backed up by a growth of smelting, supported by the considerable woodland cover. The Krakow merchants were also involved in the smelting of copper ores from Slovakia, with the Mogita site near Krakow mentioned in the late fourteenth and early fifteenth centuries. The association was a logical one in view of the export of Slovak copper northwards along the Vistula. The contacts between Poland and Slovakia appear to have grown in the fifteenth century because of a growth in demand for lead in connection with the saigern technique of extracting silver. As a major European source of lead (with competition only from Carinthia and the Harz Mountains) Poland was now able to export more widely to centres of silver production particularly in view of the silver content of the Polish ore. Lead was sent south to Banska Bystrica in Slovakia, where the Saigerhütte was mentioned in the late fifteenth century and also to Kremnica and Banska Stiavnica, often conveyed in the same carts as were used to take copper to Poland for transfer to the Vistula waterway. Other markets existed in Bohemia (Jachymov and Kutna Hora), Saxony (Freiberg) and Thuringia while the large number of small smelting companies (Saigergesellschaften) near Nürnberg resulted in a growth of investment in mining by merchants from this town. Indeed Nürnberg merchants furnish the earliest evidence of investment in drainage works in the heavily-watered Polish lead mines. The use of horse power 'round the clock' was found to be too expensive and the excavation of special drainage galleries or soughs was therefore unavoidable. Krakow interests in the Polish mining did, however, persist and the late fifteenth century furnishes an interesting case of a partnership between the Turzon family of Krakow and the Fuggers: this embraced workings not only in Poland (with drainage galleries opened up at Olkusz and Trzebenia) but also in the Harz Mountains and Slovakia, the latter brought into closer contact with Poland by means of a new road over the Carpathians.

Other industries

The glass industry demonstrated considerable capacity for growth in the shape of large-scale production.[26] Heavy timber consumption gave prominence to mountain districts like northern slopes of the Ore Mountains which spread later to the southern Bohemian side of the range. Small craft enterprises gave way to the establishment of a larger unit at Schleusingen (Langenbach) which operated from 1525 to 1589. It was founded by a Swabian and employed some thirty people in the 1560s, giving rise to a greatly expanded settlement at Langenbach. Progress at this time was stimulated by the considerable demand in the Low Countries and also by a rapid technical advance involving glass ovens (combining smelting and cooling) and also glass cutters. On the other hand the development of industry along capitalist lines was impeded by the powers of the landowners who were able to impose taxes and modify timber prices as well. For the industry does not appear to have developed with any aristocratic or princely backing and middle-class entrepreneurs had to negotiate a Privileg with the feudal authorities. The Thirty Years War imposed a heavy check on progress and although market demand (in Poland, Russia and the west) was stimulative in the late seventeenth century, when Fehrenbach and Lauscha (near Langenbach) are mentioned, the high prices charged for the dwindling wood supply prevented further growth in the Ore Mountains. Thereafter the Bohemian side of the mountains became more prominent, along with the Sudeten Mountains to the east.

URBAN DEVELOPMENT

In contrast to the Roman towns which were largely concerned with administration and the accommodation of the military, the Medieval towns of Europe were additionally occupied with commercial functions. Moreover the citizens of towns were relatively free and were not burdened by feudal obligations: thus they could take many decisions over occupation, migration or education without consulting higher authority. However Eastern Europe shared in this development only to a modest degree. There were many precedents for urban development in view of the extension of the Roman Empire into Pannonia and the Balkans but most Roman towns were simply legionary forts with canabae or trader settlements alongside. They suffered badly during the succession of invasions which accompanied and followed the demise of the empire. Although Justinian founded or restored a number of towns in the Balkans (particularly Macedonia along with Epirus and Thrace) in his attempts to reconquer the mountainous interior, urban life seems to have disappeared apart from the sheltered Adriatic ports of Ragusa (Dubrovnik) and Split: Ragusa was built on a small island and at Split defences like Diocletian's palace provided some security. On the other hand beyond the Danube there was no tradition of urbanisation at all and it is necessary to envisage the more or less spontaneous emergence of small settlement nuclei as itinerant merchants gathered or where the Germanic or Slav tribes established their strongholds. Early emperors would build castles or found monasteries, all of which were seeds that might germinate and flourish as true urban establishments. Functions might then combine for convenience: traders might agree on a gathering place or wik outside a monastery in preference to a completely isolated position, or else a function of occasional market centre might be assumed by a village. But in view of the importance of security it is likely that the castles were particularly important in mapping out the fundamentals of the urban geography. Tribal fortresses, the Burgwalle of the Germans (very numerous in Brandenburg) and the grody or hrady of the Slavs were essential as refuges during wars and even in peacetime peasants probably felt highly insecure without shelter in the immediate vicinity. Covering just a few hectares the forts usually occupied low-lying sites with river and marsh for protection supplemented by banks, palisades and well-guarded entrances. Whole systems of such forts might develop like the Polish grody, along the line of the Notec separating Great Poland from Pomerania.[27]

The forts of Great Moravia may well constitute a plausible model proto-town for Eastern Europe. The strongholds, like the one at Prague (on the site now occupied by the Hradcany Castle) observed by a tenth century Jewish traveller, would attract groups of craftsmen and traders living close enough to enjoy their protection. A small unplanned town might therefore develop spontaneously as an appendage of the castle, although where the grod was awkwardly situated the commercial quarter might be situated some distance away, perhaps on the opposite bank of a river as at Poznan and Wrocław. Nevertheless the connection was usually close and it is no accident that the Slavonic words grod and gorod are used to indicate not only a ruler's stronghold but also a town. Equally, however, there might be a planned influx of privileged western settlers that would typically give rise to a new planned town with its orderly street system focussing on to the market place. This can be seen at Krakow where the gorod (Wawel) overlooking the Vistula was complemented by both a Slav town, where privileges developed from local custom, and a planned town (1257) established zu germanische Recht (under German law, usually modelled on the practice of Lübeck or Magdeburg) which attracted settlers and merchants from the west. Such a sequence can be seen in the Czech Lands (like the Staré Mesto and Nove Mesto) emerging under the shade of the Hradcany and in Germany where the terms Altstadt and Neustadt differentiate the early trading colony from the planned town in Magdeburg or Stettin (Szczecin), although further diversification would arise from ecclesiastical as well as castle precincts.

The town evidently became a fairly standardised institution in the Medieval period by virtue of the export eastwards of German standards in law and planning. Many new towns were founded contemporaneously with the colonising movement for there was a commercial and spiritual need for central places to say nothing of the political advantages for the emerging Slav states of combining administative, ecclesiastical, economic and military functions at accessible and well-defended sites. But it is often difficult to establish whether the new towns (often dated by the year when German law was introduced) developed out of small rural settlements or whether there were some limited central place functions before the formal establishment of the town. Frankfurt/Oder was a town of German colonists (1226) with handicrafts and an important herring trade but was the earlier Slav settlement of the eleventh and twelfth centuries purely rural in character?[28] In the case of the grody established along Mieske Elbe frontier there appear to have been administrative and commercial functions supervised by the king's representative (zupan).[29] Such centres, along with others at Gdansk,

Gniezne, Kołobrzeg, Opole and Poznan, would have developed out of open tribal settlements to become part of the European trading system during the eleventh and twelfth centuries with market and merchant quarters in addition to the princely stronghold.[30] Thus at Gdansk it appears that while the German colony of the 1220s (under Lubeck law) was situated adjacent to a Slav rural settlement of ninth century origin there was also a princely stronghold, probably established by Miesko in c.975, on an island site at the confluence of the Motlawa and Vistula, where a handicraft quarter also developed by the end of the eleventh century.[31] German influence in this part of Gdansk came only in the fourteenth century when the Teutonic Knights dislodged the Poles in hand to hand fighting and went on to build the late Medieval castle of Danzig on the old princely site.

Apart from Danzig/Gdansk the largest towns of Eastern Europe were probably the Baltic ports of Stralsund and Wismar and such inland centres as Breslau/Wrocław, Erfurt, Krakow and Magdeburg. It is no surprise that this short list should pick out inland centres associated with the börde country of Germany and the equivalent loessic land in Poland at the foot of the Hercynian mountain system. For both ease of movement and agricultural potential these lands stand in sharp contrast to the heavy clay lands and marshy valleys to the north. Some towns gained additional importance through intersecting routes from the Alps and Black Sea. But although many of the more prominent towns were associated with long distance trade routes across Eastern Europe M. Malowist asserts that 'one cannot consider commercial transit as the principal factor in the great development of economic, especially urban life, in central Eastern Europe in the late Middle Ages'.[32] It was essentially the local resources that stimulated urban growth and attracted the merchants, many of them Armenians, Greeks and Jews. This was especially true in Bohemia and the whole Carpathians zone where mining was a most lucrative business and to a lesser extent along the Baltic where the relative easy movement made the potential of the farms and forests unusually attractive. Following the West European experience it is likely that many of the Medieval towns of Eastern Europe rested on very slender urban foundations. Many were entirely new in the colonial period with no history of administrative or commercial functions. Some of them certainly prospered but others were constrained from the start by vigorous local competition and subsequently by the faltering pace of colonisation, while in modern times improved circulation has given progressively greater advantages to the best placed towns. The less successful towns were mainly agricultural in function (a situation best exemplified by the towns of the Pannonian Plain), although all towns produced some of their own food by cultivating land for field crops, orchards or vineyards within a few kilometres of the walls.[33]

In several respects the mining towns are a distinct category as D. Molenda has amply demonstrated.[34] They often possessed special privileges (mining rights and tax exemptions) in addition to the normal municipal rights and the legal status of Freiberg and Jihlava in the middle of the thirteenth century became a model for other towns which either received a mining charter to supplement their existing one or else (as was usual for towns established from the late fifteenth century onwards) gained it at the outset. The generous privileges were, of course, justified in the interest of more intensive economic development and very appropriately so because in some areas mining was the initial stimulus for urban development. This applies in Silesia where the mining towns of Goldberg (Zlotoryja), Lowenburg (Lwowek) and Troppau (Opava) were established in the early thirteenth century and also in the Ore Mountains where the Wettin dukes played a crucial role in urban development in the late fifteenth and early sixteenth centuries. Another point concerns the physical aspects of development, for growth was inevitably tied to those particular places where mining could develop. Towns that were to be centres for mining regions enjoyed some flexibility in site selection and covenient layouts were therefore possible for Annaberg and Marienburg in the Saxon Ore Mountains as well as Banska Bystrica in Slovakia. On the other hand Banska Stiavnica Bochnia and Jachymov lay in narrow mountain valleys with houses forced to climb up steep hillsides. The difficulties were all the greater where spontaneous development of mines and houses had already taken place, as at Beuthen, Freiberg, Novo Brdo and Wieliczka. 'Altenberg in the region of tin ore mining was a chaotic medley of residential houses, pits, washers and foundries' and at Schneeberg it was necessary to try and put some order into more than two decades of uncontrolled development.[35] This is to say nothing of the environmental problems arising through the fumes and waste materials from smelters as well as the polluted water and subsidence problems related to the underground workings.

Population was of course extremely unstable. Kutna Hora experienced incredibly rapid development at the end of the thirteenth century when the sbeh ke Kutna (rush to Kutna) generated a town of 18,000 people. This performance was exceeded in the early sixteenth century by Jachymov which reached 20,000 in the 1530s. Migrations brought together varied mixtures of nationalities. The mining towns of Bohemia and Slovakia accommodated many Germans (from Bavaria, Franconia, Pomerania, the Rhineland, Saxony and the Tyrol) but there were also Hungarians, Poles and Swedes as well as native Slavs. And in Silesia some Dalmatians and Italians were present too. But the reverse process was also experienced: Jachymov was reduced to just 2,000 in 1600 and it is also recorded that depression in Olkusz at the end of the fifteenth century provoked a migration of three-quarters of the town's population to seek work elsewhere. Even Kutna Hora suffered from the decline of mining from the mid-seventeenth century and was reduced to a small provincial township by the nineteenth century. There are, however, some cases where the mining towns were able to assume marketing or manufacturing functions: Tarnowitz became an important regional trading centre on the borders of Little Poland and Silesia while the textile industry sustained such towns as Jihlava in Bohemia and Lowenburg in Silesia. Finally the mining towns developed their own society. Usually in control was a group of the more successful businessmen with interests in mines and smelters, as well as local forests (supplying fuel) and trade. In some cases royal officials might be included, as at Kutna Hora where they were responsible for the management of the mines, foundries and mints. And although the ownership of building plots and houses was a secondary consideration to the mining and related installations the wealthy families normally owned the best land in the centre of the town. However, the increasing complexity of mining meant that in the fifteenth and sixteenth centuries control tended to rest with outside capitalists: 'their investment became the precondition of the continued operation of mines and foundries and this in turn made them obtain appropriate privileges from the mining authority which freed them from the obligation of taking the town's citizenship'.[36] This can be seen in Banska Bystrica which became entirely dependent on companies like the Fuggers and Turzons and at Olkusz, first controlled by Krakow merchants and later by aristocratic businessmen. The inevitable result was a loss of power and prestige by the town administration as its functions were reduced virtually to labour supply. The most numerous social group comprised the workers and small contractors, the more successful of which might well progress into the ruling group and 'compensate' for the demise of some wealthy contractors ruined by mining disasters or bad business decisions. Finally there were the casual workers and the 'gentlemen of the road' who formed a 'restless mobile and turbulent group susceptible to radical slogans'.[37] They would normally be the first to leave in a depression, partly due to their mobile disposition and partly from discrimination against them by municipal authorities at times of stress.

Poland: location, ecology and hierarchy

Here as elsewhere the formal recognition of urban status involved an act of location 'which separated a settlement from the ducal administration and judiciary and brought its population under the homogenous jurisdiction of German law'.[38] This legal differentiation first occurred in 1223 in a privilege granted by the Bishop of Wrocław to the locator of Ujazd. But the act of 'location' was essentially a legal formality and did not necessarily imply the creation of a functionally urban settlement from scratch: *de facto* urban settlements already existed in many cases, with both a fortress (*grod*) and a suburb (*podgrodzie*) inhabited by handicraftsmen and traders. There would be a complex pattern of landownership involving lords and ecclesiastical institutions, although foreign merchants might be granted autonomy (under the direct supervision of a lord) on the model of the privilege granted in c.1175 to Germans from Prague. Location allowed for the emergence of the urban community as 'an autonomous ruling group' but it was then desirable that the new urban authority should be the sole owner of the municipal land.[39] And because of the enormous expense of buying up all urban land under feudal ownership it was often appropriate to build a new town on a virgin site or in some sparsely settled area where complicated ownership problems would not arise. The pre-located town then became the 'Old Town'. Large church foundations often remained outside the town radius, 'thereby not only preventing ownership conflicts and costly transactions, but also freeing the new centre from a foreign body in the form of church institutions with their immunities and exemption from the jurisdiction of town law'.[40] However in old centres 'with great traditions' where lords and clerics might continue to hold the 'located' town in a state of economic dependence, as at Krakow, Płock, Poznan and Wrocław, the newly-constituted town would have to develop on the old site and a less regular town plan would result. Exceptional difficulties must have arisen at Szczecin where the street system differed greatly from the ideal layout of Medieval planners and a central market square was never built. In Silesia Duke Henry insisted on retaining control over newly organised towns so that he could gain income from the trade links that developed with his rural domains. At Sroda this led to a new type of handicraft trade under Flemish law (previously used for new rural settlements) rather than Magdeburg law. The Bishop of Wrocław followed suit at Nysa and Ujazd. It is even possible that Flemish law was used in the first location of Krakow although Magdeburg law was adopted in 1234.

After a street system had been laid out lots were measured off for the use of the townsmen, with plots near the market squares allocated to the wealthiest merchants (for there might be separate markets for trading in fish, horses or vegetables). Craftsmen usually settled in streets carrying the name of their trade while Jews were accommodated in the peripheral areas. There would be considerable development on the edge of the town and even outside the walls, usually the hospitals and certain types of industry: the smell of tanning displaced this trade from the centre while the water power requirements of the corn mills, cutlery workshops and fulling mills also brought about dispersal. Such outlying industrial complexes marked the beginnings of another wave of suburban development, although this did not occur in every town. While some industrial areas grew sufficiently to require extensions to the walls as at Wrocław or to justify the location of new urban centres in the vicinity, as at Krakow (Kazimierz and Kleparz) and Poznan (Srodka), others continued to enjoy an abundance of land within the walls, much of which was used for gardens and pastures. The craftsmen were recruited mainly from the free inhabitants of the early 'pre-located' town, but the larger places experienced a considerable immigration of foreigners, 'generally Germans, who gained control of the guilds and determined the ethnic composition of these organisations'.[41] The Jews were tied by language to the German population and conflict between Jews and Christians was therefore an internal problem of the German community, although Jews were also granted ducal protection to bolster their security. Indeed the lords might limit the entry into handicraft industries by the native population in order to promote the immigration of skilled workers from abroad. And if the lords chose to move out, the towns might then assume an almost homogenous German character since a significant serf population would leave as well as the noble family itself. But the nobiles remained in some of the larger towns, like the Schlieffens in Kołobrzeg and the Spitemirs in Krakow, and in the smaller towns a significant proportion of municipal offices were held by the gentry. The poorer non-property-owning elements in the town often arrived on a temporary and illegal basis with their advancement inhibited by the language barrier.

The Polish urban system continued to expand in the later Medieval period with 169 new towns in the sixteenth and seventeenth centuries supplementing the 509 founded over the previous three hundred years.[42] But virtually all this development took place on the Polish crown lands, like Lipsk on the Biebrza which was founded in 1580 by King Stephen Bathory as part of a concerted effort to regenerate the economy of the royal lands. The significance of Lipsk lay in the need for a port to despatch grain and timber downstream and for a staging post on the road into Lithuania, particularly with respect to liaison between the arsenal at Tykocin and eastern territories where military campaigns against Muscovy were being planned. However the new towns were generally small. At the turn of the sixteenth century the urban hierarchy was dominated by Krakow and Warsaw, both with the population approaching 30,000 and by a group of major provincial towns with populations estimated between 10,000 and 20,000: Elblag, Lublin, Lwow (Lvov), Poznan and Torun. Below them came some 900 smaller centres, the great majority of them with less than 2,000 inhabitants. And the net result was a total urban population accounting for about a quarter of the total (falling to a fifth in Masovia and perhaps only a tenth on the eastern borders), whereas in parts of Western Europe the proportion exceeded one half. So it seems that while Polish towns may have experienced a golden age in the fourteenth and fifteenth centuries their position at the beginning of the seventeenth was thoroughly unsatisfactory for the most part. This was due basically to the failure of the towns to resist the economic and political offensive in the sixteenth century (fully discussed later in the chapter). A key factor was the preference of King Kazimierz IV to conduct his reforms in alliance with the gentry rather than with the towns. This in turn may have reflected the separatist inclinations of the Germanised population and conflict between the Rynek (town hall) and Wawel (castle): it was not easily forgotten that in 1311 Krakow resisted attempts to reunify Poland, necessitating the suppression of a rising and curtailment of the town's autonomy. But the towns were also negligent in failing to maximise their influence in national affairs. 'Lacking the appropriate political instincts, energy and above all group solidarity, the cities tended to argue among themselves over local privileges, such as staple rights and tolls, rather than undertake a joint political offensive on behalf of their entire order throughout the Polish state'.[43] On the other hand L. Kuklinska warns against too negative an approach and argues that despite the reversion to feudalism there was some continued accumulation of capital in the main cities of Poland (and also in Bohemia and Saxony) which was reflected in the industrial development of the eighteenth century.[44]

Case studies: Kalisz and Krakow

An interesting investigation has been made of the Kalisz area of Poland to demonstrate the evolution of an urban system within a small region and also to exemplify some aspects of the relocation process.[45] Kalisz itself became the main centre, situated in the Prosna Valley about a hundred kilometres southeast of Gniezno and Poznan at a point where long-distance trade routes intersected. The eleventh century stronghold of Zawodzie is seen as the first stage in an urban development process in early Medieval Kalisz, followed in the twelfth century by an industrial and trading quarter in the Stare Miasto immediately to the north. There was a reconstruction of the stronghold at this time along with the building of a collegiate church, recently discovered by excavation, where the Piast Prince Mieszko was buried. As the capital of one of the provinces of Piast Poland Kalisz was however protected by strongholds of the countryside forming a protective ring and dating back in some cases at least to the tenth and eleventh centuries. Some of these settlements then progressed from village to local market status and interestingly the names of some like

Piatek, Sobotka and Wtorek refer to the days of the week on which their market was traditionally held (Friday, Saturday and Tuesday respectively). There were close connections between all the towns in the system since they were based on German urban models and there were family ties between merchant groups as traders migrated from the older centres to the newly established markets. Thus the influence of the urban market spread to virtually all parts of the region: 'the peasantry gained buyers for their grain, flax, hemp, meat and wool while their obligations to pay rents with money were also stimulating them to enter the commercial economy. Standards of living rose, as did the expectations of a nobility increasingly disturbed by the growing prosperity of the townspeople with their rich apparel, utensils, houses and food.'[46] Disaster befell Kalisz in the early thirteenth century through hostilities and the serious flooding of the Prosna Valley. All this led to a relocation of the town to the north with the first stage of building at the Nowe Miasto (New Town). But it maintained its role as a regional centre with its own settlement hierarchy.

Of the major towns of Poland there is litle doubt that Krakow is the most remarkable.[47] Evidence of settlement on the Wawel hill dates back to the Palaeolithic era with Slav settlement beginning in the sixth century A.D. During the next two centuries the Wawel was ringed by strong embankments (in earth, wood and stone) and became the most important of a series of castle towns for the province created by the Vislanes and known in the ninth century as Little Poland (Małopolska). The settlement contained the workshops of blacksmiths and bootmakers, carpenters and potters, all probably situated in the suburb of Okol lying at the foot of the Wawel. Although the establishment of a larger state resulted in the destruction of most of the castle towns Krakow appears to have survived and prospered. A tenth century chronicle written by a Jewish merchant indicates a flourishing commercial life and close links with Prague. Armenians and Greeks were also present. Despite the rise of Lwow in the thirteenth century, at the time of Kazimierz the Great's conquests in the south, continuing economic and political importance is reflected in a wealth of Gothic and Renaissance architecture. This is best exemplified by the castle and cathedral although the Renaissance style was diffused widely through the residential areas after first making an appearance through the renovation of the west wing of the castle. But Krakow was not destined to remain the most celebrated of all Polish towns: although the Counter-reformation brought a spate of building in connection with new churches and monasteries, now using the richly ornamental baroque style, the Lublin union between Poland and Lithuania of 1569 made the city an inconvenient capital. Warsaw became the parliamentary centre and the venue for elections to the Polish throne. Kings continued to be crowned and buried at the Wawel cathedral but Krakow was abandoned completely as a royal residence in 1609. Although its trade and industry continued, symbolised by buildings like the cloth hall (Sukiennice) the loss of capital status brought stagnation. Hence the approximate demographic equality of Warsaw and Krakow around 1700.

Germany: early growth of Magdeburg and Berlin

Much has been discovered about the early history of Magdeburg in the course of archaeological work in the GDR, made possible by extensive wartime devastation.[48] Magdeburg became an important strategic and economic centre as soon as Charlemagne reached the Elbe and made war against the Slavs. By the end of the tenth century there was a fortified bishop's palace on the site of the present cathedral, with a market to the north and a settlement of Jewish merchants (probably to the south), as well as other hamlets or suburbs with mainly agricultural functions but possibly others too. Thus it would appear that the various functions were related to different sites appropriate for agriculture, defence and trade: the burg, with the cathedral and royal palace developed on a spur overlooking the river while the market was situated at the river crossing. The different nuclei would be fairly close together, presumably through common interests: 'counts, bishops, monks and landed nobility would seek proximity to centres of royal government, for example, and farmers and traders would seek to supply and be protected by their lay and ecclesiastical lords'.[49] It was this cluster of communities in Magdeburg that was then fused together into a homogenous burgher settlement of the old town (Altstadt) as a result of the successful struggles for privileges by the burgesses against the archbishop in the eleventh and twelfth centuries culminating in the grant of a charter. The fusing of separate urban nuclei can also be seen in the growth of Meissen and Rostock (and fortified tower houses reminiscent of similar structures in Italy have also been traced), but many other towns lack evidence of such early activity.

Berlin grew from the twin settlements of Berlin and Cölln which emerged out of the development of agriculture on higher ground in the twelfth century (evidence coming from graves which antedate the construction of parish churches early in the thirteenth century). Berlin and Cölln acquired significance because the ford over the Spree which they controlled acquired more than local importance with the integration of the Barnim and Teltow zones into the European trade system and the diversion of the trade route through the area (from the east towards Magdeburg) away from the long-established centre of Köpenick. While the modification of the trade route may have been logical in view of the rural colonisation process, there appear to have been political factors arising through the struggle for control of the route between the margraves of Brandenburg and Meissen and the Archbishop of Magdeburg. At any rate burgher communities sprang up around the churches of Berlin and Cölln and both communities were established as chartered towns after 1230. Only occasionally was a town created on a greenfield site with no existing settlement. Neubrandenburg is a fine example, however, established on a virgin site in 1248: conclusive evidence of the lack of any antecedents comes from archaeological evidence collected after the destruction of the old town in 1945.

Hungary: evidence of continuity

Medieval town development here must be seen in the context of Roman as well as early Slav settlement. The Danube continued to attract the greatest attention because, though the river was no longer garrisoned as an imperial frontier, it was a major line of communication between the Byzantine and Holy Roman empires and there were several attractive sites where steeply-sloping hillocks were protected by water and marshland. Hence cases arise where the same site has been used by Romans, Slavs and Magyars, probably in some cases with an actual continuity of settlement. At Györ the Roman title (Arrabona) is preserved in the Hungarian name for the river on which it stands (the Raba) and the German name for the town (Raab). The Roman military fort on the partly artificial castle hill was the site of the Medieval stronghold and it may be assumed that some houses whose ground plans originate in the Middle

Ages follow the line of the Roman wall. Györ was certainly the Avar capital in Pannonia and it may have been the first royal residence of the Magyars. By the early eleventh century the centres of ecclesiastical and secular power were established at the castle. But it is a curious feature of Medieval Hungary that there should be a sequence of royal seats, all of them clustered at or close to the Danube bend. And in the same way the residences of bishops for the dioceses of Esztergom, Vac and Veszprém as well as Györ are associated with this section of the river. 'It must be assumed that not only considerations of power but also earlier foundations and traditions determined this local concentration of bishoprics', as well as the increasing number of monasteries founded around 1000 in the vicinity of Bacs and Pécs.[50] But there is no doubt about Obuda's importance as an early seat of the Arpads. In fact, the conquering prince Arpad was buried there and with the spread of Christianity a church built over his grave became an important place of pilgrimage.

The Medieval town of Obuda coincides exactly with the legionary fortress occupied up to the fourth century, with the main street (named Kovacs) connecting the priory (actually situated within the fortress), market and harbour. Adjacent to the market lay the royal palace and the artisan quarter. The importance of defence seems to emerge through the Magyar takeover of the fortress and harbour, but without any strong tendency for settlement to extend to the canabae: practically nothing was built on the site of the civilian city in the Medieval period, contradicting the view that people would readily settle among ruins because building materials were readily available. Until modern times Obuda was a quite distinct settlement from Buda and Pest, although it is now a northern suburb of the capital city. Therefore it is important to differentiate between Obuda and the site of a subsequent royal residence at Buda where a walled town spread down the slope from the castle hill to the harbour at Kispest. Again the fortress has its links with Rome as part of the defence system of Diocletian while there is continuity again in the concentration of cross-river traffic at this point. It seems to have been the greater insecurity of the thirteenth century, in consequence of the Tartar invasions, that brought Buda to prominence since the castle hill could be stoutly defended and lay on the western side of the river well south of the bend. The review of royal residences may be completed by mention of Esztergom, developing (as at Buda and Obuda) between the castle hill and port, and the one capital not sited on the Danube: Székesfehérvar, a royal coronation city and burial place for which a strategic importance is claimed through access to overland trade routes and protection provided for the Danube towns in relation to armies advancing from the west and south. There is no Roman foundation although the site of Gorsium lies only ten kilometres to the southeast. Like Esztergom the most rapid growth appears to have been in the eleventh and twelfth centuries when there was a considerable influx of traders, both Latins (Walloon-Flemish and Lombard) and Saxons.

The Balkans: administrative and trading functions

Urban development was also an important process in the south where colonisation was geared to the settlement of empty land and the exploitation of minerals.[51] Rural settlements with a feudal regime were increasingly separated from the market town with its urban status. The Hungarian term varos is frequently used to indicate a suburb associated with industry and commerce rather than agriculture. Germans were again present, notably in the mining towns of Bosnia and Serbia where they appear as craftsmen as well as miners, but it is likely that on the whole they were relatively weak numerically and that German influence was greater through language and legal systems. Other foreigners were present in the towns. Hungarian kings encouraged Italians as well as Germans while Greeks are mentioned in Serbia, Jews in Slovenia and the influence of Dubrovnik was felt through the settlement of many of its citizens in Bosnian towns. Natives were also included in the ranks of craftsmen and some local leaders made vigorous efforts to stimulate effort. The case of one Duke Stjepan in Zeta (Montenegro) comes to mind: in 1450 he encouraged his people to produce cloth and other manufactured goods and even established a new harbour at Novi (Hercegnovi) in a direct attempt to discourage foreign traders and manufacturers from Dubrovnik, Kotor and other centres. Although the infertility of much of the karst meant that only very limited agricultural produce could be generated in an area within one day's walk of a given centre there was the stimulus of the caravan trade and the caravanserai (typically a large inn with a sizeable inner courtyard) providing accommodation for their large mobile businesses was a potential market centre. Novipazar, Pristina, Prizren and Shumen are outstanding examples. At Péc urbanisation was closely bound up with the monasteries and the patriarchate while elsewhere mining was an important force in town development.

In the Romanian Principalities again long distance trade was an important influence in urban development. The German contribution is seen in Transylvania with the Siebenbürgen, the seven towns where Saxon settlers were protected by royal privileges. These walled towns, of which considerable traces remain at Kronstadt (Brasov) and Schlässburg (Sighisoara), stand in contrast to their counterparts in the Principalities of Moldavia and Wallachia where substantial defences were not allowed under Turkish suzerainty. Hence the emphasis on refuges, often provided by fortified monasteries standing on prominent hilltops at the edges of the towns, well illustrated by the Cetatuia and Galata monasteries at Iasi. The capitals of the Principalities were both associated with the trade routes and in Moldavia the capital was transferred from the secluded site of Baia first to Suceava and later to Iasi (both on the Baltic-Black Sea route, enjoying close links with Lwow), while in Wallachia the transfer was from Cîmpulung/Curtea de Arges first to Tîrgoviste and later to Bucharest. But though some places derived importance from princely residences the towns not involved in long-distance trade and therefore dependent on local trade (perhaps combined with ecclesiastical functions) remained very small.

Dubrovnik: the classical tradition

Commercial life returned to several old Roman towns on the Adriatic coast (Bar, Budva, Kotor and Pula for example) and with some continuity of social institutions through the use of Latin as the official language despite a predominantly Slavic population. However, the outstanding trading centre in the southern part of Eastern Europe was Dubrovnik. Medieval commerce may be seen as a continuation of effort by the Roman town of Epidaurus (Cavtat) as merchants transferred to the defensible island of Ragusium some ten kilometres to the north: though the site has been substantially modified by the filling in of the shallow channel that once separated it from the mainland, the laying out of a new boulevard along the line of this channel and the building of the Rector's Palace on land reclaimed from the edge of the harbour. Dubrovnik was probably founded between 639 (when Epidaurus was raided by Avars) and 656 (when it was totally destroyed by Croats). F.W. Carter has explained how the Dalmatian townships in the Dark Ages were 'essentially border fortresses, always aware of the possibilities of attack by inland Balkan peoples'.[52] It seems that the relatively advanced civilisation of the coastal settlements prevented their absorption by the Slav migrants, but equally the numerical strength of the latter ruled out any complete assimilation. Therefore a remarkable coalescence took place between the traders of Ragusa, representing descendents of the people of classical Epidaurus, and the Slav migrants who settled on the mainland at Dubrovnik. Any survival of a commercial system is quite significant bearing in mind the hostile environment. The importance of timber for shipbuilding meant that there were numerous expeditions to the forests of Dalmatia to obtain wood for Muslim arsenals in Egypt and Syria, in the course of which Dubrovnik was frequently placed under siege. However, the same timber provided building materials for the sturdy fortifications mentioned in 866-7. And contact with people of different cultures was essential to a trading function, given the necessary political stability arising from the security of the town's defences and the overriding control of Byzantium. But it was a trading function that was closely related to Venice, the dominant Adriatic power able to propound the doctrine of *mare clausum* 'the enclosed sea thus emerges as a cultural and historical entity developing a unified civilisation around its shore'.[53]

Dubrovnik began to exploit its Balkan hinterland as a complementary effort to the Venetian emphasis on trade with the Levant. Inland penetration may have begun in the tenth century when commercial treaties were entered into with neighbouring states, but the effort was intensified after 1200, particularly with respect to Albania, Bosnia and Hercegovina. Trading privileges were granted to Dubrovnik merchants by Serbia (1186), Bosnia (1189) and the Byzantine Empire (1191). As intercourse increased there was steady migration of people finding their way to Dubrovnik. Immigrants came from various places on the trade routes, especially from Popovo Polje in Hercegovina, and there was coastwise movement involving settlers from Italy. Artisans and professionals (such as merchants and priests) were drawn to the city while unskilled people moved in to seek their fortune, pressed by famine or by the Turkish advance. Immigration into Dubrovnik was carefully controlled, for too large a population would have increased the risk of famine and reduced resources available to defence, while too varied a population would have undermined homogeneity and risked instability through political or religious differences. But it is clear that the balance gradually tilted towards the Slavs rather than the Latins. By the end of the fifteenth century Slav was the universal language, although many families were bilingual and Latin was still dominant among the governing classes. The elite incidentally comprised a coterie of some five hundred noblemen, all owners of considerable fortunes by the fifteenth century as wealth was redistributed within their ranks by the manipulation of dowries and other socially acceptable devices.[54] Altogether it would appear that Dubrovnik enjoyed the best of all possible worlds, lying under the protection of Venice yet with a considerable measure of autonomy which was respected by the powers because of the convenience of having a political mediator between the Balkans and Levant on the one hand and Western Europe on the other. This miniature sea state was able to prosper by its trade, with a sphere of influence far greater than that enjoyed by any other Dalmatian port, while remaining neutral in war.

In some respects Dubrovnik's trade was fairly passive, as can be seen in the case of contacts with Bosnian pastoralists who profited from the short summers on the high grazings of the limestone mountains and the warm damp pastures of the coastal strip in winter. The shepherds would sell their surplus animals to Dubrovnik merchants and additional trade developed in cheese, fat, hides and wool. Salt for the Bosnians was obtained from Durrës nearby but there was a long-distance trade in slaves and wax between Bosnia and Western Europe. The opening of a network of trading routes dates from the thirteenth and fourteenth centuries: these led into the interior from Dubrovnik itself or from other points on the coast which Dubrovnik merchants might reach by boat. One option was to sail north to Drijeva on the Neretva river and then cross overland to Konjic, Vrhbosna (later Sarajevo), Sremska Mitrovica and Belgrade. Another was to go south along the coast to Bar and Ulcinj and follow the caravan routes inland to Prizren, Novo Brdo, Nis and Sofia where the first Dubrovnik trader arrived in 1376. These difficult routes across rugged country made several contacts with the commercial highway from as possible.

As a result of the war-time destruction more information on on population changes was obtained. Immediately after the war a commission, *Brente Steders Regulerings* was formed to aid recovery. The commission required the preparation of maps showing changes in numbers of people, by minor civil divisions in all of Norway, for the periods 1920-1930 and 1930-1946.[8] This was the first survey of distribution since the Söderlund work of about 1920[9] and it included the latest census data of the time (the 1940 census was postponed to 1946 because of the war). It is on the commission's maps that the continual percentage gains in district populations may be seen over most of Norway, the major exceptions being in the middle of extreme southern Norway. Thus, local increase of population in recent times has been more significant nationally than local decreases and this was one reason for the selection of the sample districts.

STATE SUPPORT OF RURAL SETTLING TO THE EARLY 20TH CENTURY[10]

Farming began in Norway in the Bronze Age. Some of the places settled then still exist and are identifiable by names including *vin.* Thereafter, through the Iron Age and the period of the Sagas, the development of new farms took place slowly. But the *utmarka* (hill or forest pastures) remained largely unoccupied and eventually became state land, the King's commons. Then, in the 12th century, extensive settling started. This lasted for 250 years, during which *utmarka* were occupied, in part because of a law of 1274 which exempted a homesteader from public obligations for three years. This exemption was not automatic, however, because a new settler had to prove intent of permanence and undergo inspection at the end of the third year. By the mid-14th century farms were widely distributed in Norway although most were of the small subsistence type and only a few were large estates, called *herregårder.*

Arrival of the Black Plague in 1349 stopped the spread of farms. Inactivity continued for about three centuries, during which the government did its best to get numerous farms which had been abandoned during the plague back into use and on the tax rolls.

By laws passed in 1471, 1540, and 1557 many homesteaders acquired former farms free and only had to settle on and operate them. In the early 1600s the Danes encouraged new settling ("reclamation") by tax relief for three years, then six, and then to the death of the one who cleared the land. This led to many new small farms *(husmannsvesen)* being founded. After 1660 a number of Danish edicts promoted homesteading; the best known is a law of 1752 which provided tax exemption for 15 years if unsettled land was cleared.

After 1750 policy was different because of a growing population. Rather than increasing taxable land the desire was to take care of more people on it. Farms were divided and tenancy was encouraged so that between 1802 and 1855 the number of farms grew from about 79,000 to approximately 128,000, excluding Finnmark in the extreme north.[11] Thereafter, the numbers dropped sharply because both owners and tenants were dissatisfied with the system. Private ownership became less desirable but the state began to take steps in the 1890s to increase it.

In 1902 a state bank was founded to make loans to rural workers. These loans were for the purchase of land and the construction of houses; they went to 90°/o of a maximum allowable valuation and size and the interest rates were low. In 1917, *Småbruks- og Boligbanken* (The Small Farm and House Bank) was established. This agency, still operating, made loans for larger places so as to encourage borrowers to develop full-time farming units. Through this bank the number of small farms increased. However, the owners had to work in forestry, fishing, or other occupations to make a living. Then decline of the latter at the turn of the century forced the settlers to have more dependence upon their land, and this provoked more state aid for clearing. A loan fund for such had been started in 1857 but before World War I little had gone to small farms and the total sum available was too small for the state's needs.

Thus, by 1920 there was need for state support of new farms. This was a product of three forces: the feeling of many Norwegians that farming was a desirable way of living, the losses of population by emigration, and the hardships resulting from blockades during World War I. The attraction to farming at the present time may be less than to urban areas but it remains and is quite significant; for example, between 1967 and 1968 cultivated land increased by

14,850 decares (3668 acres) in Norway with only four of the 18 counties registering a decline[12] and it is only since about 1965 that the two programs for the development of new farms have become unused.

THE *NY JORD* SOCIETY PROGRAM

Before 1920 state support of new rural settling was only by laws and with some money. The former existed to formulate the procedures and limits of loaning and loans were available to expand the cultivated area of the nation. But not until 1920 did the state participate directly in the process. Instead it had granted funds for settling operations to one nationwide private agency, to 10 county agricultural societies, and to a few communes.

In 1908 the private organization was formed. Called *Selskapet til Emigrasjones innskrenkning* (The Society for the Limitation of Emigration) its objective was clear from its name. The Society began by purchasing a large farm and dividing it and by founding an agricultural school to train farmers for the future. However, the organization quickly felt the national need for overall guidance of homesteading. It got this charge in 1915 and changed its name to *Selskapet Ny Jord*, the full title of which was "Society for the Country's Domestic Colonization and the Limitation of Emigration."[13] By 1917 its directives were to: purchase fairly large areas suitable for homesteading (usually with group action in view); survey, build roads and ditches, and prepare plans for cultivation of an area; begin the cultivation of part of an area; lay out units so they would be full-time farms; provide aid in the construction of buildings; and make loans for purchase of the farm, this aid to be free of interest and installment payments for five years (or possibly seven years) and afterwards to be paid off like loans from The Small Farm and House Bank.

These general rules were drawn up after the Society had two experiences. In Namdalen it attempted to plan for total use, build nearly everything, and cultivate the land. In Fjotland it did the planning but built just roads and ditches. In the first area it was too much, in the second not enough, so the six directives were a compromise.[14] But they were major steps forward in many ways. They helped organize the settling process by specifying directions and limits of activity and by focusing administrative responsibilities.

They aimed at "self-sufficient" farms with 100-200 decares (25-50 acres) of cultivated land each rather than the previous maximum supportable of 20-30 decares (5-7 1/2 acres). They required detailed inventories of an area's qualities and quantities. They encouraged settling in groups but left many decisions to the settlers. They included local officials in the planning and execution of the plans. And they carefully controlled the use of state money.

With respect to the selection of settlers, the files of *Ny Jord* are rich.[15] The Society learned early that it had to search carefully for suitable persons. These had to be sincerely interested in a project, had to have some money or be able to save it or be capable of getting along on small grants and loans. And they had to work hard. Society personnel felt they could select men with some certainty but very early they determined that the female part of a new settler's family had been underestimated and that it was difficult to determine the suitability of women for new settling. As a result a great deal of attention has been given here to the women's functions and attitudes in rural settling. The selection of settlers is still a major weakness in new rural settling throughout the world and the analyses of experiences of agencies like *Ny Jord* and detailed psychological and sociological research on the topic are long overdue.

In general, *Ny Jord* did not try to form whole communities. Planning included the use of existing local buildings, such as, churches and schools. Other public and semi-public facilities were provided if the Society could not get them installed by some national or local agency first. In recent times, machines were provided occasionally to cultivate the first 50-60 decares (12 1/2-15 acres) just to save labor at a time when many things had to be done concurrently. But most often *Ny Jord* has operated as a "seeding," providing just the basic initial facilities and then encouragement and a means of bringing together new settlers and local officials.

Between 1912 and 1958 the Society founded 65 rural settlements.[16] Most of them are in three concentrations: in the Vesterålens (just north of the Lofoten Islands), on the central western coast SW of Kristiansund, and along a line from NE of Oslo on northeastward to the Swedish border.[17] Principal founding dates were the early and late 1920s and the mid-1930s. In number of farms 54 of the settlements were designed for 1-18 (of which 25 were 3-8 farms), 8 were planned for 22-28, and 1 each for 36, 45, and 89 farms. Through 1969 four more settlements were added and by then 44 were considered to be essentially developed and requiring no more of the Society's attention.[18] In 58 years *Ny Jord* developed 242,434 decares (59,881 acres) of land by the sale of 601 farms. Though all but the first 130 of these places are included in the figures for the state's homesteading program, discussed below, it is clear that the Society's effort is unique in Norway and deserves to be singled out as a model for efficient rural settling.

THE STATE *BUREISING* (HOMESTEADING) PROGRAM

The state's direct support of homesteading began in 1920. At that time the Norwegian *Storting* (Parliament) passed new regulations concerning reclamation and homesteading. These went into effect in 1921 and they were one of the major means by which food production was increased, young people were given a place in agriculture, and farm sizes were expanded.

Primary rules of eligibility for aid were that a homesteader should be between 21 and 65 years of age, that he should have property valued at 1,500-15,000 Norwegian *Kroner* (as of valuations in the 1920s but the whole requirement was dropped later), that the land of a farm be so situated that it could be operated as a unit, and that farms aided by this program should not be sold or transferred during the first ten years after aid was given without consent of the state's Department of Agriculture (to prevent speculation). Also, the farm needed to have at least 20 decares (5 acres) of arable land, of which no more than three-quarters was cultivated, and a dwelling no more than two years old when aid was requested.

Some changes in the original provisions were made mostly to parallel variations in prices until 1952 when limits on capital and income were dropped. In general, the aid is now given as a proportion of calculated cultivation expense, which includes drainage and first fertilization, and is paid at certain stages of the work; the percentage granted has been from 20 to 40 and there is, of course, an upper limit of total costs. Those persons with very little cleared land got more help by increased grants; at first this aid was double the regular allowance but since 1946 has been for 60°/o of the costs, except in the three northernmost counties where it has been

80°/o since 1952. These grants also had upper limits in the amount of cleared land which was raised in 1952 from the original 20 decares (5 acres) to 75 decares (about 19 acres).

Persons with small capital and low income also could obtain loans from The Small Farm and House Bank. *Bureisere* (homesteaders) with these loans, as under the *Ny Jord* program, got the interest and installments paid for by the state during the first seven years and they were exempt from taxation for the first five years. At first funds also were given to help build barns and in 1935 houses were added.

Farms already in existence benefited from *bureisere* support. State grants were made for the drainage of cultivated land and for the regulation of water. Further, aid was given for part of the cost of constructing roads to farms. Thus, the problem of improving agriculture was met on several fronts.

Outlining the usual procedure to become a *bureiser* shows useful checks. First, a settler applied for a loan from the Agricultural Committee for the commune where he intended to reside. Then the committee evaluated the man and his wife with respect to their abilities to develop a full-time farm. Third, the applicant contacted the *Herredsagronom* (district agronomist) to select a house plan and to propose development of the farm. Fourth, the application papers and tentative plans are forwarded to The Small Farm and House Bank.[19] Last, if the loan application was approved by the Bank the papers were returned to the local committee and were then forwarded through the county agricultural society (which rechecked the application) to the state Department of Agriculture; at this point the detailed plan for the farm was sent in. If the plan was accepted the application was approved and most of the papers were returned to the local committee where details of development were administered.

Thereupon house building and clearing began. But especially the former because the homesteader received a quarter of the money right away if house construction was started and another quarter at the half-constructed point (after inspection by the county society). As building and clearing proceeded funds were provided at certain stages (and the state Department of Agriculture kept some track of developments). After four years a *bureiser* was administered entirely through the commune.

Between 1921 and 1936 more than 11,300 farms were aided

under the state *bureising* program. Curiosity about its effectiveness prompted an official survey of this first 15 years but the war eclipsed its release in 1941.[20] Selected principal points related directly to internal migration analyses were: northern Norway had the largest percentage of new cultivated land and homesteaders; there was little land suitable for homesteading in the more favorable agricultural parts of the country; about one-half of the farms were within 2 km. (1 mile) of the nearest railroad station or bus or boat stop as well as the nearest trade center (but 16°/o had no farm road at all); of the newly cultivated acreage only 13°/o was in new farms and 87°/o was expansion at older farms; the average size of established farms increased from 137 decares (about 34 acres) in 1921-1925 to 209 decares (about 52 acres) in 1934-1936; clearing of 15-20 decares (4-5 acres) went rapidly but thereafter clearing went slowly; cultivation often went no further than was necessary for the subsistence of the homesteader's family; about four-fifths of the *bureisere* were married and nearly 70°/o were between 30 and 50 years of age; a homesteader's family was a farm's labor force; about 80°/o of the settlers had supplementary work which was usually in forestry or fishing; more than 86°/o of the *bureisere* had grown up in the minor civil division where they settled and another 10°/o had moved only within a county; water was laid into 23°/o of the dwellings and 25°/o of the barns; about a quarter of the residences had electricity; and state subsidies per farm averaged about 3,000 NK. All this pointed to the conclusion that homestead farming was essentially subsidiary to other occupations. However, it must be remembered that in the 1930s the program was also a social action to help people through the economic depression.

Weaknesses in the program resulted in some failures. The causes recognized were: instances of too rapid settling, poor location or low agricultural quality of some farms, inadequate experience of some settlers, higher income possibilities in non-farm work, a settler's lack of personal capital, and sickness.

In 1954 the excellent Borgedal report was published.[21] This noted, among other things, that by 1948 some 16,400 *bureisere* had been subsidized (though by 1954 about 17°/o of the total had had their grants cancelled after approval of applications[22]); about 5000 km. (3105 miles) of roads to homesteads were built; and about 1,900,000 decares (475,000 acres) were cleared and another 850,000 decares (212,000 acres) of previously cultivated land drained. Borgedal concluded that Norway gained much from increased earnings and greater availability of food units in relation to the program's cost. He also pointed out that homesteading depended greatly on supplementary farm income and on marketing conditions; where marketing was difficult and off-farm work was available the clearing of land stopped when the point of self-sufficiency was reached.

The state *bureising* program was most significant in the 1920s and early 1930s. Between 1921 and 1925 about 257 farms a year were aided[23] and the number increased steadily to a high of 1804 in 1936 just after loans for all residences became approvable and shortly after fishermen became eligible for such aid. Thereafter numbers declined. In 1939 it was 1180 and between 1946 and 1949 a yearly average of 230. In 1962 there were only 21 new *bureisere*, in 1965 16, through 1968 less than 7 each year, and in 1969 only 1; in the four sample areas of this study no *bureiser* started after 1963 excepting 2 in the Pasvik Valley in 1970.[24] In short, Norway's *bureising* program has ended. Through 1969 a total of 18,514 farms were approved in 49 years of activity. With respect to the nation's internal migration, between 1921 and 1948 about 16°/o of Norway's population increase was at least partly absorbed by the program.

In several parts of the country the program was especially significant locally. In the southern half of Norway, for example, 14 *herreder* (districts) had more than 20°/o of their farms in 1941 occupied by *bureisere* while in northern Norway there were 24 such.[25] In total numbers per *herred* through 1963, the higher ones in southern Norway were in the more accessible areas where districts like Trysil had the maximum of 270 homesteaders in comparison to a usual 20 to about 60; in northern Norway these totals were larger, often from 50 to 100 and more with the three sample districts being 181 in Hattfjelldal, 235 in Målselv, and 159 in the Pasvik Valley.

The total effect of the state *bureising* program to the present time has been truly significant geographically, socially, and economically. But some of its lasting effects may now be in jeopardy. In Norway's rural areas which have higher degrees of isolation (as described below) the great percentage of residents in older age groups and the absence of younger people signals abandoning is in force; this was not yet apparent in the Trysil area in 1970. Many such areas in Norway were settled as a result of *bureiser* support.

RECLAMATION OF BOGS

Both the state and *Ny Jord* programs have received considerable aid, sometimes indirect, from another source. This is *Det Norske Myrselskap*, The Norwegian Bog Association. It is a semi-public organization, founded in 1902 and very active since the early 1930s, whose task was to sponsor the proper use of Norwegian bogs and peat. The Association is composed of citizen members but the state provides grants for its research.

That the society had a large and complex objective is clear. The state's policy has been to encourage the production of food for people and animals and to make farming as attractive as other occupations.[26] With less than three per cent of the country being farmed and so much of it in mountains, it was recognized in the early 1930s that bogs needed to be studied and, if possible, used. But they totalled about 3 million hectares (7 1/2 million acres) and in an area of former mountain and continental glaciation swamps were found in all sizes and shapes, at widely varying elevations, and with considerable range in physical properties. So the Association began an inventory in 1934 under the able leadership of its director, Dr. Aasulv Løddesøl.[27]

Results of the Bog Association's efforts were significant and surprising. Multiple use, in various stages, was proposed and carried out at some localities where industrial processing of the peat (for as long as 20 years) preceded incorporation of the bog into local agricultural production. Elsewhere large bog areas were drained by relatively inexpensive methods[28] and it is still startling to see cattle grazing in areas which were open swamps three or four years previously. In only a few places outside Norway, of which Newfoundland is one, have the experiences of *Det Norske Myrselskap* been applied.

MEASURES OF ISOLATION

To these national trends of settling and populating there needs to be added an understanding of Norway's differing degrees of isolation. After all, the country is nearly 1800 km. (1100 mi.) long, starting at latitude 58°N., and is composed of many divergently oriented and shaped valleys and mountain ranges. Accessibilities vary from place to place and season to season and certainly bear on the possibilities of internal migration. There is, therefore, need to classify and map the differences in isolation.

Initiation of understanding is by recognition of primary measures of isolation. The three employed here are: (1) the number of neighbors within minimal straight-line distances, (2) the number of local transport routes available between neighbors, and (3) the the number of transport routes near enough to a home to be used for shipment of materials in and products out of a region (Table 1).

MEASURES OF ISOLATION

REGION, ZONE, TYPE	POPULATION DISTRIBUTION PATTERN	NUMBER OF ROUTES PROVIDING ACCESS*								SYNTHESIS: RELATIVE DEGREE OF ISOLATION	
		RAILROAD		ROAD		WATER		AIR			
POLEWARD ↑		INTER-REGIONAL	LOCAL	INTER-REGIONAL	LOCAL	INTER-REGIONAL	LOCAL	INTER-REGIONAL	LOCAL	REGIONAL	LOCAL
UNPOPULATED	None (No population)	0	0	0	0	0	0	0	0	Very High	Very High
DISCONTINUOUS SETTLEMENT											
4. Outermost Fringe Zone	Spots									Very High	High
Inland Type		0	0	0	0	0	0-1s	0	0		
3. Outer Fringe Zone	Clusters of Spots, Occasional Short Lines									High	Moderate
Inland Type		0	0	0	1-2	0	0-1s	0	0-1		
Coastal Type		0	0	0	1-2s	0-1	1-3	0	0-1s		
2. Middle Fringe Zone	Groups of Clusters, Short and Long Lines									Moderate-Low	Low-Moderate
Inland Type		0-1	1-2	0-1	2-3	0	0-1s	0-1	0-1		
Coastal Type		0-1	0-1	0-1	1-3	1-3	1-4	0-3	0		
1. Inner Fringe Zone	Interrupted Areas, Clusters of Groups									Low	Low
Inland Type		0-2	0-2	0-2	3-4	0	0-3s	0-1	0-1		
Coastal Type		0-2	0-3	0-2	3-4	1s	1-4s	0-3	0-1		
CONTINUOUS SETTLEMENT	Uninterrupted Areas	1-2	2-4	1-3	3-4	0-3	0-4	0-3	0-4	Very Low	None

*—Within approximately 10-20 English miles of each permanent resident.
S—Only summer access on some or all routes.

Table 1. The Measures of Isolation for determination of regions of settlement and fringe of settlement zones.

The first measure is of the proximity of a settler to neighbors for emergency or short-time help. Assumptions are that such aid must be no more than one hour's foot-travel time away and that throughout the seasons the average speed in that hour is three miles (of course, this is modified by the use of skis and the presence of communication equipment). The measure is the number of major directions, to a maximum of six, from any residence to other homes within three miles by direct measurements. The cartographic view of this is obtained by drawing circles on a map with 1-1/2-mile radii centered at every permanently occupied residence. Where the resulting pattern is individual spots (under Population Distribution Pattern on Table 1) no one is close enough to reach another home within an hour so the places are said to have maximum local isolation (as well as maximum discontinuity of settlement). If the pattern is narrow lines then settlers in each house, excepting end ones, might be helped from two directions. In clusters a few inner residences might be reached from up to six major directions and in ascending order of size of agglomeration the number of such houses increases through groups of clusters to interrupted areas to a maximum in uninterrupted areas which are tens of miles in size.

The second measure of isolation reflects a dwelling's accessibility by means other than on foot. This is determined by the number of different classes and types of transport routes within 10-20 miles of a home. Such a place that close to only one railroad and a road is noted to have measurably greater isolation than a dwelling equally close to two railroads and three roads. Further, each class of route is divided into interregional and local types in order to specifically designate the former which are generally all-weather lines over which bulky or heavy goods may be moved directly, quickly, and regularly, into or out of a Discontinuous Settlement Region; the index is the number of major directions, to a maximum of four, for each sub-type of transport available to a home.

The combination of these two measures leads to a general designation of settlement regions. Their minimum sizes are usually one to two hundred miles in both major directions in order to lead to small-scale mapping of large areas so as eventually to obtain worldwide comparability. Three regions which may be recognized are: (1) that of Continuous Settlement where there is no isolation by these measures, (2) that of Discontinuous Settlement where there are four different combinations of isolation separated into fringe of settlement zones, and (3) the Unpopulated Region with neither permanent habitations nor, usually, transport facilities. Synthesizing the characteristics of these regions and their zones provides the adjectives needed to express the various degrees of isolation (Table 1, Synthesis).

THE CONTINUOUS SETTLEMENT REGION

In Norway the Continuous Settlement Region is a southern coastal strip (Fig. 1). On the west coast it is about 40 km. (25 mi.) wide but near the mouth of the Oslo Fjord it doubles in width. The region includes most of Norway's oldest settled areas and there are large sections of close permanently occupied residences in many directions. From Stavanger northward they are broken by the fjords but eastward they generally are uninterrupted excepting near the Swedish border (Fig. 2).

This is the region where most internal migration eventually ends. Within it the absorptive qualities vary, in part because population densities already are so different (Fig. 2). Near the cities of Bergen and Stavanger and along the western side of Oslo Fjord there are more than 48/km.^{2} (125/mi.^{2}) and from the southernmost point northeastward they are 20-48/km.^{2} (50-125/mi.^{2}) but there are inland parts of the region where the densities are less than 10/km.^{2} (25/mi.^{2}).[29] The three urban areas included have Norway's first, second, and fourth municipalities in size: Oslo with nearly 488,000 inhabitants, Bergen with over 116,000 and Stavanger with nearly 81,000.[30] The growth of all the region's cities in the past three decades, plus emigration to the United States of America and overpopulation in relation to the resources available, have combined to foster population losses, especially in the south between Kristiansand and Stavanger.[31]

The region's good to excellent accessibility aids population movements. From Stavanger northeastward all residents are 19-21 km. (12-13 mi.) from a railroad, usually the interregional type (Fig. 3). There, too, the road net is dense although interregional highways are found only around Oslo and east of Oslo Fjord. Every dwelling is within 8-13 km. (5-8 mi.) of local roads going in at least three major directions (Fig. 4). North of Stavanger only Bergen is served by railroad, also interregional, and most of that coast has local roads. This land transport is supplemented by considerable freight and passenger traffic the year round on water and in the air. Oslo, Kristiansand, Stavanger, and Bergen are major ports for international merchant marine traffic and only Kristiansand is not a

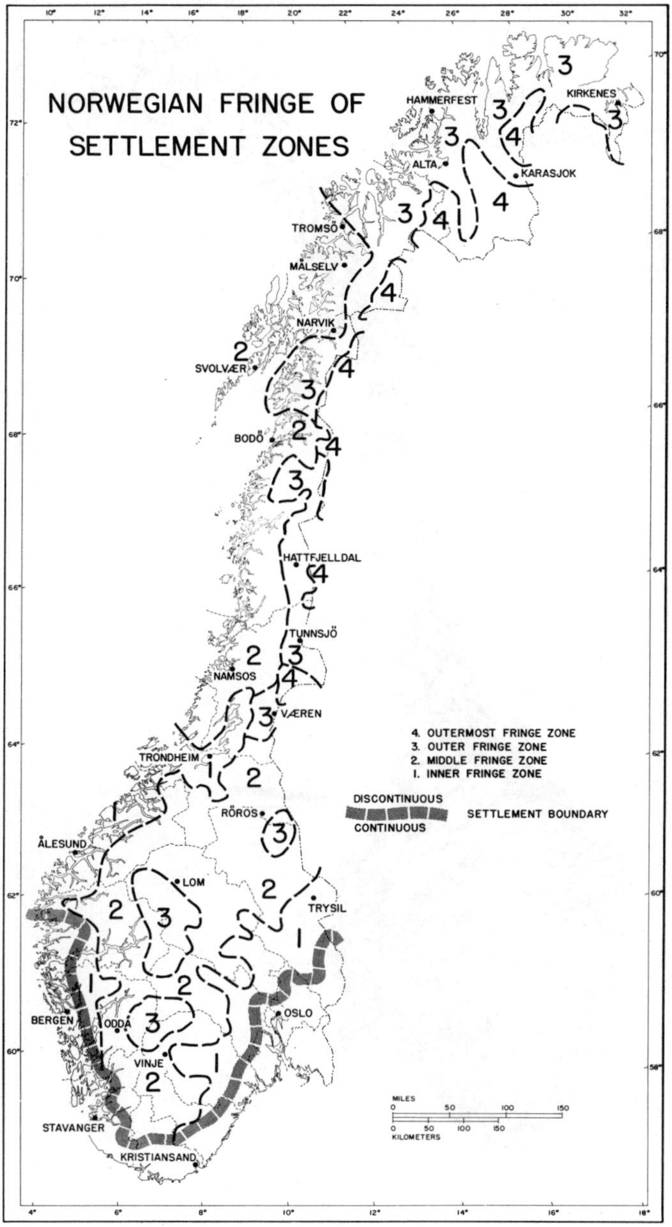

Fig. 1. Norwegian Fringe of Settlement Zones, based on the Measures of Isolation.

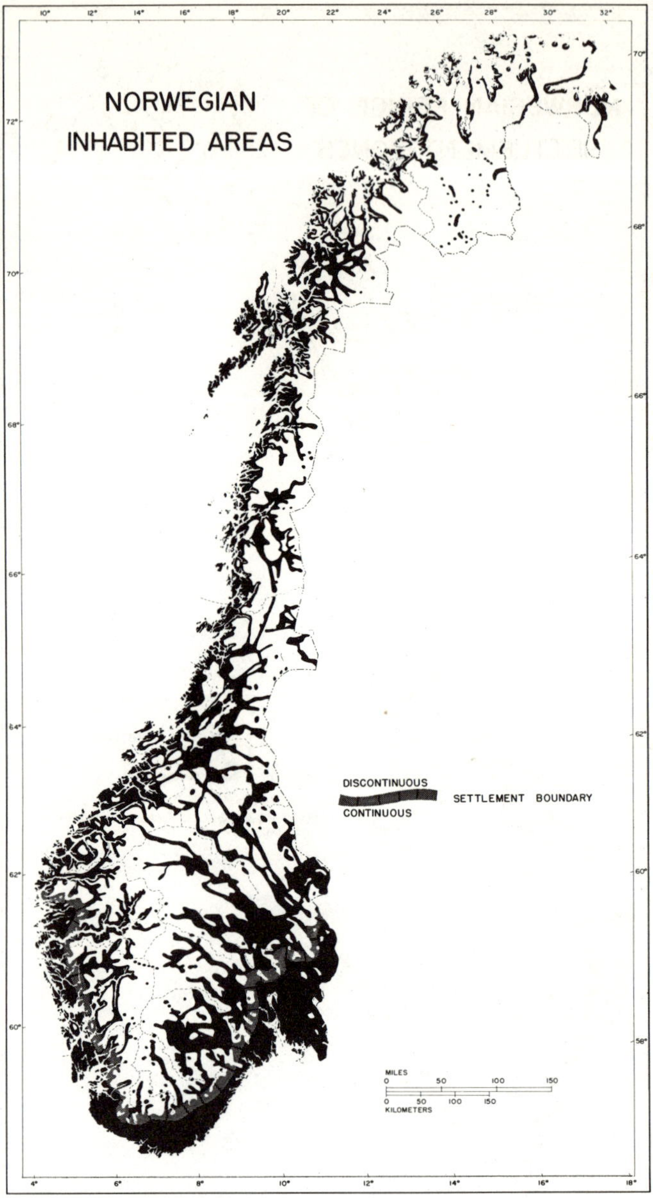

Fig. 2. Norwegian Inhabited Areas. Black portions represent areas within 2 1/2 km. (1 1/2 mi.) of permanently occupied residences.

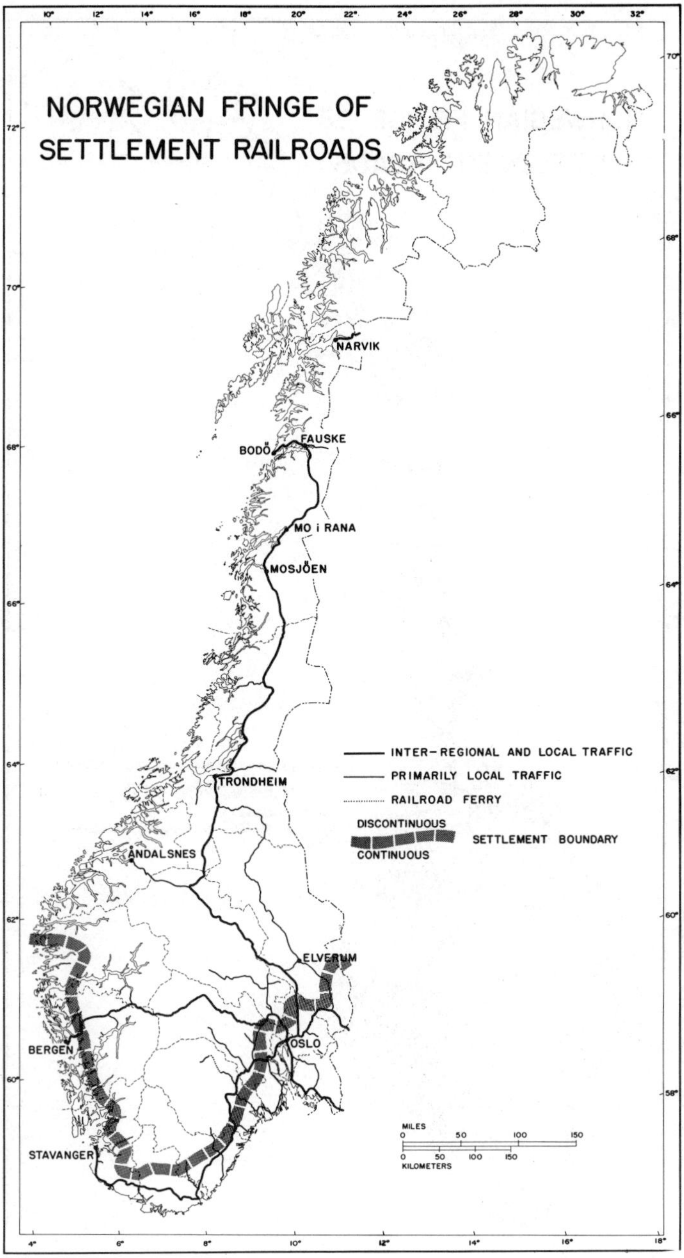

Fig. 3. Norwegian Fringe of Settlement Railroads.

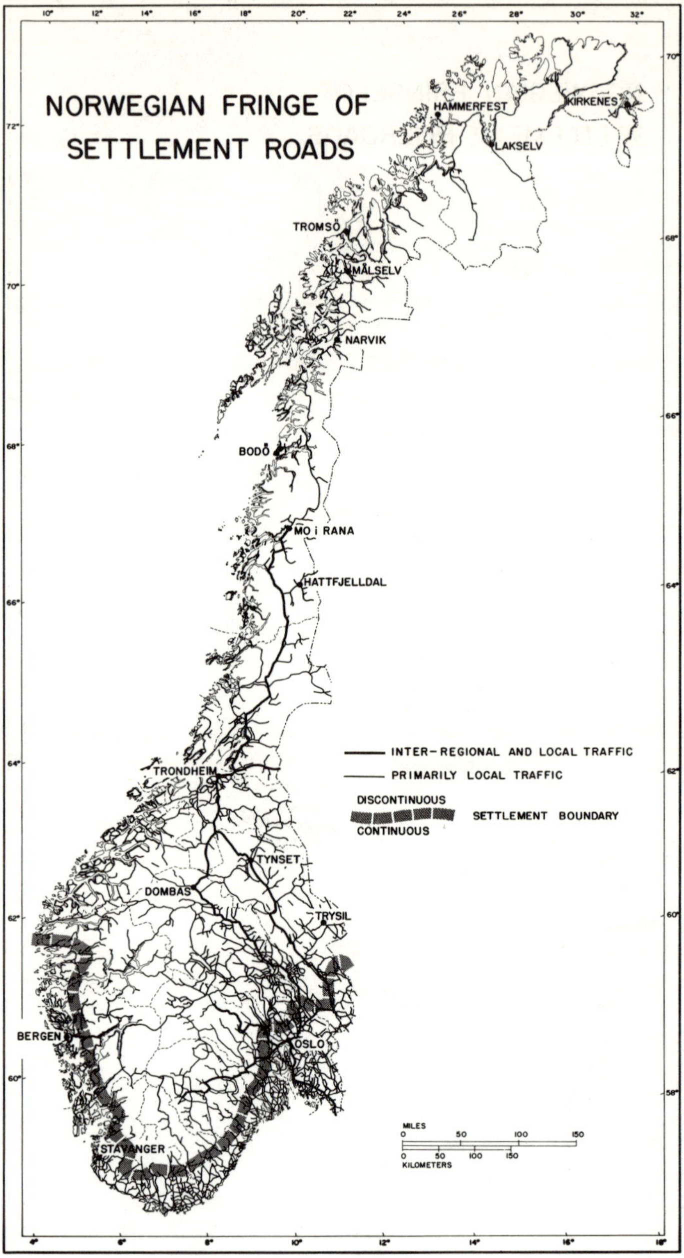

Fig. 4. Norwegian Fringe of Settlement Roads.

primary air traffic center as well. In addition, local boat traffic supplements all movement and, especially along the western coast, makes up for the lower numbers of and breaks in land routes.[32]

Thus, this part of Norway has little or no regional or local isolation. Even where they are dependent mostly upon water transport people in the region can get and give aid quickly from or in several directions and at nearly any time of the year. With the additional national economic development expected and the government's encouragement of the production of food and feed for domestic use, it is likely that farms throughout the Region will remain occupied and become larger, while some of the rural population is lost for good. Of course, cities may be expected to grow more so the problem of finding housing in them will continue. This is not so in the region to the north.

INNER FRINGE ZONE

North of the CS Region is that termed the Discontinuous Settlement Region. This is the source of nearly all Norway's internal migration. The region has two sections of Inner Fringe Zone. These are 80-160 km. (50-100 mi.) apart and each is 40-120 km. (25-75 mi.) wide with a main axis oriented NE-SW; the eastern part is about 440 km. (275 mi.) long while the western extends about 645 km. (400 mi.) (Fig. 1). The latter is primarily a coastal area and the eastern one is entirely inland. However, both have highly irregular internal boundaries which are sharply defined.

Each section has interrupted (i.e., discontinuous geographically) inhabited areas (Fig. 2). In the eastern part there is a general linear pattern, oriented NW-SE, which becomes strong near the inland side of the zone. There dwellings are on the bottoms and sides of deep valleys. In the western part the inhabited areas are more interrupted, mostly by water bodies, and lineation is dominant where houses are on strand flats or in valleys (Fig. 5). Thus, many of the inhabited areas there are parallel to and adjoin the coast and some are at right angles to it.[33]

Although the population of the IFZ is predominantly rural the urban is sufficiently large to attract migrants. The eastern section's largest municipality is Hamar with about 19,600 people (in 1965) and others like Elverum with 7000, Gjøvik with 16,000, and Notodden with 10,000. But the western part's cities are larger with

Trondheim having more than 108,000 residents, Ålesund and Kristiansund more than 19,000, Molde nearly 15,000 and Steinkjer about 8500.

Fig. 5. Representative strand flat rural settlement in the Inner Fringe Zone of western coastal Norway. Northward from town of Ålesund to western tip of Ellingsöy on 22 June 1956.

The transport facilities of the IFZ zone hold regional and local isolation to low degrees. In the eastern part, most people are less than 19-24 km. (12-15 mi.) from a railroad, three of which are interregional on which the CS Region can be reached in two hours or less practically any day (Fig. 3). There, too, are four interregional highways and, in the inhabited areas, a network of local routes so dense that most dwellings are less than 5 km. (3 mi.) from three or four and most of the rest are within 8-10 km. (5-6 mi.) of roads running in two to three major directions (Fig. 4). But the western section is much different; in that part just one interregional and one local rail line go through the Trondheim Fjord basin and one local line barely touches the zone at Åndalsnes. Interregional highways serve the basin sector north-south and eastward and the rest of the zone has some local roads, most of which follow the shores or major valleys and must be used in conjunction with ferries, while some of the other routes farther inland are closed for short periods in winter by snow. Further, interregional and local air transport is available at Trondheim and Ålesund. But the saving grace of this western part of the IFZ is the boat travel. *Hurtigruten* (express-route) vessels call at the principal ports daily on runs between Bergen, Trondheim, and Kirkenes (in extreme NE Norway). Into all places from ports to farmsteads go many small craft regularly to collect and deliver passengers and all sorts of freight.

In this zone *Ny Jord* founded six farming-forestry colonies between 1929 and 1953 in the northern section of the eastern part and between 1918 and 1945, 15 farming-fishing colonies in the western part, especially north of Molde.[34] The *bureising* program was received very warmly in the northern portion of the eastern IFZ and also by many farmer-fishermen throughout the western part. The result of both programs was a significant attraction for potential migrants to agricultural settling in the zone.

THE TRYSIL DISTRICT: IFZ SAMPLE

Trysil District is in southeastern Norway about 175 km. (105 mi.) NNE of Oslo (Fig. 1). It is on the western lower slopes of Kjølen Mountains in an area of stony morainic soils, irregularly distributed swamps, and a thick cover of predominantly Scotch pine. The district is a part of Hedmark *Fylke* (County) which was described and analyzed rather thoroughly in 1955 (Fig. 6).[35]

Modern settling of the district got its real start in the late 18th and 19th centuries and several of the early settlers were Finns who came by way of Sweden. But the significance of the Trysil District in this study is the combination of its location, the large number of *bureisere*, the concentration of *Ny Jord* colonies, a predominant occupation of farming-forestry, and a low-middle income per capita.[36] In addition, it has experienced a slow but steady decline

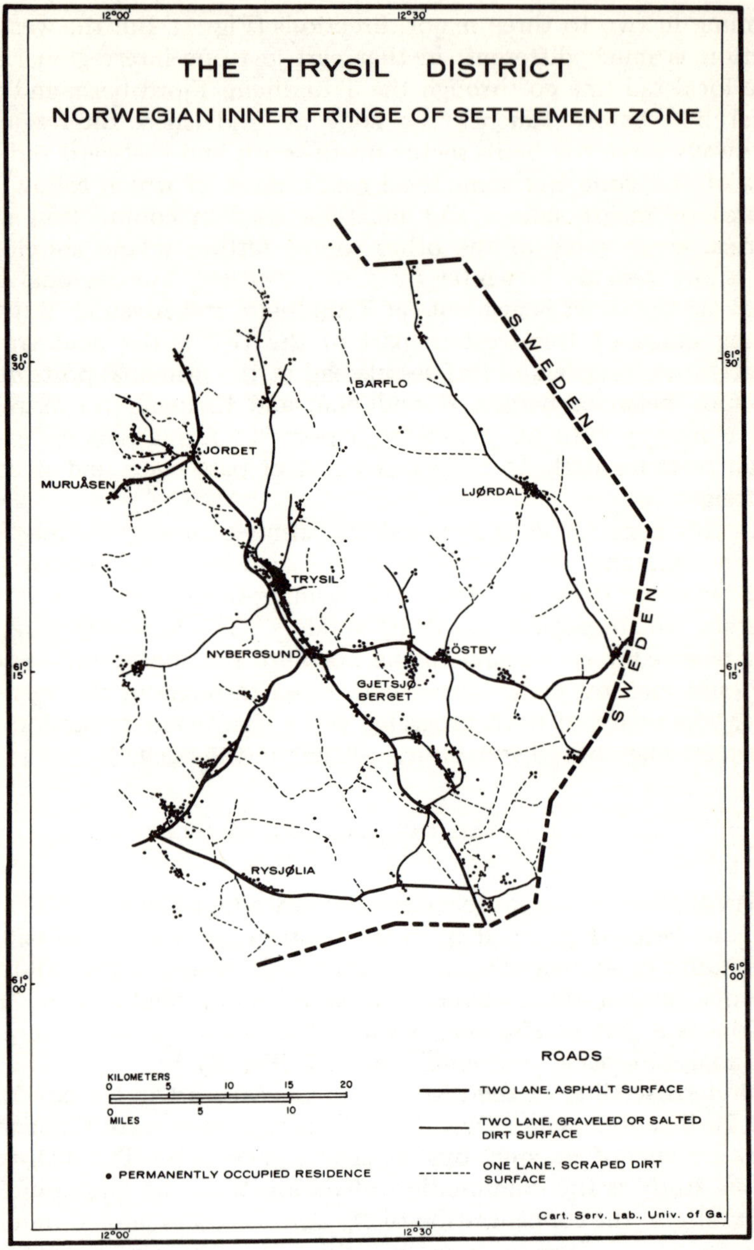

Fig. 6. The Trysil District.

of population in recent years, dropping from 8410 people in 1950 to 7841 in 1965 to 7479 in 1970.

The start and the rates of growth and decline of the *bureising* program in Trysil District were representative of much of southern Norway. But the number of homesteaders was the greatest for any *herred* in that part of the country. The first support was given to one applicant in 1922, the numbers rose to 18 grants in 1930, through a maximum of 25 in 1936, until 1941. From 1942 through 1944 there were 5-15 a year, in 1945 and 1946 only one each, and from 1947 through 1952 there were 5-10 new *bureisere* a year. After that the numbers dwindled to one or two annually and since 1960 there has been none. These changes reflect the early desire to provide farms for people as a social benefit, then the big need for aid during the depression years, a continued need during the war period of the early 1940s, and the desire of young married people to get on to farms in the post-war era. But more recently the trend has been for the young, unmarried people in the district to move out with the increased opportunities for work in the cities and in rural industry in nearby municipalities.

Many of the *bureisere* opened new farms in the district (Fig. 7). Certainly the percentage of freshly broken places was much higher than the average of 13°/o for the country although the specific figure is not known. Several of them were formerly the *seter* (summertime hill pasture) type or were new clearings at somewhat higher than average elevations 630-690 meters (2067-2264 feet) above sea level because the lower land, along the southeastward-flowing river that splits the district in half, had already been taken.

The *bureisere* were scattered all over the district by 1939.[37] Most were single farms but several clusters of three to six farms were noted in 1943.[38] As more of these were introduced county officials felt the need for a survey and instituted one in 1950.[39] Items of immediate interest in the report on that survey were: *bureisere* farms were small (averaging 93 decares or 23 acres), most of them were new farms, for only half was there room for expansion, houses were small and poor (as a direct result of war-induced restrictions and difficulties of procurement of materials), 32.5°/o of the farms contributed little to the families' support, the most difficult period of homesteading was the beginning, some of the land and some of the people selected were unsuitable, the larger the family at the start the more likely the farmer would have to perform off-farm work (71% of the *bureisere* in Hedmark worked off their farms at least part-time), building costs were about 10,000 NK per barn and 5000 NK per dwelling, cultivation costs were about 500 NK per decare (1/4 acre), and state support had been about 4810 NK per farm.

Fig. 7. A state-supported homestead in the eastern Norwegian Inner Fringe Zone. Representative of a milk-and-timber producing farm in the Trysil District. About 4 km. (2 1/2 mi.) north of Ljördal on 15 July 1958.

The report's major conclusions were that the homesteading ought to have given a somewhat better result,[40] that the state should do more developing of a farm (i.e., build the dwelling and clear 25 decares of land) before selling it to a *bureiser*, that homesteading took too much time, and that there was room for more in the county. Yet, many articles have been written about the county in the vein that a living cannot be made from farming or that the forest-farm income to be expected there is about 10 to 1. And now there is a declining and aging population in the district.

An interesting exception in the program was the group settling of Muruåsen. This area, near the northwestern corner of the district, had seven homesteaders arrive in 1948. At each of the seven the state cleared 25 of the 280 decares (6 1/4 of the 70 acres) and paid for most of all of the work (using local, privately-owned clearing equipment). Electricity was brought in about 1950 and telephone lines were strung later; almost all farms had electricity but only a few telephones by 1958. The water supply at some of the farms was problematic due to high iron content. Of considerable importance was the fact that in the beginning there was much cooperation between homesteaders. An eighth farmer started in 1952 in the same area and soon was working very closely with the others, especially with respect to draining and clearing. Once everyone had a good start there was a noticeable decline in the cooperative efforts but it is recognized by each settler now that the ability to work together is present.

The five *Ny Jord* settlements cover a variety of settling circumstances. Founded over a span of 18 years they range in size from 6 to 29 farms (Table 2). Most of the farms were in previously unoccupied areas so each settlement represents a spot of advancing edge of occupied land.

TABLE 2. *NY JORD* SETTLEMENTS, TRYSIL DISTRICT, 1958[41]

Name	Date Founded	Total Farms	Newly Created Farms	Residence Built	Farms for Sale	Total Size (Decare)
Osskogen	1934	6	2	2	0	3200
Rysjølia	1936-37	18	13	13	0	6132
Grönåsen and Gjetsjøberget	1936-38	29	22	15	3	8470
Toråslia and Formoteigen	1942-52	15	3	1	7	8530

The two larger settlements demonstrate the time necessary for development. Rysjølia was a completely new group of farms, in the extreme southern part of the district, started in 1939 when two houses were built. By 1941 there were three but most of the remaining farms could not be started until after World War II. In 1952-53 *Ny Jord* began to use machinery more and by 1958 about 210 decares (52 1/2 acres) were cleared there. The settlers were not paid for their work in the clearing and draining. In 1958 draining of lower fields was still in progress and the land was being limed for seeding to grass. A poor first crop but a useable second one was expected on the land drained during the previous year. In 1957 electrical service was available but not until 1959 did telephone lines reach the area and only since about 1962 could it be approached by road from the east as well as the west. By 1958 16 houses had been built, accompanied by 13 rather small barns, but the general feeling was that the southwest-facing slopes were too steep at the easternmost three farms for completion of the farms there to be expected. The income at all of these farms was largely from the forests and the state figured it got its grants back from the sale of the wood; about 8500 NK were given at each place, the total state cost was about 10,000-12,000 NK per farm, and individual farmers borrowed about 20,000 NK each. There was no major change there between 1958 and 1970 except improvement of the road and the addition nearby of three summer cottages (Fig. 8).

Grönåsen and Gjetsjøberget, the largest *Ny Jord* settlement in Trysil, was started in 1936. It is in the south central part of the district. The bridge and road into it were begun in 1938 and there, too, settling was delayed by the war. But by 1958 only three farms remained to be sold, settlers were developing different ways of removing the boulders from the morainic soils (Fig. 9; at costs of 2000-3500 NK per hectare), some farms had as much as 10 hectares (25 acres) of cleared land, potatoes were being raised successfully, and daily milk pickups were being made for hauling to the Nybergsund dairy. Additional land was being cleared and some of the farmers were near the end of the first stage of settling so they were considering improvement of land already cleared or buildings already erected.

While settling under the two programs was going on other developing in Trysil District supported it. Road construction was one.

Fig. 8. A representative small two-building farmstead at the base of a slope and a barn and telephone lines along the road, in the eastern Norwegian Inner Fringe Zone in the middle of *Ny Jord's* group settlement at Rysjølia in the Trysil District on 18 June 1970.

In kilometers built per year it was: 15,300 in 1929, 6,523 in 1934, 14,987 in 1937, 5,945 in 1938, and less than 20 annually since.[42] Thus, by 1938 this road building program provided the primary and secondary access network as it exists, in improved form, at the present time (Fig. 6);[43] although several houses in the district are 5-10 km. (3-6 miles) from the nearest road most are much closer.

Fig. 9. A *Ny Jord* farm in the eastern Norwegian Inner Fringe Zone. Representative of the difficulties of removal of boulders and stumps, of the house-and-one-barn farmstead, and of the forested area in the Trysil District. At Gronåsen on 14 August 1956.

Erection of electrical lines began about the time extensive road construction was ending. A power plant established in 1938 at Sagnfossen, in the southern center of the district, opened the way for local power distribution. This proceeded immediately along most of the primary roads and to the principal villages on secondary roads.[44] Since the war several extensions have been pushed into areas with higher degrees of local isolation in spite of the fact that some farms in those localities had their own private generating facilities.

Telephone lines were installed even more recently and in a much closer distribution pattern than roads and electric lines. The telephonic trunk route was put in along the road from Trysil Village southward in 1943 and in 1944 eastward to beyond the village of Östby. In 1947 another line went southwestward from Trysil and in 1950 the district's easternmost valley was tied in. By 1955 the main line was run northward from Trysil Village with a side line up Flendalen in 1956. Otherwise only short extensions have been built north of Östby in 1957 and to Rysjølia in 1959. However, the recency of this construction program was of little significance to the new settlers because individual phone service is considered expensive and several farms are still without it.

Two recent rural population trends have been decline and increasing age of the people on farms. The former is representative of areas with moderate to high degrees of local isolation throughout Norway. The reason is that younger people are going to more accessible places by a series of short moves. Some of the migrants are unmarried men and women in the late teens and others are married middle-age people so older folk are left behind.

This movement means, too, that there are spots of abandoning. Actually there are more with respect to farming than is apparent at first. Many a *bureiser* farm, which was previously a *seter*, was not on better agricultural lands and had a higher degree of local isolation than older farms near the villages. So the movement of young people left older ones in more isolated situations and with increased age they have left the farms for institutional living or a cemetry. But because of the extension of roads or electrical or telephonic lines abandonment often did not follow; rather the place became a privately-owned summer-or-winter-time recreational hut. This change is in keeping with the well-known decline of the *seter* in numbers and in importance during at least the past two to three decades.[45] Increased industrialization, especially more mechanization of woods work, and trade as well as increased mobility of individual Norwegians is likely to cause local migration from farms in the other fringe zones to increase in the years ahead.

Norway's Middle Fringe Zone is in two segments. The first is a southern inland section, between the two parts of the IFZ, and the second is in the middle of the western Norwegian coast. The first begins sharply between Stavanger and Kristiansand and extends northeastward about 563 km. (350 mi.) and averages about 200 km. (125 mi.) in width but is interrupted in three places; the second section starts at Trondheim Fjord and extends along the coast, including the Lofoten and Vesterålen Islands, for about 805 km. (500 mi.) as a strip about 120 km. (75 mi.) wide (Fig. 1).

Fig. 10. Westward over the village of Dombas in a representative part of the southern section of the Norwegian Middle Fringe Zone on 19 August 1958.

Inhabited areas here are predominantly long lines in the southern part, separated by uninhabited uplands roughly 11-24 km. (7-15 mi.) apart and of varying lengths from a few tens of kilometers to about

150 km. (95 mi.). An occasional village has a thousand or more people but most places have fewer than 300 and are local shopping or shipping centers for the farmer-foresters (Fig. 10). By contrast, the west coastal section's dwellings are distributed mostly in groups of clusters and short lines (Fig. 2). Further, the urban population is greater proportionally and in the size of its groups, ranging from Tromsö with about 24,000, through Bodö with 23,000, Mo and Narvik with 18,000, and Mosjöen with 10,000, to Namsos with approximately 6500, and to many centers with 1000-2000 residents. All are transport foci and places for either fish collection or processing or for ore reduction. Towns and cities of such size and importance in areas of relatively low density are quite attractive to possible migrants in the zone.[46]

Both regional and local isolation are moderate in the southern part. There are only three railroads, two of them in the interregional category, which go through to Bergen and Trondheim (Fig. 3). Two interregional roads also go through the zone to Trondheim and a third just reaches its southern districts (Fig. 4). Though it is common for the residences to be on or within 1 1/2 km. (1 mi.) of a road the movement over some roads may be slow at any time or completely blocked seasonally (Fig. 11).

The west coastal portion also has moderate degrees of isolation. In its southern section is *Nordlandsbanen* (the Northland Railroad) which serves the ports of Mosjöen, Mo i Rana, and Fauske and in 1961 was extended to Bodö;[47] two other ports have rail connections, too, Namsos via a local line from the east and Narvik by an interregional route through Sweden (Fig. 3). Paralleling the railroad in the southern sector is an interregional road as far as the steel center of Mo i Rana but on northward it is a local road. A few other local roads run eastward from this highway, some going through the mountains into Sweden, but north of the latitude of Bodö the roads are interrupted by ferries, limited to individual islands or fjords, and are subject to being closed seasonally. Thus, they do not provide an all-weather net connecting the inhabited areas.

However, sea and air routes do provide such a net. The express route includes coastal ports northward to Bodö and then insular centers northward through Tromsö. This is fed by a multitude of smaller-vessel runs, some seasonal, which include centers of less than 100 people. Meanwhile, daily air service by an interregional route goes from Bodö to Oslo and in the summertime local seaplane service is available from Bodö on northward through the islands.

Fig. 11. A single residence, on an island in a mountain enclosed lake, representative of a high degree of local isolation and a moderate degree of regional isolation in the southern section of the Norwegian Middle Fringe Zone. Near Myrdal on 16 October 1955.

New 20th-century rural settling within the MFZ was widely scattered but in significant numbers was concentrated geographically. *Ny Jord* colonies, some among the largest of that type, were established mostly in the Vesterålen Islands, and in the Målselv district.

In general, rural settlement of the MFZ has great sensitivity to changing conditions. Major decreases of rural population between 1930 and 1950 occurred in southern districts, along the western edge of the zone, and in its northeast.[48] There was a similar loss in the northern MFZ, but there, too, World War II bombings and Nazi reprisals destroyed many towns as well as individual farm homes. The recovery demonstrated strong nationalistic feeling and stubborn individual effort -- the price paid was high. But losses characterize recent years.[49]

As a whole, Middle Fringe Zone rural settlement is rather delicately balanced, the kind of situation where local emigration starts easily. On the map of inhabited areas there may appear to be much space for new settling but this is misleading. Great care must be taken, if decision is to develop more, not only to protect new settlers but also not to upset the economics of those now there, as is clear from the details of recent settling in the sample area.

THE MÅLSELV DISTRICT: MFZ SAMPLE

Målselv is in northern Norway near both the coast and the northern end of the Middle Fringe Zone (Fig. 1). However, the area extends so far inland as to be partly in the Outer Fringe Zone also. Administratively it is the Målselv District and adjacent areas in the southwestern center of Troms Fylke (County), an area analyzed economically and described historically in the middle 1950s (Fig. 12).[50]

Though the very earliest settlers near the north Norwegian coast are lost in early history, the first modern Norwegian settling of the Målselv District commenced in the 1780s.[51] These were people from the two major valleys of southeastern Norway, farming districts where there were big floods in 1770. That they were clever farm and woods people has been demonstrated by the continuous occupying of many holdings in the five valleys comprising the settled parts of the sample area. But its importance here is in the association of being a high-latitude (69°N.) position, astride a zonal boundary usually characterized by little or no recent settling (or by abandoning), an area of one of the larger numbers of *bureisere* in northern Norway, where there are two *Ny Jord* colonies and a nearby *bureisere* group settling experiment, a predominant occupation of farming (dairy) supplemented by off-farm construction work or hunting or fishing, a group of people with low income, and an area of recent new settling.

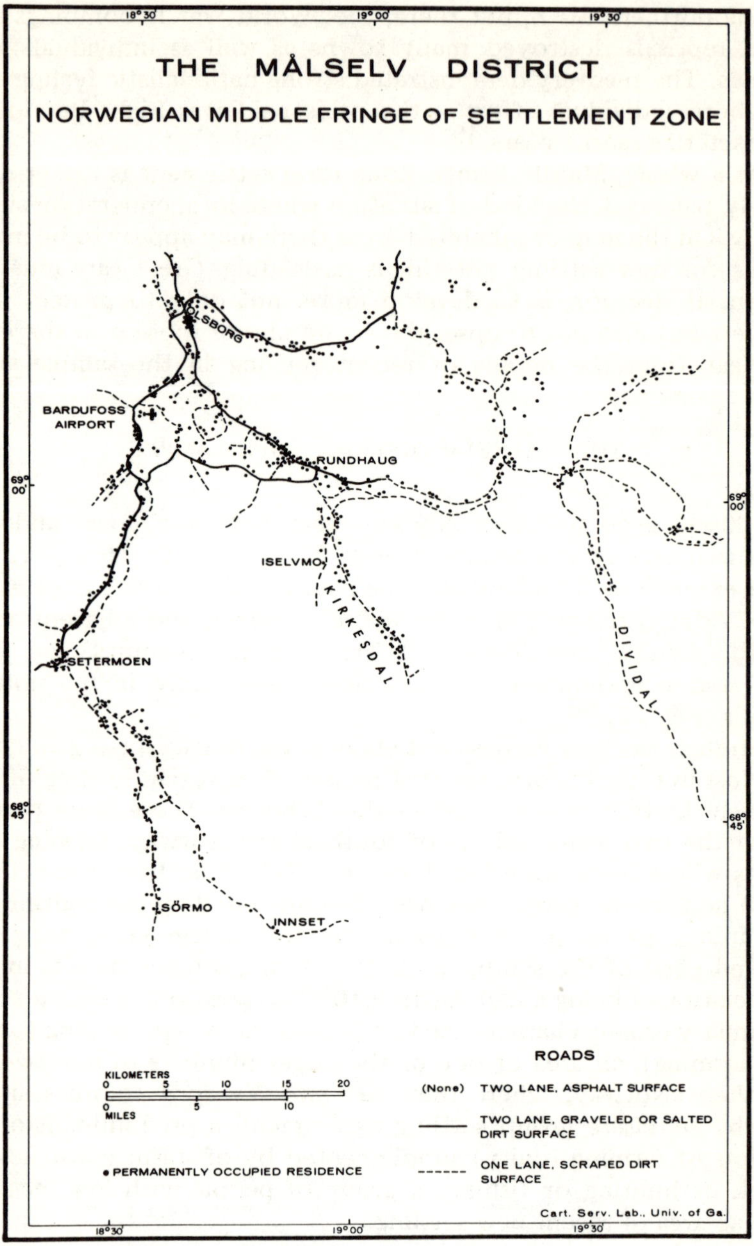

Fig. 12. The Målselv District.

The growth and decline of *bureisere* in the area is roughly representative of other parts of Troms County which had larger numbers of homesteaders. First in the district were five farms approved in 1922 and annual additions were about that until 1931. Then the figure went to 14 and remained about the same through 1936 when it went to the maximum of 21-23 per year for 1936-1938. Thereafter it plummeted to 3 in 1940 and remained insignificant through the war years. Since 1944 a total of 19 homesteading grants have been made in seven different years with the last being two in 1957 and one in 1962. Yet, throughout the Målselv area not only was no abandonment observable through 1964 but many new dwellings were evident (Fig. 13); certainly some were reminders of reconstruction of places destroyed during the war but this must not have been more than a quarter of the newer buildings present. These homesteaders were scattered all over the area.[52]

Fig. 13. State-supported new farms in north Norway's Middle Fringe Zone. Exemplary of the river terrace sites selected in the mountains of the Målselv District. At Sörgård on 5 August 1964.

Most of the new farms were formed by splitting off pieces of existing farms (a practice discouraged by a national law passed in 1955) so the *bureisere* were close to other settlers in at least two directions. Farmsteads were placed on either existing roads or those newly built by the state for the purpose (Fig. 12). Everyone interviewed volunteered comments on the indispensability of good roads, especially to the marketing of fresh milk produced on so many of the places. Agreement was general on the need for a telephone at each farm and that the state phone service was often too expensive compared to the average low income; this was solved in at least two sub-areas by local cooperatively-established phone lines between the residences. There was complete agreement that most of the farms were too small; averages of 300-400 decares (75-100 acres) under a program aimed at full-time and mechanized farming[53] produced impossible situations, especially where the cultivation limit is about 300 feet above sea level. Electricity was not considered so essential in the late 1920s and 1930s but now it is and often by those who thought it not so earlier; lines were brought in to several of the valleys between 1960 and 1962.

In timing of settling activities there was general agreement that clearing should be done first and often that barn building should be the second action; this reflected the requirements of cattle raising as well as the possibility of living in a barn or a temporary house at first. Usually the house was built as small as possible in order to save money and because many of the houses were constructed without state support. Many of the homesteaders felt the state should do more clearing, draining, and erection of buildings than was done, a reflection of the pressures felt in the early stages of homesteading; yet, local officials warned against doing too much for financial and psychological reasons.

Reactions concerning the selection of settlers showed agreement between homesteaders and officials. Most of the former moved only within a district or to adjoining districts and favored settlers having local knowledge but one official called for the reverse to encourage the introduction of new ideas. And at the same time most homesteaders insisted it would be best to have agricultural school training before homesteading. Meanwhile most interviewees agreed that the settlers approved ought to be in their low 30s, married, in good health, with some money, experienced in farming and with great interest in doing it in the area, willing to work hard and long, and that the wife's attitude and ability were very critical to a family's ability to stay.

The *bureiser* experiment in group settling was started northwest of Målselv in the eastern central part of Senja Island. Named Grasmyrfelt, this was a state-planned operation on land purchased from individuals and which has been active since 1953 (though laid out much earlier). The experiment was begun to create an example for the improvement of local farms and depended first upon considerable draining and road building by the state. By 1964 the *prøvebruk* (experimental farm) and six others were being developed according to a detailed plan for a total of 34 farms to be grouped closely. But recent interest in the settlement has been low because farm work is considered hard and results too few as a result of agriculture there being limited primarily to potatoes and hay even after the draining. Of course, few applicants might have been expected because the planned farm sizes only average about 220 decares (55 acres).[54]

The other group settling efforts in the Målselv area have been two *Ny Jord* colonies. These are off the west side of the mouth of Målselva (The Mål River) in drained swampy areas. The older, to the west and called Fugelmo, was started in 1926-1927 to create five new farms about 200 decares (50 acres) each; work is completed there and in 1958 some 189 decares (47 acres) were cleared.[55] The newer place, Homen, was started in 1935 with space for 9 farms, also about 200 decares each and by 1958 there were 182 decares (45 acres) cleared and only one farm was left open for purchase. Here again, as at Grasmyrfelt, farms were so small that it is clear that much of a settler's income was expected to come from off-farm work, most likely fishing.

All of the *bureiser* program in the Målselv area received extra impetus from the regional development program.[56] Under this the war damage was cleaned up, the improvement and extension of transport routes took place,[57] industrial development was fostered, electric and telephone lines were put in (Fig. 14), and local markets for local foodstuff expanded.[58] Also, a military training base was established near Bardufoss airport, about 12 km. (7 mi.) southwest of Moen village. All this was accompanied by a growth of population; in Målselv District, for example, the 1950 population of 5079 was by 1963 up to 5572 and by 1965 even higher to 7067.[59] This is especially significant because the district includes only a few villages. It is this growth, rather than abandonment, which makes this part of the Middle Fringe Zone out of the ordinary. For it the state may take a good share of the credit, though the cost has been great.

Fig. 14. State-supported new farms at road end in the north Norwegian Middle Fringe Zone. Small two-building farmsteads and electric lines at Sörmo on 31 July 1964.

Norway's Outer Fringe Zone occurs in six separate sections which are distributed throughout the Discontinuous Settlement Region in a complex pattern (Fig. 1). In the southern part of the nation the four sections are inland and are generally oval shaped with one axis about 55 km. (35 mi.) long and the other from 40 to 160 km. (25 to 100 mi.). North of the latitude of Namsos the fifth part is inland and linear, being 40-80 km. (25 to 50 mi.) wide and merging over the border with the same zone in Sweden. But the last part, to the north of Bodö, is both coastal and inland, has a width of 65 to more than 160 km. (40 to 100 mi.), a length of 725 km. (450 mi.) NE-SW, and also is tied to Swedish counterparts to the east (Fig. 15).

The sharpness of the edges of most of these six areas is a reflection of the zone's moderate regional and high local isolation.[60] The distributional pattern of residences is generally clusters of spots and short lines but there are a few long lines, too (Fig. 2). Settlers often have someone near in two or three directions but as often it may be only one or two. And many homes are without telephones.

Furthermore, the zone's accessibility is poor. Interregional railroads cut through two narrow sections, southeast of Bodö and east of Narvik, but otherwise the zone is without rail service (Fig. 3). No part has an interregional highway and many sections are at the ends of widely spaced and short routes, some of which are usable for only six to eight months in a year (Fig. 16). Furthermore, several portions of the zone have no roads at all; where these are inland and inhabited, settlers must resort to travel on foot, on skis, or with the aid of an animal. In the coastal parts the roads, if present at all, are narrow and short and nearly everyone depends on small boats for movement. Two exceptions are the cities of Hammerfest and Kirkenes, each with roughly 7000 inhabitants, where longer roads are present (Fig. 4), where *hurtigruten* vessels call daily (and at a few other small centers as well), and where, respectively, there is summertime and all-year local air service.

The OFZ usually is unsuitable for settling. However, in parts of this zone in Norway it is occurring anyway. This is largely because the Norwegian government wants settling there for combinations of political, economic, and, possibly, military reasons. The country is, after all, long and narrow, with much of its area in mountains and little in agriculture but with a coast open to shipping at all times, good fisheries, some mineralized areas, and sites suitable

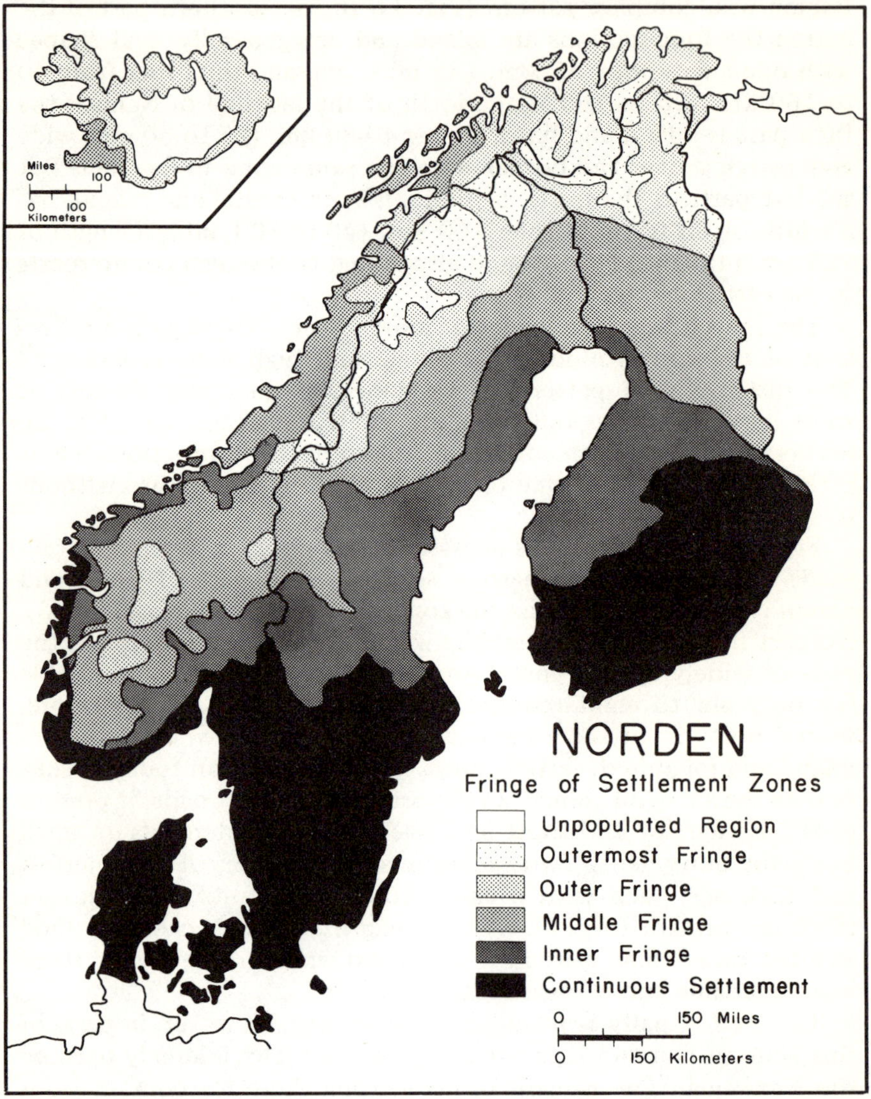

Fig. 15. Norden, Fringe of Settlement Zones, based on the Measures of Isolation.

for hydroelectric generation. Development could be expected. The mining of low-grade iron deposits near and the concentrating of them at Kirkenes, started at the beginning of this century, required the development of port facilities and a city. Old places like Hammerfest have long been major centers for the fishing industry, and still other areas were opened agriculturally to support the regionally isolated cities and villages of the zone. Most of the farming is part-time, in combination with fishing along the coast or forestry inland, and much of the post-1920 increased acreage in farming was a result of the *bureising* program.

Fig. 16. A representative single farm in north Norway's Outer Fringe Zone. The site is characteristic of those selected for farming-forestry. On State Highway 50 about 4 km. (2 1/2 mi.) south of Torhop on 15 June 1956.

Major expansion occurred at four places: in the Hattfjelldal sample area, just southwest of Narvik, just east of Tromsö, and in the vicinity of Kirkenes; at least two of these were accompanied by new settling. Even though much of Finnmark's settlement was levelled during World War II, redeveloping at the same sites began immediately thereafter, then later there was the governmental development program.[61] And developing and new settling continue. In this zone, then, there has been a forced growth which accelerated after 1951 and is worthy of detailed study at two areas to measure the costs and the permanence of new settling.

THE HATTFJELLDAL DISTRICT: OFZ SAMPLE

Hattfjelldal is a small village at about the geographical middle of Norway. It is the center for an administrative district with the same name but herein the area includes some of that and a part of the *herred* on the west. All of this is an inland section of the southern division of Nordland County, considered by Norwegians as the beginning of "the North."[62] This qualified the area for special aid for settling after World War II. Also, the location is one within the Kjølen Mountains where settlement is concentrated in the forested floors of six valleys whose pattern is that of an I and E connected across the top (Fig. 17); most of the area is in the Outer Fringe Zone but it extends westward into the MFZ and eastward to the OMFZ.

Norwegian settling of the area began in about 1680.[63] By 1742 there were four inhabited places with 10 farms in Hattfjelldal district and two more farms in Fiplingdal, the valley of the western part of the area. Through the rest of the 18th century settling was slow and much was the *seter* type for seasonal pasturing. In the 1800s settling continued to be slow, in part because of a big fire in the 1830s and in part because a large section of the area was owned between 1866 and 1899 by an English firm, interested only in the timber there. Yet, most of the present-day farmed areas originated in places started in the 1800s, particularly after 1850 (Fig. 18). However, the significance of the Hattfjelldal area to this study is the combination of its being mostly in the Outer Fringe Zone, in an inland high-latitude position (c66°N.), where there have been so many *bureisere* that it is the highest percentage per district in all Norway, where some of the farming approaches full-time farming

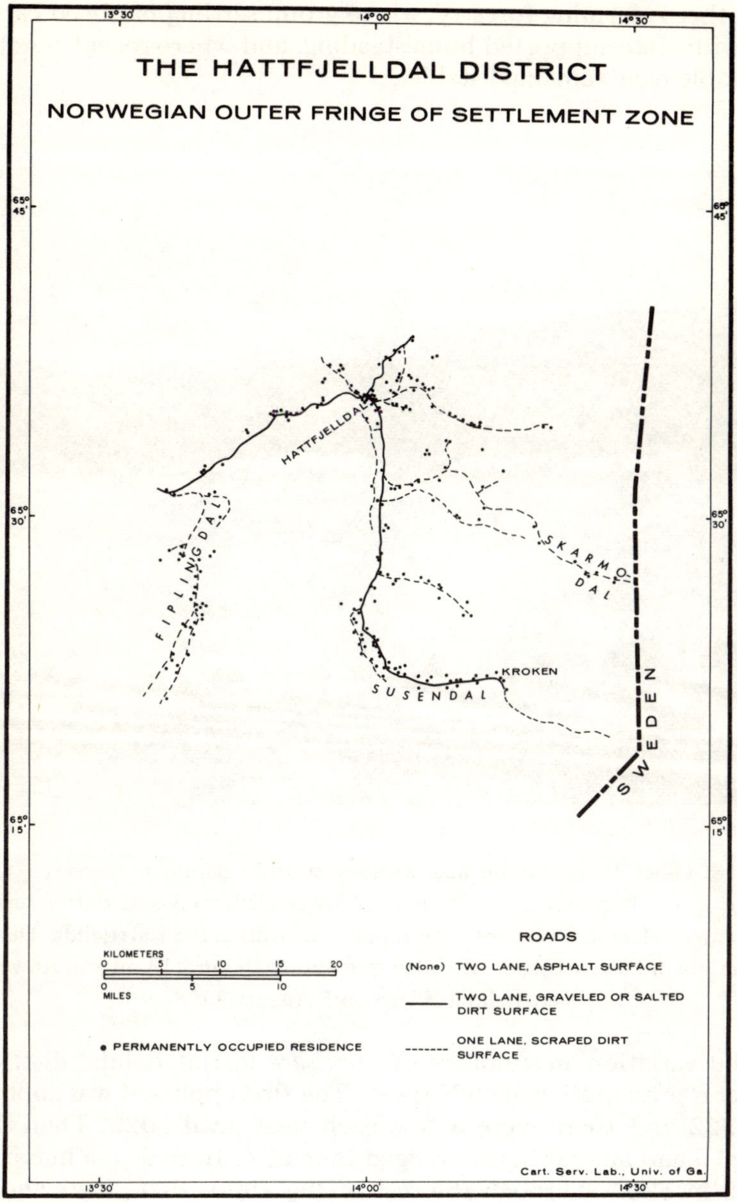

Fig. 17. The Hattfjelldal District.

and other is farming-forestry, where group settling has been carried out with state-supported homesteading, and where recent numbers of people have remained stable.

Fig. 18. Older farms established without subsidy in north Norway's Outer Fringe Zone. Representative of sites, at lower elevations and flatter surfaces near water, selected for recent state-supported farms in the Hattfjelldal District. At the northeastern corner of Unkervatn about 25 km. (15 mi.) southwest of Hattfjelldal village on 5 August 1958.

The variation in numbers of *bureisere* in Hattfjelldal district is rather representative of all Norway. The first applicant was approved in 1922 and there were a few each year until 1929. Then there were 16 and annual figures ranged thereafter from 6 to a maximum of 19 in 1934. Through the rest of the 1930s there were about 8 per year. In 1941 and 1942 there was none but from 1943 to 1946 as many as 10 per year. After that 2 or 3 was an average annual figure for some years until 1958 when, as for all of Norway, the program for homesteading began to taper off, and for this part of the country meant no *bureisere* at all through 1966.

The unusual feature about the Hattfjelldal area is that it is one where there has been recent local advance of settling (Fig. 19).

Fig. 19. A representative farmstead on a two-year-old state-supported farm near a road end in the north Norwegian Outer Fringe Zone. Barn under construction to left of the residence, potato field in the foreground. About 11 km. (6 1/2 mi.) ESE of Hattfjelldal village on 8 August 1958.

This was in spite of its high regional and local isolations and even though there was Nazi occupation during World War II. In part this is due to much settling being delayed until a time when state support was available. In part it was because the Nazis built an airport near Hattfjelldal village and tried to win local support by careful control rather than ruthless rule (and so there was relatively little destruction in the area). And in part it may be due to the woodworking plant set up in the village since the war.[64]

Settler reactions to the homesteading program carried out in the area were similar to those elsewhere in Norway. In general they favored the state's program and were pleased with the attention and advice given by the officials but there was disagreement as to whether enough financial aid was available for either buildings or clearing, especially where the latter was done in stony areas. Most of the newer farms were formed by the purchase or grant of part of an existing farm;[65] the farms were too small from the beginning, being perhaps 400 decares (100 acres) with 20-75 decares (5-19 acres) cleared and supporting three to five cows. Most of the farmsteads now are accessible by a seasonal road but several were not on such when started; the principal share of the area's roads was built in the latter part of the 1920-1952 period. Most of the *bureisere* were in their late 20s or early 30s when they went to the area, were married, and came from nearby valleys (both wives and husbands who did not were easily recognizable during interviewing by their noting the area was isolated and that they desired to move). The high degree of local isolation and the amount of work required of the woman on the farm emphasized the essential nature of her contribution to permanence in this area more than in either the Trysil or Målselv districts. Commonly female interviewees stressed the desirability of telephonic communication early in the settling process but almost all the homesteaders had to begin without either telephones or electricity; at several places neither was available even 10 years after the starting time. And most places received mail only three times a week when the roads were passable.

Some non-agricultural work characterized most of the homesteaders. It was common for half the annual income of a family to come from forest work, wood sales, or off-farm employment. A significant part of this centered on the wood processing plant at Hattfjelldal village. This factory, which began production in October 1957, was located there to use the hangar at the Nazi-built airfield, to be close to a source of birch which predominated after the the spruce was taken out by the English timber firm, to take advantage of governmental funding, and to use the good local labor supply (because the farms were small). By the end of the first year of production, which was quite successful, 43 farmers were employed and some indicated the work to be much easier than the usual farming-forestry of the area. The stimulation of such a plant on the economy of an area with such degrees of isolation is worthy of continued and penetrating study.

In the timing of settling actions almost all the homesteaders began with their houses, usually the permanent type, and proceeded to the barns and then to clearing. One modification was making the barn only temporary in order to get to clearing at least in the second season and a further departure was first clearing a small bit of land, perhaps 4-6 decares (1-1 1/2 acres), and then erecting permanent buildings in the usual order. This succession depended, of course, on the amount of money, machinery, and experience a homesteader had; most had enough of the last, too few had the first two in sufficient amounts.

Most of the settling of Fiplingdal was different. There 21 farms, at least seven of which were completely new, were introduced on state-owned land. Some 16 began in 1943, a difficult time. Settlers were selected by the usual process (approval of application for loan) but as a state-sponsored operation more roads, major ditches, and clearing were available for homesteaders settling separately. There, too, over half of the farms were larger than those in Hattfjelldal, some being nearly 600 decares (150 acres). By the fall of 1957 a total of 468 decares (117 acres) of land was cleared in the valley; at five farms no land was cleared and at nine others less than 5 decares (1 1/4 acres); all homes but three and all barns but five were completed.[66]

As usual in the *bureiser* program, district and county agronomists were major elements in the settling of Fiplingdal. They governed much of the state's part and provided advice on all phases to the settlers, especially concerning the siting of houses, barns, and fields. In general, the 19 families interviewed in the valley had favorable reactions to the aid given with any possible exceptions usually being persons who were not originally from the local area. But a major additional strong point was the presence of an exemplary farmer. This man was a homesteader but one who had had special college-level agricultural training. To him the local agronomists brought the newest ideas and the application of these by a local farmer was most effective on the other homesteaders. This is a technique that can bear repetition elsewhere in the world.

In general, some of the Hattfjelldal area's moderate to high local and regional isolation has been conquered. It took the will of its settlers, good fortune during wartime, industrial ingenuity, and the state's encouragement. The result is evident. One was in recent population numbers remaining stable; between the beginnings of 1963 and 1965 the 2110 people changed to the equivalent of 2116;[67] the total declined by 82 persons to 1 January 1967.[68] In another way, roads have been improved and a new one built in the mid-1960s eastward up Skarmodalen to the Swedish border (Fig. 17). But clearest is the absence of any areas of abandoning and, in fact, of single unoccupied places. Of course, the normal life and death of a rural landscape means there will be a few places that appear run down and little used because of advanced age, illness, accidents, or disinterest of the owners -- the Hattfjelldal area has its share of these but there are no indications that the numbers are abnormal nor that abandoning is likely to be localized in the anticipatable future. So the area is unusual -- it has had significant recent local advance of settling and is at least stable now. But it is not the only such area in the country.

THE PASVIK VALLEY DISTRICT: OFZ SAMPLE

Pasvikdalen (The Pasvik Valley) is a similar example. It is at the extreme northeastern corner of Norway and is a finger of Outer Fringe Zone extending southward from the town of Kirkenes to almost touch some Outermost Fringe Zone (Fig. 1). It is the Norwegian, or western side, of the lowland of the north-flowing Pasvik River, the boundary between Norway and the Soviet Union. But it is only a part of the Sør-Varanger *herred* which includes coastal and inland parts quite unlike the valley in rural settlement form and rural settling process.[69]

Modern Norwegian settling of the Pasvik Valley began about the middle of the 19th century.[70] In 1801 the 163 Lapps in Sør-Varanger made up most of the population with some 31 Norwegians also reported. Only Lapp growth was noted until 1845 when of a total of 690 people there were 78 Norwegians and 75 Finns. But in the next 20 years the population nearly doubled with the Lapps increasing to 667, the Norwegians to 194, and the Finns to 339; by then, too, there were 39 who were mixtures of Lapp and Norwegian or Finnish blood. In 1900 further growth in the district was evident from a sum of 1912 people being made up of 698 Lapps,

396 Norwegians, and 818 Finns. The increase of the Finnish element was significant; these people had shorter trips and less adjustment than the Norwegians who were encouraged, especially in the 1890s, to come from the eastern valleys of southern Norway. However, this changed.

In the late 1860s a taconite-type iron ore was discovered south of the present site of Kirkenes town. In 1906 a company was formed to mine the ore, construction of the facilities to concentrate and move the ore began in 1907, and processing began in 1910.[71] By 1910 the population of the *herred* was 3320 and by 1920 had increased to 4798. Then came the *bureising* program under which most of the settling of the Pasvik Valley area took place, giving it a special significance.

Rural settling in the Pasvik shows what can be done if a national government wants and encourages developing in spite of odds against it. The Valley has the highest degrees of regional and local isolation of any of the four sample areas considered herein; its latitude is nearly 70°N., no movement eastward is possible, and the one road dead-ends about 120 km. (75 mi.) southwest of Kirkenes (Fig. 20).[72] Much of the area's settlement was destroyed during World War II. But in spite of these the numbers of homesteaders through 1966 increased continually to one of the higher totals in northern Norway, these *bureisere* are farmer-foresters, they have a relatively high income per person, and in population the area has continued to grow or remain stable through 1967. This is, indeed, a rare combination.[73]

The *bureiser* program of Sør-Varanger *herred* has been a steadily continuing program to the present time as well as one of the greater in total persons settling with state aid. The beginning was in 1922 when 7 homesteaders were approved. Starting in 1925 there were annual additions for 17 years; they were about 6-8 a year in the late 1920s and mid-1930s and rose to a maximum of 10-16 per annum in 1937-1939. During the destruction and reconstruction of 1942-1948 there were only 2 homesteaders (in 1944). But thereafter just three different years had none through 1964, and from 1950 through 1955 there were 32 new *bureisere* (10 of which started in 1954 alone). And, while the program was rapidly decreasing throughout Norway in the 1960s the district had 7 new homesteaders in 1963 and 1964 and four more thereafter. Thus, by 1970 there had been 166 farms started by *bureisere*.

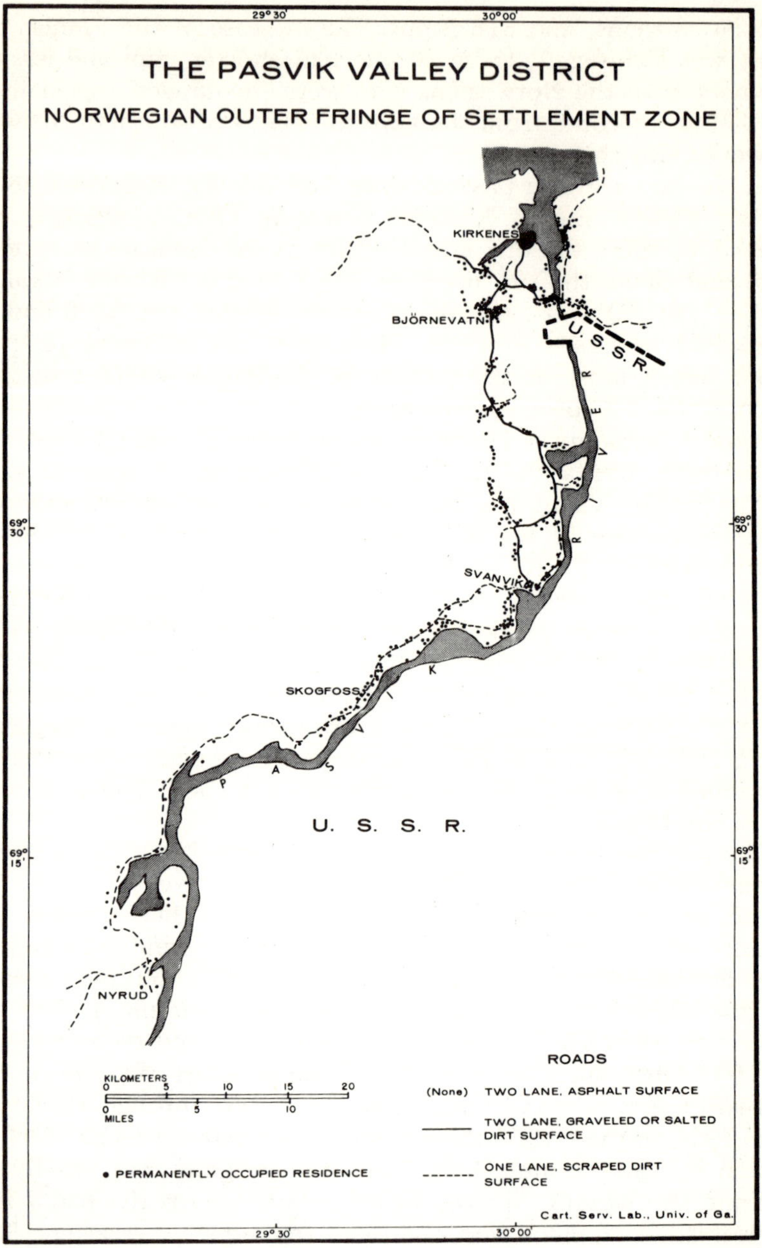

Fig. 20. The Pasvik Valley District.

An overwhelming majority of these was in the Pasvik Valley area. Elsewhere in Sør-Varanger there were eight areas organized for new state-sponsored rural settling; five were started after 1950, none had more than four farms by 1958, and only three were planned to have more than 20 farms each when completed. But the Valley was different. Downstream from Svanvik village were older farms, upstream (southward) was the big state area. This was started about 1930 and administered directly by the agricultural department in Oslo through two local officials. The land involved extends from the end of Langfjorden southwestward through Svanvik about 65 km. (40 mi.) to the Finnish border and is the settled section on either side of the road. The plan was to have 130 farms of about 200-300 decares (57-75 acres) each as well as space for more. Land prices were low, subsidies were somewhat more easily obtained than elsewhere, transport and machinery were made available cheaply, a demonstration farm was set up in the area, and roads and main drainage ditches were installed. All these were to attract Norwegian settlers, particularly in the late 1920s and early 1930s, so as to counter Finland's announced program of growth in the north; the more rapid increase of Finns than Norwegians in the area prior to 1920, as noted previously, prompted this concern and spurred the formation of this state area shortly after the *bureising* program began.

The early interest in this state area was great. However, many of the people who came in the 1930s were adventurers and were not accepted. Still, by 1958 there were more than 60 farms in this part of the Valley and about half were completed according to the original plan. Considering that destruction during Nazi occupation was 80-100 per cent in the Valley (including bridges, utility poles, and churches as well as farmsteads and cities[74]) the program has been strong; this is easily observable by land being cleared and farmsteads under construction or newly built (Fig. 2). And all this in spite of the great geographic weakness of settlement being too scattered and along a single dead-end road in an area of high regional isolation.

Road building was essential to all activity in the area. Around Kirkenes and from the southern end of Langfjorden to Svanvik roads were put in about 1870. Between 1919 and 1929 the main road from the ore quarries at Bjørnevatn to Svanvik was built to eliminate water travel via the fjord or the river to get to the village.

Then between 1931 and 1940 the present road route southward was constructed. The most recent significant addition was the completion of a second road from Svanvik southward which runs next to the river and joins the older route about 10 km. (6 mi.) southwest of the village. Inasmuch as the river is unsuitable as a transport route the only circulation line in the Pasvik area is the road (Fig. 20). This is one lane wide, with passing points, has a surface of gravel, and, unfortunately, is closed at some times.[75]

The explanations of the local advance of settling involves direct and indirect relationships with other elements of the Valley's landscape. The continual increase in production of iron ore at Kirkenes [76] is an example. In the 1920s some of the miners tried to be homesteaders as well; it did not work and by 1958 there was no farming-mining combination. Yet, the miners and the workers in the plant at Kirkenes provide markets of real value to the farmers in the Valley.

Related to the increasing production of iron ore is a second example, the hydroelectric development of the Pasvik River. This began in 1958 when the Norwegian and Soviet governments agreed to mutual use of the river for generation of much-needed electricity. The river was divided into three parts for different uses: the upper (southern) boundary section for the Soviet mine and plant at Nikkeli, the central portion at Skogfoss for Norwegian use, and the Boris Gleb part still farther north for Soviet purposes. It is that at Skogfoss which is significant here.

The falls of Skogfoss are about 42 km. (26 mi.) southwest of the town of Kirkenes. This location, near the exact middle of the Norwegian boundary on the river, is 16 km. (10 mi.) southwest of Svanvik village and, therefore, well within the state settling area previously discussed (Fig. 20). The falls, like most on the river, were low being about 10 meters (33 ft.) before the dam was built. At that point the flowage capacity was known to fluctuate between 120 cubic meters (4,238 cu. ft.) per second and 200 (7,063 cu. ft.) and at flood stage to reach as much as 500 (17,657 cu. ft.). To increase the amount of fall to 20 meters (66 ft.) and to develop a water storage area a 3/4-concrete-and-1/4-earth dam was built across the river at a point 300 meters (984 ft.) wide. This formed a lake about 40 km. (25 mi.) long and 1 km. (0.6 mi.) wide. All this was planned to be done in two years and by early 1965 work was completed and the generators were working.

As a result the concentrating plant in Kirkenes got more electricity and could increase production, so there were more workers and a bigger market for local farm products. Too, half the increase in power was for the area's residents and the cost per unit to them was reduced. So more heat, light, and people plus reduced costs of an essential were elements of encouragement to settling.

But there were losses, too. Namely, ten farms. These were on their way under water in 1964 (Fig. 21). At some points the

Fig. 21. A new state-supported farm in northeast Norway's Outer Fringe Zone. Representative of the two-building farmstead, with electricity, on flatter forested land adjacent to the Pasvik River (background) and adjoining the one north-south local road. About 12 km. (7 1/4 mi.) SW of Svanvik village on 14 August 1964.

road had to be moved. The farmers displaced were offered new places with cultivated land; in 1958 the ten were discouraged and only one planned to accept the offer while the rest wanted total reimbursement in cash. For some the loss of a farm was tragic as no amount of repayment seemed sufficient for years of inconvenient living and hard work.

This damage is similar to what occurred in several places in northern Sweden. However, much of the forced movement there was in Outer Fringe Zone areas where abandoning was in progress.[77] In the Pasvik Valley it has been largely the reverse. There has been little or no abandoning other than the 10 flooded out. On the contrary, the appearance is one of a viable area which will absorb the loss and which has profited from the opportunity to work at construction so as to be able to invest more in the farms.

The viability is displayed in part by the Sør-Varanger district population figures. By 1930 there was a 10-year growth of more than 58°/o to 7590 people; in 1946, even after all the war-induced losses, it was up to 7993. By 1950 another 1000 people were there, in 1958 the total was 9,767, and between 1963 and 1967 it grew by 71 to 10,456. Of course, much growth has taken place in Kirkenes where the town, which was levelled by bombing in the early 1940s, was replanned, reconstructed, and now has more than 5,000 inhabitants. So much of this has been supported by the rebuilding and growth of the iron ore industry. But with more ore being discovered, a growth in the number of tourists, the generation of more electricity, and reflections of strong feelings of nationalism by governmental sponsorship of growth along this border, a stable to locally advancing Outer Fringe Zone may be expected here for some time to come.

In such an area it was deemed especially desirable to determine the attitudes and suggestions of local farmers and officials concerned with new farming.[78] The most important conclusion was that though most of the farmers spoken to were born outside the area, and some outside of northern Norway, only one or two showed desire to leave. Most recognized their lot to be hard work, nearly all acted as though they expected it. Otherwise, reactions were quite similar to those in the Hattfjelldal sample area: necessity of a quick start, the need for machinery, the desirability of a large barn quickly, the necessity for much larger farm sizes, the desirability of telephonic service at first and electricity as soon as possible, the advisability of helping people on older farms in an area where *bureisere* are being introduced, and the clear-cut need for adjustments to local conditions. Examples of the last in the Pasvik Valley were farmers who raised mountain reindeer at first and others who spaced drainage ditches or selected building sites more conservatively than advised by local leaders.

Local officials also had recommendations concerning rural settling procedures in the Pasvik. One felt a state area should be developed around five points: 1) road and main drainage ditches established first, 2) plan total development in relation to a detailed plan of a community center, 3) cultivate about 20 decares (5 acres) with machines on each farm before the settler brings his family and starts building, 4) introduce electricity and telephone with the start of settling rather than 10-20 years later, and 5) the individual farmer needs a house before a barn. The last is undoubtedly in response to those *bureisere* who recommend a large permanent barn first (though they were usually balanced in the interviews by a wife's countering that the house must be built first!). Another official very close to the homesteaders in the Valley agreed with these and added: 6) the need for a qualified "leader-type" farmer (as noted in Fiplingdal), 7) careful presettling study of availability of water, 8) the desirability of concentrating cultivated land so as to use machinery efficiently, 9) farm sizes should be much larger, 10) building materials should be nearby each place, and 11) the requirement of a total overall plan for an area to be developed.

The most interesting omission in all interviewee's answers and comments was any suggestion as to how to select the settlers for a project. Though the action is by and for people only a few persons have approached the problem more than obliquely. Yet each insisted on careful inventories of all other elements of a landscape. Why so many people dislike the discussion of judging others is puzzling, especially in view of the fact that most persons are making significant judgments of family, colleagues, and employees regularly. But in this respect the Norwegians in the Pasvik Valley are no different than people in other countries.

OUTERMOST FRINGE ZONE

Along Norway's eastern border and north of the latitude of Namsos is the Outermost Fringe Zone of settlement (Fig. 1). Of the seven areas, four are very narrow extensions of the zone in Sweden. Two of the others are parts of the OMFZ in Finland and only that S and SW of Karasjok is primarily Norwegian (Fig. 15). It is two-pronged and has maximum dimensions of about 160 km. (100 mi.).

The zone is characterized by both high regional and high local isolation. Only a few hundred people are present, all Lapps, most of whom are in that small minority now dependent upon the raising of reindeer. Inhabited areas are some widely spaced dots (Fig. 2) which represent single dwellings (often sod and rock tent-shaped structures and always near water) or poorly defined clusters of two or three families. But even these are becoming fewer in number as the Lapps move to nearby Outer Fringe Zone villages, like Karasjok and Kautakeino (about 400 and 300 inhabitants, respectively), where markets, churches, schools, and amenities encourage them to settle permanently and give up the nomadic life.[79]

Probably 85 to 90°/o of the zone is uninhabited. All of the area is hills, much is covered with swamps and lakes. No part of the zone is reached by mechanized transport routes except along a snowmobile way from Karasjok westward to Masi and Kautakeino and occasional summertime travel on a road southward from Kautakeino into Finland. Thus, travel times are both unpredictable and long and inasmuch as there are no phones closer than the two OFZ villages most settlers are dependent upon themselves in case of need.

As elsewhere, the OMFZ is the one of maximum difficulty just to maintain the settlement that is there. Were it not for the Lapps, the area might be uninhabited. This is perhaps what it should be.

PERSPECTIVES

Internal migration is complex dynamics. Usually it is a series of currents and counter-currents. And these are of varying strengths in unsynchronized periods. So it is in Norway.

Norwegians increased in numbers to 3.8 million in 1969. Recent growth to this has been steady but slow, the average annual rate being 0.8^{o}/o. Within the long and narrow nation the distribution of people has been unequal: more in the south than in the north, more on the coast than inland, more on water than not, and more in the lowlands than on the uplands. Now it has become still more uneven for since World War II there have been more people in the urban parts than in the rural.

In spite of these changes, rural residence has remained significant. Some Norwegians preferred it. Others remained rural because it was, and is, difficult to find housing in most urbanized areas. And still others went to new rural sites because of governmental encouragement.

This state action has been for multiple reasons and in various ways. Administrations have favored rural living in order to produce more food locally, or to have people in political "buffer" areas, or because of moral persuasions. They have done it by indirect and direct actions, more important among the latter being the support of the national homesteading program, the *Ny Jord* Society, agricultural research organizations, and special provisions in war reconstruction acts. Through these several tens of thousands of Norwegians have been aided in new rural settling, either to open new agricultural areas or expand existing ones.

New rural settling is now stalling in Norway. The homesteading program is practically ended. Other colonization is minimal, being mostly consolidation of previous efforts rather than new ones. So the process is presently a small counter-current in Norway's internal movement of people. But this is the short-time view; in the immediate past local movements to rural sites were significant and in the future they are likely to be so again. The old reasons for new agricultural settling are still good, they are just relatively less important at the moment.

Thus, the sample areas are important to the near future. When and if the population increases more rapidly and when cities surely grow, and especially if nervousness about potential conflict in the neighborhood increases, the lessons of recent movements to new farms will be very helpful. Right now the four sample areas are living demonstrations of the effects of state policies and detailed programs operating where there are great measurable differences in regional and local isolations. One may see in each area the advisability of complete overall planning tied realistically to international events, national desires, and local human and natural resources. In greater detail are demonstrated the needs for both specific guides as well as flexibility in the selection of settlers, the timing of actions, clearing of land, construction of buildings, financing, draining, the building of roads, the erection of communication facilities, the creation of multiple sources of income, the provision of educational and religious facilities -- these and the rest of the multitude of necessary operations tempered to the characteristics of the people involved.

Norway is near the center of a most fruitful region for research on the movements of population. To the west Iceland has emigration from the country as well as a local rural-urban change. To the east Sweden has rural losses in large rural areas and intensive urban growth. Farther east Finland has declining colonizing in the north but increasing urbanization all over and growing rural densities in the south. To the south Denmark also has a slowly increasing population with a high degree of urbanization but much of its rural population in a widely spread intensive agriculture. There is, therefore, a regional laboratory within which each of the countries can provide something of value to its future and that of the others and there is also the potential for significant contributions by comparative studies.

NOTES

1. H.W. Ahlmann, The Geographical Study of Settlements, *Geographical Review,* v. 18, 1928, pp. 93-128, especially pp. 118-124, and K. Larsen, *A History of Norway,* New York, 1950, *passim.*

2. Much of this section on emigration is based on J.E. Bacher, Norwegian Migration, 1856-1960, *International Migration,* v. IV, 1966, pp. 172-185.

3. Statistisk Sentralbyrå, *Statistisk Årbok, 1964* (Statistical Yearbook, 1964), Oslo, 1964, p. 5, and ----, *Folketallet i Kommunene, 1965-1967,* Oslo, 1967. The rural-urban movement required more adjustment in Norway than in some countries for which see P.A. Munch, *A Study of Cultural Change, Rural-Urban Conflicts in Norway,* Oslo, 1956.

4. J. Tuck, Jr., Geographical Changes in an Area of Rural Settlement: The Salten Region of North Norway, 1946-1967, in progress, Fig. 1 and Table 1, Appendix.

5. G. Jahn, Norway's Population Problem, *American Scandinavian Review,* v. 25, 1937, pp. 118-128, and J. Doublet and H. Palmstrom, Problèmes démographiques en Norvège, *Population,* Oct.-Dec. 1946, pp. 650-662.

6. Statistisk Sentralbyrå, *Statistisk .... 1964, op. cit.,* p. 18 and O.J. Adamson (ed.), *Industries of Norway,* Oslo, 1952, particularly pp. 11-19.

7. K.H. Stone, Regional Abandoning of Rural Settlement in Northern Sweden, *Erdkunde,* in press.

8. Copies of these maps, four sheets for each period, on a scale of 1/1,000,000 and done in 1948, are in the library of the Statistisk Sentralbyrå in Oslo.

9. A. Soderlund, *Befolkningens Fordeling i Norge* (Population Distribution in Norway), Kristiania (Oslo), 1923, with two maps, scale of 1/1,000,000 (data for towns based on the 1920 census and data for rural areas based on 1910 census returns modified by questionnaires and field work in 1917 and 1918).

10. Considerable material in this and the following two sections is from three references: Statistisk Sentralbyrå, *Bureising med stattstøtte, 1921-1936* (Homesteading with State Grants, 1921-1936), Norg. Off. St. X, Oslo, 1941; E. Gjelsvik, *Bureising* (Homesteading), Oslo, 1939; P. Borgedal, *En vurdering av statensstøtte til nydyrking og bureising i Norge* (An Evaluation of State Grants for Land Reclamation and Homesteading in Norway), Gjøvik, 1954.

11. In 1850 tenant farms made up about two-thirds of the farms in all of Norway.

12. Litt on nydyrkinga i 1968, *Ny Jord,* v. 56, 1969, p. 127.

13. The story of the society is abstracted from details given in Selskapet Ny Jord, *Selskapet Ny Jord, 1908-1958* (The New Land Society, 1908-1958), Oslo, 1958, in P. Borgedal, *op. cit.,* item 15, and recorded in my notes of several discussions in the field with administrative personnel, especially Secretary G.H. Paulsen.

14. One of the more interesting discoveries during the research for this study was the *Ny Jord* policy on house building. Before the society had constructed 130 homes it learned that it was too expensive in money and, above all, in settler dissatisfaction. It stopped building the houses in 1924. Yet, 11 years later when preparing for the Matanuska Valley colony in Alaska United State's planners repeated the error -- and produced the same results.

15. But they have not been searched specifically for guides on this point.

16. Selskapet Ny Jord, *op. cit.,* pp. 132-133.

17. We have all the Ny Jord settlements plotted on a manuscript map, scale of 1/1,000,000, according to date of founding and number of farms.

18. *Ny Jord,* v. 57, 1970, p. 60.

19. Most homesteaders operated with a loan, a state grant, and private funds; the administration of the homesteader's commune was required to underwrite the loan.

20. Statistisk Sentralbyrå, *Bureising....*, *op. cit.* However, a geographer preceded this with the first published maps on the effect of the program, showing the per cent of 1939's cultivated area which was newly cultivated between 1918 and 1939, in L.H. Hertzberg, Nydyrkingen i Tre Østlandsbygder, 1918-1939, (New Cultivation in Three Eastern Areas, 1918-1939), *Norske geografiske selskab* (Ad Novas No. 2), Oslo, 1944, maps on pp. 10 and 11.

21. Borgedal, *op. cit.*

22. Letter from Secretary Olav Ringstad to K.H. Stone, Oslo, December 19, 1957.

23. One article, prepared early in the program's life, notes that between 1903 and 1927 there were 74,483 families either newly settled or improved by state aid and tied to agriculture whether dwelling in rural or urban areas: J. Frost, Landwirtschaftliches Siedlungswesen in Norwegen, *Reichsminister Ernahrung von Landwirtschaft, Berichte von Landwirtschaft,* N.F. 11, 1930, pp. 280-288. This is more than four times the total number of *bureisere* determined during this study with the use of original records for the period 1920 through 1963. If the figures given by Frost are correct it is another example of how terms may be used in varying ways and thereby produce incomparable results.

24. Data obtained during interviews of Secretary Olav Ringstad by K.H. Stone in Oslo on May 6, 1964 and June 17, 1970.

25. A series of 88 manuscript maps has been prepared of the geographical characteristics of the *bureisere* program. There are two maps for each year from 1920 through 1963 showing the number of new *bureiser* in each of the country's smallest civil divisions, *herreder* (the districts). In addition, a summary set of 10 manuscript maps has been prepared showing the percentage of farms in 1949 occupied by *bureiser* and classified as 0-10°/o, 10-20°/o, 20-30°/o, 30-40°/o, and more than 40°/o.

26. G. Gronbech, Agricultural Policy in Norway, *Foreign Agriculture,* v. XVI, 1952, pp. 50-53 and map on back cover.

27. A. Løddesøl, Det Norske Myrselskaps Myrinventeringer (The Norwegian Bog Association's Bog Inventory), *Meddelelser fra det Norske Myrselskap,* 1941, pp. 1-22; A. Løddesøl, Bog Inventory in Norway, *International Peat Symposium,* Section B1, Dublin, Ireland, July 1954, pp. 1-3; A. Løddesøl, *Myrene i Naeringslivets Tjeneste* (The Bogs in the Support of Life), Oslo, 1948, pp. 42-58; and A. Løddesøl and J. Lid, *Myrtypen og Myrplanter* (Bog Types and Bog Plants), Oslo, 1950. Field mapping for the inventory was done at scales of 1/10,000 to 1/50,000 during which the bogs were classified according to predominant vegetation, degree of humification of peat, and other physical properties. Estimates were prepared of the possibilities of draining and utilizing them. This research was carried on in upwards of eight per cent of Norway's bog land.

28. Two methods of creating tributary drains, for example, employ waste pine slabs from small sawmills and a third uses a new machine that creates a tube underground by compaction around a missile-shaped object at the end of a thin rod.

29. A. Sømme (ed.), *The Geography of Norden,* Oslo, 1960, map 9.

30. Statistisk Sentralbyrå, *Statistisk Årbok, 1969,* (Statistical Yearbook, 1969), Oslo, 1969, pp. 7 and 8.

31. Ø. Rödevand, Avfolkning av Avsidesliggendes Norske Bygder (Depopulation of Remotely Located Norwegian Districts), *Kulturgeografi,* v. 7, 1955, pp. 65-69 and Å.B. Tschudi, Avfolkningen i Vest-Agder og Nedlegningen av Heiegårdene, Saerling i Sør-Audnedal og Spangereid (Depopulation in Vest Agder and the Preservation of Upland Farms, Especially in Sør-Audnedal and Spangereid), *Norsk Geografisk Tidsskrift,* v. 5, 1934, pp. 207-248.

32. In Norway there is great dependence of the inhabitants upon local scheduled small boat service and that of buses, as well as other usual forms of transportation. Therefore, the schedules of every transport agency in the country are published monthly or quarterly and sold at newstands.

33. See Statistisk Sentralbyrå, *Bosettningskart over Norge* (Settlement Map of Norway), 1/400,000, Oslo, 1955, 15 sheets; divisions of population numbers are on the basis of different symbols for each 25 people up to 300 and then proportional-area circles for places with more than 300 residents. See also L. Sommers, Möre og Romsdal County, Norway: Population Distribution, *Journal of Geography,* v. 50, 1951, pp. 309-317.

34. We have prepared a manuscript map, scale of 1/2,000,000 of all *Ny Jord* colonies founded between 1908 and 1955 from data in (No author), *Selskapet Ny Jord* (The New Land Society), 1908-1958, Oslo, 1958 and from information provided by Secretary G.H. Paulsen of that society; to several other administrators of that organization we are indebted for field experience and for specific data about certain colonies.

35. Kontoret for områdeplanlegging i Hedmark og Oppland, *Hedmark, en Statistisk-økonomisk analyse* (Hedmark, A Statistical-Economic Analysis), Hamar, 1955.

36. As disclosed by Øivind Rødevand's manuscript maps, of average income per capita by herreder for 1946, on file at the library of the Statistisk Sentralbyrå in Oslo.

37. L.H. Hertzberg, *op. cit.,* map on p. 81 as well as lists of *bureisere* by location and date obtained from local officials.

38. L.H. Hertzberg, *Innberetning fra reise i Trysil sommeren 1943 for Dr. A. Sømme* (Report on Travel in Trysil in the summer of 1943 for Dr. A. Sømme), Oslo, 1943, 31 pp., mss.

39. A. Vatnebryhn, *Bureisingen i Hedmark, 1922-1950,* (The Homesteading in Hedmark, 1922-1950), Hamar, 1951.

40. *ibid.,* p. 24.

41. Selskapet Ny Jord, *op. cit.,* p. 132.

42. Data copied from official record in the County Road Office in Hamar on July 6, 1958.

43. J.W. Cappelens Forlag, *Norge Bil- og Turistkart* (Norway, Auto and Tourist Map), scale 1/325,000, Oslo, 1965, sheet 3-4.

44. A manuscript map of the dates of erection of electric lines, since 1937, in Trysil District was prepared in manuscript form for this research on a base of sheets II and III of Hedmarks vegkontor, *Vegkart over Hedmark Fylke* (Road Map of Hedmark County), scale 1/200,000, Oslo, 1954.

45. D.E.H. Hayward, Transhumance in Southern Norway, *Scottish Geographical Magazine,* v. 64, 1948, pp. 71-81 and A. Coleman and S.H. Beaver, Dale-i-Sunnfjord; a study in changing geographical values, *Geographical Journal,* v. 121, 1955, pp. 51-63.

46. For recent data on population changes in Norway's three northern counties see R. Mook, *Flyttinger i Nord-Norge etter 1950* (Movements in North Norway after 1950), Studieselskapet for Nord-Norsk Naeringsliv, Skrift No. 35, Bodö, 1967.

47. The significance of rail transportation to local people in north Norway is demonstrated amply in J. Broch, *Ole Tobias Olsen og Nordlandsbanen* (Ole Tobias Olsen and the Northland Railroad), Oslo, 1945.

48. Ø. Rødevand, *op. cit.,* p. 66.

49. R. Mook, *op. cit., passim.*

50. Kontoret for områdeplanlegging, *Troms, en Statistisk-økonomisk analyse* (Troms, A Statistical-Economic Analysis), Oslo, 1953 and N.A. Ytreberg, *Troms Landbruksselskap gjennom hundre år, 1855-1955,* (Troms Agricultural Society through a Hundred Years, 1855-1955), Tromsø, 1955.

51. E. Gjelsvik, *op. cit.,* p. 7 and I. Seater, *Maalselvdalen* (The Maal River Valley), Oslo, 1926, pp. 21 ff.

52. To determine reactions to and recommendations concerning the *bureisere* program there, the owners (often the resident woman as well as the man) of 25 farms were interviewed in 1958 for this study; these were concentrated in the more nearly full-time agricultural parts of Målselv District itself. In addition six local officials were interrogated in 1958 and in 1964 most of the farms, plus several tens of others, were observed again. A summary of the comments emphasizes the significance of the measures of isolation adopted for this study and indicates recommended processes of settling.

53. R.S. Yohe, Norway Is Developing the Agriculture of Its Northland, *Foreign Agriculture,* v. VII, 1953, pp. 183-187 and Kontoret for områdeplanlegging, *Troms,....., op. cit., passim.* The story of the long struggle to expand the cleared land on a farm in the area is demonstrated nicely in M. Allfresde, Un Exemple de Mutation dans la Vie pastorale sub-arctique Norvégienne: La Ferme de Bratti (Troms), *Revue de Géographie de Lyon,* v. XL, 1965, pp. 77-99.

54. (No author), *Bureisingsfeltet, Gressmyrskogen-Høgli,* scale 1/8000, copy of manuscript map (made in Tromsø?).

55. Ny Jord, *Ny Jord, op. cit.,* p. 133.

56. Kommunal- og Arbeidsdepartmentet (U. Olsen), *Om Gjennomforeningen av Utbyggingsprogrammet for Nord-Norge* (On the Accomplishments of the Program for the Development of North Norway), St. Meld. No. 48, Oslo, 1958, *passim,* and Utbyggingsfonder for Nord-Norge, *Utbyggingsprogrammet for Nord-Norge, 1952-1960,* Bergen, 1961.

57. See also C. Bernard, Problemes de Communications en Norvege du Nord, *Revue de Géographie de Lyon,* v. XXXV, 1960, pp. 317-333.

58. Statistisk Sentralbyrå, *Folkemengden i Herreder og Byer, 1 Januar 1964 og Foreløpige tall 1 Januar 1965* (Population in Rural Districts and Towns 1 January 1964 and Provisional Figures for 1 January 1965), Norges Offisielle Statistikk A 119, Oslo, 1965, pp. 44-45.

59. Kontoret for områdeplanlegging i Nordland, *Nordland, En Statistisk-økonomisk analyse* (Nordland, A Statistical-Economic Analysis), Bodø, Oslo, 1954.

60. Note that the types of isolation are reversed from the ones usually characteristic of this zone. This is another reflection of the complexity of the Norwegian Outer Fringe Zone, especially in the north where the government has taken special efforts to foster the continued populating of the area.

61. Kommunal- og Arbeidsdepartmentet, *op. cit.*, and Utbyggingsfonder for Nord-Norge, *op. cit.* See also T. Lloyd, The Reconstruction of North Norway, 1945-1955, Technical Report, ONR 438-63-04, 1956, mimeo.

62. Kontoret ..... Nordland, *Nordland ....., op. cit.*

63. Some of the history of settling the area is condensed from many parts of J.M. Ingebritsen, *Storjorden, Hattfjelldalens Bebyggelse* (The Big Land, Hattfjelldal's Settlement), Mosjøen, 1923; I am deeply indebted to Mr. Karl Helmerson of Hattfjelldal for loaning his copy of this out-of-print item so that a reproduction could be made for this work. Also liberal use has been made of historical information obtained from local officials during interviews.

64. To provide bases for understanding these circumstances 53 interviews of selected local persons were carried out in 1958. The summaries are divided between that for Hattfjelldal *herred* and that for the state group settlement in Fiplingdal, the western part of the area.

65. Letter from Fylkeslandbruksjefen (The County Agricultural Director) Bjarne Hovde to K.H. Stone, Bodø, Nov. 30, 1956.

66. From data obtained at local district offices in 1958.

67. Statistisk Sentralbyrå, *Folkemengden i Herreder ....., op. cit.*, pp. 40-41; allowance needs to be made for the transferring of a part of Hattfjelldal district to another district in January 1964.

68. Statistisk Sentralbyrå, *Folketallet ....., op. cit.*

69. For the variety of the county see Kontoret for områdeplanlegging (H. Luihn), *Finnmark, En økonomiske analyse* (Finnmark, An Economic Analysis), Oslo, 1952.

70. S. Mosling, Pasvikdalen i gammel og ny tid (The Pasvik Valley in Old and New Times), *Sør-Varanger 100 År,* Supplement to Sør-Varanger Avis, 13 September 1958, pp. 7 and 16, data from interviews with local officials, and figures from various censuses taken since 1801.

71. T. Lloyd, Iron Ore Production at Kirkenes, Norway, *Economic Geography,* v. 31, 1955, pp. 211-233, especially pp. 218-223.

72. For several years it has been proposed to extend this southward to connect with the Northern Finnish road through Ivalo; such a connection existed before World War II by way of the Petsamo district now claimed by the U.S.S.R.

73. Another rare combination is that of local citizens who did so much to aid this study. Many gave much but those in Kirkenes who went out of their way several times to provide all kinds of help, and to whom we are specially grateful, are: Captain A. Rygg, Royal Norwegian Navy and Boundary Commissioner, Engineer B. Helskog of Sydvaranger Company, Fylkelandbrukssjef A. Bartholsen, and Feltbestyrer A. Mostad.

74. The destruction and reconstruction of the Pasvik Valley and Kirkenes areas are presented in many references. See, for example, M. Allefresde, Villes arctique....., *op. cit.;* T. Lloyd, *The Reconstruction....., op. cit.,* T. Lloyd, *Reconstruction of Transportation in North Norway*, Technical Report ONR 438-03-06, Hanover, N.H., 1956, mimeo.; D.H. Lund, The Revival of Northern Norway, *Geographical Journal,* v. 109, 1947, pp. 185-197.

75. A specific problem regarding the use of this road is that the distances involved in delivering milk are so great that a farmer does not get his cans back before the next pick up. Thus, each farmer must have two sets of cans which is rather expensive.

76. T. Lloyd, Iron Ore....., *op. cit.,* p. 230.

77. K.H. Stone, Regional Abandoning....., *op. cit.*

78. More than 20 farmers and another 20 local officials were interviewed and have been corresponded with over a period of 13 years.

79. Note the distinction between the sea-Same, the reindeer-Same, and the agricultural-Same described so clearly in G. Gjessing, *Changing Lapps*, London School of Economics and Political Science, London, 1954, chapters V-VII.